ecpr PRESS

Series Editors:
Dario Castiglione (University of Exeter) and
Vincent Hoffmann-Martinot (Sciences Po Bordeaux)

schools of democracy

how ordinary citizens (sometimes) become competent in
participatory budgeting institutions

Julien Talpin

ecpr PRESS

First published by the ECPR Press in 2011

The ECPR Press is the publishing imprint of the European Consortium for Political Research (ECPR), a scholarly association, which supports and encourages the training, research and cross-national cooperation of political scientists in institutions throughout Europe and beyond. The ECPR's Central Services are located at the University of Essex, Wivenhoe Park, Colchester, CO4 3SQ, UK

Typeset by ECPR Press
Printed and bound by Lightning Source

British Library Cataloguing in Publication Data
A catalogue record for this book is available from the British Library

Paperback ISBN: 978-1-907301-18-6

www.ecprnet.eu/ecprpress

Publications from the ECPR Press

ECPR Monographs:

Causes of War: The Struggle for Recognition (ISBN: 9781907301018)
Thomas Lindemann

Citizenship: The History of an Idea (ISBN: 9780954796655) Paul Magnette

Coercing, Constraining and Signalling: Explaining UN and EU Sanctions After the Cold War (ISBN: 9781907301209) Francesco Giumelli

Deliberation Behind Closed Doors: Transparency and Lobbying in the European Union (ISBN: 9780955248849) Daniel Naurin

European Integration and its Limits: Intergovernmental Conflicts and their Domestic Origins (ISBN: 9780955820373) Daniel Finke

Gender and Vote in Britain: Beyond the Gender Gap? (ISBN: 9780954796693) Rosie Campbell

Globalisation: An Overview (ISBN: 9780955248825) Danilo Zolo

Joining Political Organisations: Institutions, Mobilisation and Participation in Western Democracies (ISBN: 9780955248894) Laura Morales

Paying for Democracy: Political Finance and State Funding for Parties (ISBN: 9780954796631) Kevin Casas-Zamora

Political Conflict and Political Preferences: Communicative Interaction Between Facts, Norms and Interests (ISBN: 9780955820304) Claudia Landwehr

Political Parties and Interest Groups in Norway (ISBN: 9780955820366) Elin Haugsgjerd Allern

Representing Women?: Female Legislators in West European Parliaments (ISBN: 9780954796648) Mercedes Mateo Diaz

The Personalisation of Politics: A Study of Parliamentary Democracies (ISBN: 9781907301032) Lauri Karvonen

The Politics of Income Taxation: A Comparative Analysis (ISBN: 9780954796686) Steffen Ganghof

The Return of the State of War: A Theoretical Analysis of Operation Iraqi Freedom (ISBN: 9780955248856) Dario Battistella

Urban Foreign Policy and Domestic Dilemmas: Insights from Swiss and EU City-regions (ISBN: 9781907301070) Nico van der Heiden

Widen the Market, Narrow the Competition: Banker Interests and the Making of a European Capital Market (ISBN: 9781907301087) Daniel Mügge

Please visit www.ecprnet.eu/ecprpress for up-to-date information about new publications.

contents

list of figures and tables

list of abbreviations

AMPAs:	Associacion de Madres y Padres de Alumnos [Spanish PTA]
ATTAC:	Association pour la Taxation des Transactions financières et l'Aide aux Citoyens
CFDT:	Confédération Française Démocratique du Travail
CGT:	Confédération Générale du Travail [French]
CNDP:	Commission Nationale du Débat Public
DS:	Democratici di Sinistra [Left Democrats]
FCPE:	Fédération des Conseils de Parents d'Eleves [French PTA]
HLM:	Habitation à Loyer Modéré [French Social Housing]
IU:	Izquierda Unida [United Left]
NC:	Neighbourhood Council
PB:	Participatory Budget
PC/PCF:	Parti Communiste Français [French Communist Party]
PLU:	Plan Local d'Urbanisme [Local Urban Plan]
PS:	Parti Socialiste [French]
PTA:	Parent Teacher Association
PSOE:	Partido Socialista de los Obreros Espanoles [Spanish Workers Socialist Party]
RC/PRC:	Partito della Rifondazione Comunista [Italian Party of the Communist Refoundation]

| acknowledgements

People often think writing a book is a lonely adventure. This is not how I lived it however. I was constantly surrounded by people, both academics and friends, without which this enterprise would not have been possible. I want to tell them how grateful I am.

I am aware how lucky I have been to have had the opportunity to spend four years at the European University Institute in Florence. I'd like to thank the programme EGIDE and the French Ministry of Foreign Affairs for the Lavoisier grant I was awarded for the three first years of my PhD, as well as the European Union for the last year of the grant. I want to thank as well the Spanish government, who provided a Salvador de Madariaga grant for my Spanish research that was of great help.

I'd like to thank first of all Donatella Della Porta, my thesis supervisor, without whom nothing would have been possible. She was constantly supporting, trusting me and letting me free enough to let my work develop. Without being directive, she always knew how to drive me onto the good path. Then, I know all I owe to Yves Sintomer, my co-supervisor, for his always wise advice, his thorough criticisms, his constant support. I want to tell him that I am grateful for what he did for me.

Then, I'd like to thank all these professors and colleagues I had the chance to cross along these years, that I regularly bothered with my work and whose advice were crucial in the development of my thoughts and arguments. I'd like to thank Loïc Blondiaux, who always took the time to read the papers and chapters I sent him, always making sensible remarks and well-thought arguments. I want to thank, as well, Bernard Manin, for his rigorous and bright mind, which enlightened me many times, in both seminars and private conversations. Thank you to Jürg Steiner, for his lively seminars and straightforward criticisms. I'd like to thank, as well, Luigi Bobbio, with whom I had a short but very intense intellectual exchange, that had a clear and distinct footprint on this book. Thanks as well to Daniel Céfaï, both source of inspiration and critical reader, without whom this thesis would have probably been different. I have also a particular intellectual debt towards Nina Eliasoph and Paul Lichterman, whose theoretical approach and empirical insights were the greatest source of inspiration over these years. Thanks for their careful reading and their brilliant minds. I am also very grateful to Giovanni Allegretti, for having introduced me to the field of participatory democracy in Italy, his good mood, nice jokes and beautiful words make of him a unique scholar.

Thanks as well to Marie-Hélène Bacqué, Marion Carrel, Paula Cossart, Robert Goodin, Jean Leca, Laurence Monnoyer-Smith, Daniel Mouchard, Derrick Perdue, Marc Sadoun, Isabelle Sommier, Stéphanie Wojcik.

If professors have a strong influence on your thesis, the specificity of the social sciences, and especially of ethnographic research, is to lead you on the field, to observe and talk with "real people". In my case, I have spent quite some time in Rome, Seville and Morsang-sur-Orge, and met extraordinary people, who have been critical in the development of my thesis and were genuinely committed to the deepening of democracy and welcomed me like a friend.

Thank you to Luciano Ummarino and Eugenia for their kindness, Elena for all she did for me, as well as all the people from the Casale Garibaldi, without whom my Roman fieldwork would have been impossible. Thanks, as well, to all the participants, all those I bothered with my intrusive questions, strange remarks and awkward looks, especially thanks to Valentina and *Action* people, and Antonio for his straightforwardness.

My thoughts also go to Virginia, who did all she could to make of my Sevillan fieldwork a success, always giving me smart advice, introducing me to the right people, and explaining to me how things actually worked. Thanks as well to Joaquin, Javier, and all the people from the *Presupuestos Participativos* Office, who were always so welcoming to me. Thanks as well to Fausto, Ana and Joaquin no2, for their warm support and great food.

Last, but not least, I'd like to thank the House of Citizenry of Morsang-sur-Orge, where I spent four months that I am not ready to forget. Thank you to Marie-Claire, for all she did for me, all the good time we had gossiping or analysing the behaviour of the people around us, and for the nice political conversations we had. Thanks to François too, despite our strong disagreements, for his continuous support. Thank you as well to Anita, Christine, Béa and Françoise, who made of this participant observation experience, a real pleasure. Despite the hour drive to get there everyday, I was always glad to enter the office in the morning, having coffee, commenting on the daily news or simply gossiping. That was great! Thank you as well to Marjolaine, Francis, Patrick and all the municipality of Morsang-sur-Orge for its openness.

I'd like to thank as well Federico, Laurent, Nadia, Pedro, Philippe and Roland, without whom this work would have probably been different. Finally I'd like to thank my family, without whom I wouldn't be who I am. Thanks to my sister Alice, for being such an attentive ear. My last word goes to my parents, to whom I owe everything. Thank you for having given me a passion for politics and an incomparable love of intellectual joys. Thanks for their constant support, despite my reluctance and silences sometimes.

| introduction

> I discovered a passion for politics. [...] I enjoyed this experience in the
> participatory budget so much that I wanted to keep on at a higher level.
> [...] This is new for me, I always voted but I have never been really active
> in anything. But when the mayor offered me to be on the list for the local
> elections, I was really honoured, and I said yes, of course.
>
> Floriana, participant to Rome Municipio XI participatory budget

For years, Wallon neighbourhood council had known a small attendance, a lack
of dynamism and enthusiasm from the population. Considering this local apathy,
the elected official in charge of the organisation of the participatory process was
extremely directive. She spoke the most over the meetings, defined the agenda,
and framed the discussions in a rather authoritative manner. And when you frame
discussions in a participatory setting, you have a strong influence on final decisions. In a word, Wallon neighbourhood council (NC) had little autonomy from
Morsang-sur-Orge municipality. Things started to change in the fall of 2005 however. Encouraged by the citizenry administration's boss, a few participants started
to get more involved in the organisation of the meetings. Preparation meetings
were thus planned before each neighbourhood council, which were attended by at
least five regular participants, while the elected representative did not. These citizens were therefore able to define the agenda of the neighbourhood council, to prepare small introductions on the issues to be discussed collectively, and in the end,
to moderate the meetings directly. The change in the power-relationship of the NC
was embodied in the very scenography of the meetings. While the elected official
and the public functionary used to be at the centre, it was now this small group
of citizens at whom all the other participants were staring. The meetings were no
longer introduced by the elected representative, but by one of the members of the
organising committee. Discussions were still framed, but by different actors, ordinary citizens motivated by the fate of their community, who increasingly gained
new skills and competences. They learnt to speak in public, to organise a meeting,
to administrate a public budget, to arbitrate between conflicting public goods or to
mobilise the population.

The evolution of the organisation of Wallon NC is pretty telling on the type of
collective learning and empowerment processes that can take place with repeated
political participation. A leftist will probably not become a right-winger, a neo-liberal will not convert to statism and a black block activist might not become a WTO
advisor, but they might be affected, to a certain extent, in their civic practices and
public discourses. The people I met over my fieldwork in participatory budgeting
institutions, were committed to the fate of their community; they took participation seriously and felt they were involved in something meaningful to them and

others. Speaking regularly in public assemblies and, for some of them, negotiating with local representatives, arguing with civil servants, mobilising their neighbours and friends, arguing with municipal technical services and urban planning experts, going around the district in search of all the small problems to be solved, they felt they had gone through an enriching experience that did not leave them immune.

Others, many of them, left the boat on the way. Disappointed by the lack of tangible results, by the manipulation of the politicians or by the narrowness of the power they were granted, tired of the conflicts regularly emerging in the public assemblies, or of the arrogance of the technicians, or by the selfishness of their neighbours, they merely stopped participating. Those were probably little affected by their participation, apart from a growing cynicism resulting from such a dull experience. For many of the participants anyway, participatory budgets (PB) offered a first channel of involvement in local government, a first contact with the world of politics that was so remote from them so far. This does not mean they all discovered a passion for politics – like Floriana above. Some just discovered that they were part of a broader community; that their pavement could not or should not necessarily be rehabilitated this year with regard to more crucial needs of the city, that their arguments could make a difference in changing their daily life, that the construction of a new parking lot could be detrimental to the environment or that recycling was important. They also learned to speak in public, to listen as well, to make compromises between different interests or to negotiate from a position of strength with powerful authorities.

These details about ordinary people in civic practices could appear insignificant or even trivial. Why should social scientists pay attention to them? Why should people interested in the functioning and the future of democracies care about the masses, while we all know that politics is about power, domination and conflicts of interests among elites? In the end, representative government's bottom line is all about the ballots people cast on Election Day. Political scientists should therefore focus on the mass media, elites' discourses and eventually social mobilisation, not on what lay citizens do when they talk about politics. What could be learnt indeed from people who are so ignorant about the functioning and the stakes of complex modern polities? The dominant approaches in the social sciences oscillate, therefore, between macro, often structuralist or functionalist perspectives, and micro-designs based on the aggregation of individual answers through large survey research.

This type of elitist narrative is no longer in fashion however. People have understood – some of them centuries ago – that the quality of a democracy largely stems from the quality of its citizenry. Non-participation and apathy are no longer seen as optimally functional for a democracy. On the contrary, most commentators deplore the decreasing electoral turnouts, the fall of political party membership rates, or the decline of social capital as symptoms of the crisis of representative government. The apathy of the public is now seen as a problem for democracies. While education is considered a pre-requisite to constitute a free people able to decide of its own fate, the increasing educational level of the public did not result in a more vibrant civic life. Even if education is necessary to get a healthy democracy, composed of voters competent enough to make sound choices, it would no longer be sufficient. The structural transformations of capitalism have pushed national educative systems to specialise increasingly to form a workforce able to compete on the international labour market. And it is not sure that the production of efficient agents goes hand in hand with the nurturing of a competent citizenry. Furthermore, if schools can provide individuals with the basic cognitive skills to decode the complexity of modern societies, they are not thought to form competent voters or political beings as such.

The basic skills necessary to make enlightened choices about the future of one's community have to be learned. Some are born in families where politics is important and makes sense; they therefore receive a primary political socialisation that probably marks them for the rest of their lives. Others, a vast majority, given the decline of traditional intermediary agents like trade unions and political parties, do not receive such a primary socialisation. They might get acquainted with politics along their personal, professional, educational trajectory, given the persons they meet and interact with. But they might not as well. They thus have a high chance to never understand anything about politics and to end up stepping back, letting competent people decide in their name. This, as some argued (Crozier, Huntington and Watanuki 1975), can be functional for democracies. It pacifies them. Most social scientists and political actors consider, however, that the political apathy and disengagement of a vast majority of the public is problematic for modern democracies. It raises problems of legitimacy when those who decide only represent small portions of the electorate. It also raises problems of power and domination: those expressing themselves and deciding in the end being often those with the higher economic, social and cultural resources and they might end up promoting their own interests at the expenses of the most modest fringes of the population.

For people who consider political apathy as a problem for democracy and social justice, different interpretations of the phenomenon have been offered, as well as different solutions. One of them, especially popular among civic republican philosophers, is to praise and push forward citizen participation at all levels of government. Only direct participation could nurture the basic skills and habits necessary to make enlightened and just political choices. The history of political theory, from Machiavelli and Tocqueville to Dewey and Pateman, has been marked by recurrent calls for increased citizen participation. Most of them, in different schools of thought and fields of research, have seen participation in local government or associations as the cradle of democracy. The anthropological foundations of democracy would thus be at stake. The relationship between the character of a citizen and the nature of the regime has indeed been at the core of political theory for centuries. Plato wondered, in *Alcibiades*, whether (civic) virtue could be learned. Machiavelli praised the Italian Republics for nurturing a spirit of honour and liberty. Tocqueville argued that American vibrant civic life stemmed from the skills learned in local associations and town meetings. For Marx, it took the form of consciousness-raising of the dominated classes: how can the working class become aware of its common interests? How can the working class move from being a class in itself to become a class for itself? Gramsci offered a subtle interpretation linking class-consciousness to revolutionary praxis. Interrogations over real socialist experiences linked to Marxist ideology led, nevertheless, to question potentially totalitarian ambitions to create a new man. Critical and social theories consequently moved their focus towards radical democracy; democratic praxis being a condition to promote social justice and ensure social change in a pacific manner. As Arendt (1995) argued, social change requires the emergence of a common world, a public space of interaction in-between human beings, rather than the creation of a 'new man', which would be a totalitarian enterprise.

The critical conceptualisation of social change is also due to the structural evolution of society: given the increased fragmentation of social classes and the blurring of identities resulting from it. It has become harder for individuals to make sense of their interests, as they became more complex and contradictory. The problem of apathy and disinterest for politics has, therefore, been understood as a question of subjectivation (Rancière 1995). A new subject, or a new language, has to be created to allow citizens to relate to politics meaningfully. From this perspective, the mobilisation of a territorial identity required by participatory democracy, with the character of the resident or the neighbour encompassing different identities, appears capable of overcoming fragmentation and allows individuals to reach a greater awareness of their interests. Deliberative and participatory theorists of democracy have therefore made of deliberative institutions the necessary intermediary bodies between citizens and the state, where individuals can form their opinions, interests or consciousness. By changing the rules regulating interactions between human beings, and thus creating new institutions, democratic citizens could be nurtured at the same time. If politics exists in the space in-between human beings, not in their interiority, the norms regulating the public space should shape human interactions with the world rather than their inner self. The relationship between the democratic system and the nature of the citizenry has therefore come at the forefront of contemporary political theory debates, along with the rise of deliberative democratic theory.

Despite the recurrence of the calls coming from different sides of the theoretical spectrum, little empirical research has been carried out to assess and analyse the social processes at work under the school of democracy hypothesis (Mansbridge 1999). Under what conditions and to what extent can actors be affected by their experiences of participation? What are the favourable conditions for the emergence of a competent citizenry? What are, on the contrary, the hurdles on this democratic path? If people change, how do they change? Do they think, act or speak differently? What happens inside participatory institutions that could explain how people's behaviour and discourses are shaped? Are schools of democracy also places of politicisation of the public or, on the contrary, forums depoliticising collective issues?

One might wonder however, why this book focuses on urban democracy to answer these questions and assess the school of democracy hypothesis. Participation can change people they say, but not any type of participation. Radical social movements, considering the level of mobilisation they require, the emotional commitment they imply, the risks sometimes taken by the participants, create dramatic personal and political changes, the trajectory of groups and individuals being affected for the rest of their lives (McAdam 1988; Polletta 1998; Goodwin *et al.* 2001). But participatory democracy institutions do not imply such radical political involvement. On the contrary, they are made of relatively consensual public meetings; deal with local issues with little political potential, gather rather conservative than critical individuals. So why would participatory democracy change people's lives? Why would participation in that kind of public bodies affect them at all? In a nutshell, why studying participatory democracy when one is interested in consciousness raising and the nurturing of a critical citizenry?

The main answer to these questions lies in the political potential of grassroots democracy. While involvement in participatory democracy institutions is less intensive and challenging than participation in radical social movements, it presents the specificity of being more than just occasionally, and has the potential to concern the whole of the citizenry. While social movement mobilisation might just be an outburst, concerning a small fraction of highly politicised individuals, participatory democracy could (potentially) involve millions of people, especially among the less politicised and more dominated fractions of the population (Fung and Wright 2003). The territorial dimension of participatory democracy, by encompassing different identities, allows the gathering together of people with different backgrounds, different interests and visions, which is less and less common in increasingly fragmented societies. If the aim were consciousness-raising, what would be the point of studying already committed people? Why focus on a Lilliputian *avant-garde* while participatory democracy could affect those generally excluded from political participation arenas? Participatory democracy could potentially represent a different way of organising contemporary societies and, as such, it embodies an interesting political phenomenon.

From a philosophical perspective, participatory democracy has the ambition to institutionalise a space where people can speak and act together, an Arendtian common world where people can communicate despite their inherent diversity. While, as Arendt argued, the emergence of politics – understood as a space of communication and participation between people – has been rather exceptional in history, participatory democracy could set the grounds for regular communication between lay citizens and allow a direct control over their lives. Arendt (1965) contends that politics emerges only in times of crisis, during revolutions or popular insurrections, and often takes the form of soviets, popular assemblies and councils. The emergence of politics would therefore mean the uprising of grassroots democracy. The ambition of participatory democracy is, in the same line, to institutionalise emergent public spheres, where diverse individuals and groups can talk, cooperate and argue about what to do together, without reproducing the revolutionary spontaneity of leftist groups and by putting the emphasis on procedural designs and fair deliberations.

If politics requires contention and exception to emerge, is the will to institutionalise spaces of public deliberation doomed to fail? Is there a paradox of politics, expression of human liberty but independent of human will? Spaces of political discussion are increasingly needed given the growing moral pluralism of contemporary societies, but politics could only emerge in times of exception. The institutionalisation of politics might indeed reify the common world and confine its radical potential. As Rancière (1995) argues, the emergence of democracy requires a '*mésentente*', which is not an institutionalised space of consensual discussion, but the apparition of the plebeians – the '*sans-part*' – in the public sphere, from which they have traditionally been excluded. What matters then is not so much the discussion, than the redefinition of the distribution of the parts, of the rules of the game. Social change and the emergence of politics, far from requiring collective deliberation, would require contentious interaction. Political practice cannot be envisaged by simply making pre-constituted identities deliberate, but in constituting those identities in confrontation (Mouffe 2000; Young 2001). While conflict and contention are necessary for both the emergence of the common world and individual change (as social movement scholarship showed), the institutionalisation of participatory democracy – aspiring to extend these potential virtues to all – would therefore undermine its political capacity. While the institutionalisation of participatory democracy offers a fascinating political potential for reaching traditionally excluded citizens, it also represents a serious challenge for self-change as a whole. As an institutionalised form of civic engagement, participatory democracy might not favour the emergence of conflict and dissent, which appear crucial conditions for the self-transformation of activists in the case of social movements. It is precisely the contentious nature of collective actions that made them such intense experiences for actors.

Some political and social theorists – in the pragmatist tradition – have also emphasised the importance of conflict and contention in the formation of a public (Dewey 1927; Boltanski and Thévenot 1991). Inspired by these theoretical approaches, some social scientists, studying the involvement of citizens in scientific and technological controversies, have highlighted the importance of conflict to spur mobilisation in the first place and allow self-change and the hybridising of knowledge in participatory forums (Callon, Lascoumes and Barthe 2009). If conflict and dissent are so important for self-change to happen, how can an institutionalised body make it possible? This crucial dilemma at the heart of participatory democracy (institutionalisation vs. creativity of conflict) is also at the core of this book. Can participation in local democratic bodies change people? Are social movement activists and ordinary citizens affected in the same way? What type of politicisation process might eventually result? This books ambition, therefore, is to reconstitute the process of self-change of individuals engaged in participatory institutions.

Having conducted comparative ethnographic studies over 18 months in three participatory democracy institutions in different southern European cities, I managed to follow the trajectory of some participants over time. At first anonymous strangers to me, some of them became friends, acquaintances or simply objects of research that I met regularly, in public settings or not, to talk about them, their life, their engagement, their impressions about the participatory process and about other people. I saw some of them changing. Not in the same way, not for the same reasons. Overall, I accumulated enough material to offer an empirically grounded and solid analysis of the school of democracy phenomenon. The results might partially be context-dependent; they nevertheless enlighten the understanding of participatory democracy, the construction of civic competence and the effects of deliberation at a micro-level. The ethnographic approach, based on direct and participant observation, and life history interviews, allowed the reaching of a certain depth in analysis and description, and thus opened up the black box of a crucial social and political phenomenon, namely the construction of a democratic citizenship.

The argument starts at a general level, as chapter one offers a systematic review of the theoretical and political stakes at question in the construction of civic competence. Analysing the philosophical origins of a question that crossed the history of modern political thought, I show how it recently re-emerged following the development of participatory institutions, in Europe, Latin and North America. Then, I show the interest of developing a pragmatist perspective on self-change. Based on an analysis of the social science literature on the construction of the self, identity and civic competence, I argue both against rational choice approaches, and more broadly against the concept of preference, opting for what I call a pragmatist perspective, centred on the mutual shaping of individuals and contexts in interaction. This perspective justifies both the methodological approach (the comparative ethnographic work) and the focus on micro social phenomena like speech norms and discursive interactions (Eliasoph and Lichterman 2003) within PB institutions.

Chapter two presents the main object of this research, namely participatory democracy institutions in Europe. I thus offer a detailed analysis of the functioning of the three PB experiences studied in this book: Morsang-sur-Orge, a small suburban city in the Paris *banlieue*, Rome 11th district in Italy, and the city of Seville in Spain. These cases have been chosen as they embody three of the most ambitious PB experiences in Europe, devolving an important decision-making power to citizens. I show how such radical participatory experiences have emerged and developed strict procedural rules, thus giving specific opportunities of participation to citizens. The question of the impact of citizen participation on public policies is also tackled, stressing that in most European cases, PBs fail to foster social justice significantly as it did in Brazil.

Beyond formal procedures, chapter three focuses on the informal rules regulating interactions in PB institutions. It is therefore articulated around a three-tiered conceptual architecture. On the one hand, it is argued that a participatory grammar has emerged in the last decade around the world, praising the involvement of citizens in the discussion of public policies at all levels of government. The participatory grammar is then translated at the national level, taking different forms given the political culture and civic traditions with which it is hybridised. Finally, this national understanding of the participatory grammar is also declined at the local level. Given their past civic habits, elected officials and municipal agencies translate the participatory grammar in contrasted ways, which give rise to different group styles in Morsang, Rome and Seville PBs, thus offering different opportunities for self-change.

Going down to the micro-level in chapter four, I introduce the main characters of the story: the public of participatory budgets. I try to construct the different characters active in PB institutions and to sever out the type of competences they are able to mobilise in the participatory process. Chapter five then offers an analysis of the discursive interactions taking place in PB assemblies, and tries to determine the favourable social, political and institutional conditions for the emergence of deliberation and its effects on individuals. I show that despite the hope of the deliberative literature and the centrality of public discussions in PB assemblies, deliberation is scarce, and has little impact on individuals.

The last chapter describes the process of self-change experienced by certain participants. This process is made of three phases, described in turn. First, individuals have to learn the grammar of the institution, i.e., to respect the discursive norms of PBs. At the end of this first step, a large number of actors stopped participating, being excluded symbolically, refusing or not being able to master the official language of the institution. Others, a minority, kept on participating, and could therefore acquire new skills and competences with time. The rest of the chapter focuses on the long term consequences of engagement in participatory budgeting institutions. People who passed the first step can then acquire knowledge, skills and competences. These new skills and competences embody resources in a process of politicisation that might convert into adhesion to a political party, an association, a social movement, or even integration into the local government council. In this regard, engagement within participatory democracy institutions can translate, after years of intensive participation, by significant bifurcations of individual trajectories. These individual consequences also have political effects, as these new politicised actors can play a decisive role in re-boosting the local political and associative scenes. This transformative process is however extremely demanding for individuals, so much so that few participants were affected in the end. I conclude on the social, political and institutional conditions of the construction of civic competence, and on the consequences for the democratisation of the public sphere.

chapter one | entering the black box of civic competence: a pragmatist perspective on self-change

> The origin of human freedom does not lie in man's interiority – be it his will, his thought or his feelings – but in the space in-between that only emerges when a plurality of men gather together and can only last as long as they stay together.[1]
>
> H. Arendt, Qu'est-ce que la politique ?

Participation in the public sphere could have deep transformative effects on individuals. Deliberative institutions and civil society organisations have thus often been labelled 'schools of democracy'; individuals gaining political and civic skills, and becoming more public-spirited by participating in the public sphere. Inclusive democratic institutions would thus have the potential to create 'better citizens' (Elkin and Soltan 1999). An implicit assumption shared by many political and social theories is, therefore, that citizens are not naturally born competent or public-spirited; they have to become so by participating. If schools of democracy are needed it means something is missing; a lack (of competence, information, sophistication, or consciousness) has to be filled. Behind these interrogations lies therefore, the question of the construction and mobilisation of civic competence in modern societies. While this theme has pervaded political theory since Aristotle and Plato, it has become especially salient in the social sciences in the last twenty years. Deliberative theorists, neo-Tocquevillians from the social capital paradigm, social movements' scholars, neo-republican and communitarian thinkers, all try to understand how active citizens can be nurtured.

While research initially tried to assess whether ordinary citizens were politically competent or not, empirical studies showed convincingly that most individuals had low levels of political sophistication and knowledge (Converse 1964; Gaxie 1978; Verba *et al.* 1995). These results were confirmed by the decline of voting turnouts in most Western democracies, and more generally, the growing apathy of the public (Hibbing and Theiss-Morse 2002). Far from the ambitions of classical theories of democracy, most citizens do not care much about politics. As Walter Lippmann argued:

> Although public business is my main interest and I give most of my time watching it, I cannot find time to do what is expected of me in the theory of democracy; that is, to know what is going on and to have an opinion worth expressing in every question which confronts a self-governing community. And I have not happened to meet anybody, from a President of the United States to a professor of political science, who came anywhere near to embodying the accepted ideal of the sovereign and omnicompetent citizen.

(Lippmann 1925: 20–1)

While there are competing interpretations of this phenomenon, its evidence led to a reformulation of the question at stake, which thus became: how can citizens develop a minimal understanding of politics and participate in the public sphere despite such low levels of interest and knowledge? These interrogations have been formulated almost simultaneously by political scientists (Kinder and Sears 1985; Ferejohn and Kuklinski 1990; Sniderman, Brody and Tetlock 1991; Zaller 1992; Blondiaux 1996), social psychologists (Moscovici 1976) and linguists (Chomsky 1977), in relatively similar terms. One of the common interpretations of this phenomenon is that civic competence is derived from the institutional context in which it is expressed, and therefore, that citizens can become competent if offered the appropriate social, cultural or institutional conditions (Marcus and Hanson 1993; Elkin and Soltan 1999). The recent development of participatory institutions could, therefore, offer training grounds for citizens, and thus allow for the systematic evaluation of the school of democracy hypothesis.

Participatory institutions have indeed (re)-emerged in the last thirty years to answer this growing apathy and the rampant crisis of representative government (Macedo *et al.* 2005; Stoker 2006; Rosanvallon 2008). Considering the declining election turnouts and political party membership, the increasing distance between politicians and the masses, and the breach of trust by citizens with political elites in general, it appeared that participatory democracy, as being rooted in proximity, starting with personal, local or ordinary issues people face on a daily-basis, could re-enchant democracies and spur interest in the life of the community (see chapter 2). One of the expected benefits of local participation – for both elected officials and political theorists – is indeed the nurturing of a competent citizenry.[2] Participatory institutions could foster civic competence and the construction of 'better citizens'. As Mansbridge (1999a: 301) argues in a seminal article:

> Participating in democratic decisions makes many participants better citizens. I believe this claim because it fits my experience. But I cannot prove it. Neither, at this point, can anyone else. [...] Those who have participated actively in democratic governance often feel quite strongly that the experience has changed them.

While this lack in the literature has partly been filled for evaluating the short-term impact of participatory experiences – right after a deliberative poll or a citizen jury for instance (Fishkin *et. al.* 2002; Goodin and Niemeyer 2003) – the long-term consequences of civic engagement in participatory arenas have not been assessed so far, especially when it comes to institutions gathering more regularly and for a longer time than mini-publics, which have received most of the attention of deliberative democrats interested in the self-change hypothesis.

Before engaging in such an empirical endeavour, a theoretical investigation appears however necessary, to better understand how self-change through participation can work. Five different theoretical explanations have been offered in the literature and will be presented in turn. If they all share the assumption that political participation can make 'better citizens', they differ in their understandings and conceptualisations of this hypothesis. Their definitions of the 'good citizen', of public-spiritedness or politics in general, depart from one to the other. More importantly, their ontological and epistemological positions on central sociological issues like structure and agency, the separation between the public and private realms, and more broadly, their theories of action, lead them to different interpretative paths. To understand self-change, it appears indeed necessary to start by offering a consistent definition of the self. What does holding a political preference mean? What is and is there anything like personal preferences? What is personal and collective identity? Should the research focus on the 'inner self', through the psychological analysis of 'real interests and preferences', or on its 'outer expression' through the analysis of arguments, practices, and their structural determinants?

It will be argued that the focus on preferences and opinions, central especially in the deliberative democracy literature – and derived from social choice theories – is partly misguided. Often based on experimental methods, such research designs grant social scientists the illusion they can access 'true selves' and the personality of individuals. The argument presented in this chapter holds that the social sciences – especially when dealing with the public sphere – cannot and should not aim at reaching anything like an 'inner self', but should on the contrary, have the ambition to understand how individuals interact in public arenas. While the social sciences cannot enter actors' minds, they can in contrast, scrutinise their external expression, i.e., the practices actually observed in situation. Evaluating the individual consequences of participation therefore requires assessing whether individual practices (public discourses, civic engagement, political mobilisation, voting, etc.) evolve through time. For both methodological reasons – how could the social sciences reach what people really think ? – and pragmatic ones – what matters is the consequences of what people think, i.e., their actual practices –, it appears more fruitful to opt for a praxeologic perspective on self-change. It is through the detailed observation of interactions, speeches, practices and vocabularies of motives taking place in public arenas that one can grasp the impact of participatory experiences and the possible emergence of public-spirited citizens.

After having presented a critical review of the different epistemological perspectives on self-change, I will argue against the concepts of preferences, to then defend a pragmatist perspective on participatory practices. Through the reconstruction of 'the grammars of public life' (Céfaï 2001) regulating the activities of participatory arenas, it will be possible to offer a comprehensive approach of what speaking in public, as a good citizen, actually means.

Understanding the process of self-change

Over centuries, philosophers and social scientists have offered competing accounts of the social and psychological processes leading to self-change. Five explanations of self-change through participation have thus been traced back, imputing it to conviction, information, self-interest, publicity or emotions. Each of these interpretations of the self-change process is presented in turn, based on the arguments of their main proponents, before evoking their theoretical and empirical flaws. While they offer different accounts of self-change, they are not mutually exclusive however. It is precisely by drawing theoretical and empirical insights from the publicity and emotional hypotheses, that I construct my own pragmatic understanding of self-change.

The deliberative hypothesis: the power of arguments

The deliberative hypothesis put the emphasis on language as the source of self-change. The force of arguments should be sufficient to make people change their minds. Collective argumentation would eliminate self-centred and irrational opinions, thus constructing more informed preferences and more competent citizens. This theoretical tradition has its roots in Ancient Greece, where mutual conviction and rhetoric were at the centre of the political system (Castoriadis 1998; Finley 1973). It has recently come to the forefront of political theory with the emergence of the deliberative democracy paradigm. For the latter, fair, collective agreements in complex and multicultural societies have to be the result of a process of argumentation and mutual conviction (Cohen 1989; Gutmann and Thompson 1996; Habermas 1996b). In this process, individual preferences are refined and enlarged, as participants discover new interests and arguments, and evaluate them comparatively. Preferences would, in the process, become more reflexive, as being the result of a thorough evaluation process more than of individuals' guts. Moreover, in order to appear convincing, speakers would tend to put forward arguments upon which everybody could agree (Elster 1995). Deliberation would therefore operate as a filter, expelling unsatisfactory (self-centred, egoist or narrow minded) justifications to focus on more embracing ones.

These theoretical assumptions have since then been evaluated empirically. One of the most ambitious projects from this perspective is that of 'deliberative polling', directed by James Fishkin and his colleagues.[3] Individual preferences are evaluated through questionnaires before, during and after the deliberative process, to test the influence of discussion and information on policy preferences. The results seem to confirm the hypothesis: Fishkin and his colleagues show that the deliberative process produces opinion change, preferences becoming more informed and robust. These results have nevertheless been severely criticised: participants would be partly unrepresentative of the American population (Mitofski 1996), change only marginally their minds (Mitofsky 1996; Merkle 1996), and their preferences remain mostly stable in the long run (Hansen 2002).

Another limit of Fishkin's approach is its quasi-experimental design. Results might indeed differ widely in a real world and non-experimental context, especially when power relationships and real binding public decisions are at stake. Would people really change their minds if their arguments and decisions had an impact on their tax level or property value for instance? These problems are nevertheless partly solved in other empirical research. Button and Mattson, who studied deliberative forums in America – whose procedural organisation is relatively similar to that of deliberative polls –, reach the same conclusions as Fishkin: mutual conviction enriches people's preferences (Button and Mattson 1999).[4] It is not sure however, whether it is collective deliberation itself, i.e. argumentation, the publicity of the process, the new information gathered through discussion or the direct interactions between diverse actors face-to-face that affected participants' viewpoints. Goodin and Niemeyer went a step further, showing that in the citizen juries they studied preference change occurred mostly due to the new information gathered by the participants and through a process of internal deliberation, rather than as a result of collective and public argumentation (Goodin and Niemeyer 2003).

Despite these promising results, the deliberative hypothesis faces these serious empirical criticisms. First of all, recent scholarship attests that beside exceptional situations like citizen juries, persuasion is a rare phenomenon in contemporary societies (Gamson 1992; Conover *et al.* 2002), as people prefer to keep their opinions to themselves. And when it occurs it does not necessarily produce more public-spirited preferences. James Kuklinski and his colleagues (1991), who studied the formation of tolerance judgements – understood as one of the forms 'better' or enlightened preferences can take – did not find that deliberation promoted them. Comparing preferences derived from both unreasoned survey answers and more thoughtful ones (respondents were asked to think about the consequences of their positions), Kuklinski and his colleagues found that 'the people explicitly asked to consider consequences actually expressed less tolerance, on the whole, than did those who reacted from the gut'. (1991: 23) They explain these results by showing that once people start to think about the consequences, they see the risks of tolerating groups such as the Ku Klux Klan, they also begin to evaluate the potential consequences of their judgements for themselves and, consequently, express fears about close-to-home threats. This experience appears however rather idiosyncratic, as usually the consideration of the collective consequences of a certain course of action, the listening to the other side on a given issue, the enlargement of the repertoire of arguments and opinions about a topic fosters more reflexive, considered and public-spirited judgement, on issues such as the death penalty, social security or the tax system (Fishkin 1997). It is indeed difficult to defend purely self-interested positions in a public context (Elster 1994).

If deliberation does allow the construction of enlightened preferences, how lasting are they however? Most of the empirical research on deliberation is based on the study of mini-publics (Fung 2003; Dryzek and Goodin 2006; Rosenberg 2008), who gather randomly selected citizens for, at best, a couple of week-ends to produce a non-binding policy opinion. While preferences might be affected in the short run, a few weeks after the experience, do they hold after a few months or years? Very little research has been carried out to study the long-term consequences of deliberative experiences. It has however been shown that, after a year participants remember very little of what they learnt from the deliberation (Talpin and Wojcik 2010). Furthermore, while producing more-informed preferences is important, affecting actual practices appear crucial too. While declaring, 'I will take care of the environment more in the future' after a consensus conference dealing with global warming, is an important move, it appears as more solid evidence if the actual transformation of individual practices (recycling, consumption, voting, etc.) in relation to the environment, is evaluated. There is, however, very little research assessing the impact of deliberation on individual practices. This is precisely the aim of this book.

Given the number of critiques it faces, the deliberative hypothesis has often been complemented – or replaced – by a cognitive perspective putting the emphasis on the new information learnt in the process of participation. The transformation potential of deliberation would not stem from mutual conviction – that rarely happens – but from the new information learnt in the course of discussion.

The cognitive hypothesis: several heads think better than one

The cognitive hypothesis puts the emphasis on the new information learned through participation, especially when it involves public deliberation. One of the starting assumptions of the cognitive hypothesis is that preferences are caused and unstable. People only partially know what they want; they have conflicting desires, because they draw them from a limited set of information (Manin 1987; Sunstein 1991). Participation should therefore allow the gathering of new information, data and examples, thus enriching individuals' perspectives. As collective deliberation is supposed to be open to a diversity of viewpoints, people would necessarily learn something and leave the room better informed. In a word, the motto of the cognitive hypothesis could be 'several heads think better than one' (Mendelberg 2002).[5] This idea emerged with Aristotle, before being reinterpreted recently by some prominent democratic theorists and tested empirically by social scientists.[6]

In some regards, Fishkin's deliberative polls are also aimed at testing the effects of information input on individuals' policy preferences. During the sessions, participants watch documentaries, listen to panels of experts, and have the opportunity to question MPs representing different political parties. What are the effects of this information input? Opinions change, becoming more informed and considered. Goodin and Niemeyer, distinguishing between the information phase (where the jurors were offered information by questioning experts, technicians and community representatives) and the discussion phase, found that preferences changed much more after the information phase than after deliberation (Goodin and Niemeyer 2003). They asked participants to rank the factors that could explain their opinion change – between learning, listening, and discussion – and three-quarters of the jurors answered that information was the main cause of their shift. They therefore conclude that the cognitive aspect of deliberation is the most important one for personal change. A central problem with Goodin and Niemeyer's approach however, is the method they use: Is self-reporting reliable to assess the learning impact of deliberation? It could indeed be socially more desirable for respondents to answer that they changed their minds thanks to the new information than due to other participants' influence. They could as well be unaware of the process that actually led them to change their mind. Jacobs and his colleagues (2009: 123–131) have shown, however, that participation to a mini-public on the reform of social security increased both subjective and objective evaluation of individuals' knowledge on the topic.

The detailed scrutiny of small group dynamics by social and political psychologists shows as well that, despite the hopes evoked above, public deliberation does not always mean improved cognitive capacities. The contrary can even be true. While it appears trivial that the discovery of new information might increase the reflexivity of actors' preferences, it is not sure whether public deliberation allows individual discovering new information. Different small groups' dynamics might, on the contrary, hinder the epistemic virtues of deliberation. First of all, individuals increasingly interact with people similar to them. Manin (2005) defines this phenomenon as the 'balkanization' of contemporary societies, linked to the development of both residential segregation and 'selective exposure' behaviours (i.e., the propensity to expose oneself selectively to media messages and interpersonal interactions consonant with one's own views). Balkanization translates in the decline of both cross-cutting communication (among different social or cultural groups) and exposure to opposing political views, in both Europe and the United States (Huckfeld and Sprague 1995; Mutz and Martin 2001). The probability of encountering new information is therefore, quite low.

Then, even if diverse people actually meet – some participatory institutions as being highly inclusive (or sometimes randomly selected) claim to reach such diversity – this does not mean that a diversity of views will be expressed or that it will be perceived as such. Social and political psychology experiments show, on the contrary, that people holding a certain position tend to interpret new information as confirmatory of their own view, even against all evidence (Schultz-Hardt *et al.* 2000). This phenomenon is known as 'the confirmatory bias'. People tend to misperceive the information brought to them as additional support for their own previous opinion (Stasser and Titus 1985; Gigone and Hastie 1993; Winquist and Larson 1998). The phenomenon known as 'group polarisation' seems to indicate, as well, that small group discussions tend to radicalise individuals' opinions in an irrational manner (Sunstein 2000; 2002). The group median position shifts after the discussion to a more extreme position. A group slightly opposed to gay marriage will for instance end up with a more extreme anti-gay marriage stance after the discussion. This stems from both social comparison processes – individuals tend to conform with the dominant norm existing in the group, seeking approval of others and trying to avoid conflict (Noelle-Neumann 1993) – and the mere effect of mutual conviction, the initial prevailing opinion in a group having highest chances to be heard and thus to convince and radicalise participants. As Manin argues, the problem with group polarisation is not so much radicalisation in itself, that can be legitimate, than the fact that shifts occur systematically, regardless of the issue at stake.

Social psychology experiments seem therefore to invalidate the cognitive hypothesis: several heads do not systematically think better than one. One of the greatest limitations of the empirical assessments of the cognitive hypothesis is that they stem from experimental designs however. Real-world deliberations – where political interests are at stake – might work differently. Considering that people will change their preferences in the light of the new information provided, can be seen as a naïve argument. Can preferences change so easily? Are not they more deeply entrenched in people's social positions? Are preferences completely detached from interests? The cognitive perspective appears overly confident in the power of deliberation and information, and in some regards overly idealist, as it forgets the power of interests and the structuring of individual preferences illustrated by electoral studies. While new information might re-orient opinions at the margin, people's preferences are deeply embedded in their life conditions and in the structure of their interests. Interestingly however, it seems that civic virtue could stem from self-interest itself.

The interest hypothesis: when civic virtue stems from self-interest

The interest hypothesis is based on the idea that the driving force of human behaviour is the maximisation of private interests. In this regard, civic virtue is understood as a way to promote self-interest through other means. As Machiavelli already argued, in certain contexts (a republic for instance), it might indeed be in the interest of citizens to defend and promote the common good (Viroli 1990; Skinner 1998). The argument was to be fully developed by Tocqueville, for whom town meetings and local associations were the cradle of democracy, in which citizens discover that it is in their interests to be virtuous, responsible and to promote the public good.[7] More recently, the idea of the interest in being virtuous was developed more systematically by Pierre Bourdieu. Considering that no act can ever be 'disinterested', in the sense that there are always reasons and interests backing them up, he analysed disinterested and virtuous behaviours as the interested adaptation to the rules of the social field in which actors are embedded:

> Thus for the question of knowing if virtue is possible, one can substitute the question of knowing if one can create universes in which people have an interest in the universal. Machiavelli says that the republic is a universe in which citizens have an interest in virtue. [...] Thus groups reward conduct that conforms universally (in reality, or at least in intention) to virtue. They particularly favour real or fictitious tribute to the ideal of disinterestedness, the subordination of the I to the we, or the sacrificing of individual interest to the general interest, which defines precisely the passage to the ethical order. Thus, it is a universal anthropological law that there are benefits (symbolic and sometimes material) in subjecting oneself to the universal, in projecting (at least) an appearance of virtue, and adhering externally to an official rule.

> (Bourdieu 1998: 89–90)

For Bourdieu, certain social fields, the scientific one but also the political sphere under certain conditions – he evokes the republic of Machiavelli – are ruled by norms rewarding disinterested, universal and virtuous behaviours. Social groups reward virtuous behaviours and, one might assume, sanction and exclude self-interested ones. Then, Bourdieu argues that actors have a personal interest in respecting those rules. Individuals can draw symbolic gains, probably good reputation and social integration, and eventually material ones, from disinterested behaviour. The French sociologist even concludes with a 'universal anthropological law' of the interest to act virtuously.

While the first claim is convincing, the second one, related to the actor's motivations, appears more dubious. Why do actors follow these rules? Do people only follow the social norms prevailing in public arenas because of self-interest and symbolic pay-offs? It appears – as is developed below – that a more pragmatic and empirically based sociological analysis of this phenomenon is possible and required.[8] In this regard, the focus should not be put on the individual only, thus drawing an (overly)-ambitious 'universal anthropological law', but on the social conditions of the interactions taking place in certain institutional and social settings, allowing virtuous and disinterested behaviours to blossom. Self-interest is not sufficient – and remains largely unproven – to understand why people follow the rules. Closer attention should be paid to the public status of the groups Bourdieu refers to. One of the central features of a public arena is indeed the force of publicity it imposes on actors. Interestingly, deliberative democrats themselves emphasise the importance of publicity for disinterested deliberation.

Jon Elster probably offers the clearest analysis of the interest of disinterested behaviours in public assemblies. According to him, when entering into the public world, actors have to bracket their own interests and generalise their personal positions. Publicity thus operates as a pragmatic filter on individual preferences:

> The conceptual impossibility of expressing selfish arguments in a debate about the public good, and the psychological difficulty of expressing other-regarding preferences without ultimately coming to acquire them, jointly bring it about that public discussion tends to promote the common good.

> (Elster 1998a: 12)

Elster tries to understand why actors searching for the promotion of their private interests feel the need to use a discourse of the common good (Elster 1994). He thus discovers that a strategic use of public argumentation is possible.[9] The public hold normative expectations regarding what representatives are supposed to say. One of these expectations is that any overt reference to mere self-interest, in the course of justifying their position, would be seen as unacceptable (Elster 1998b: 101–2). By using a rhetoric of the common good, the speaker strives at convincing the audience, and especially the neutral groups, that his position is the soundest one. 'Small group of impartially minded individuals might induce many others to mimic their impartiality out of self-interest' (Elster 1995: 249). Individuals find it much more persuasive to couch arguments in terms of the public interest rather than in term of the self-interest that might actually motivate them. The discourse of the common good would therefore only be a form of hypocrisy.

Independently of the motives of the common good discourse, one of Elster's pivotal conclusions is that hypocrisy itself has a 'civilizing force' (Elster 1998a: 12). Once individuals have justified their position in terms of the public good, they cannot switch to another view unless they can justify such a departure. They are subject to a consistency constraint (Elster 1998b: 104). Otherwise, they lose face. However, it is not only a matter of avoiding losing face, but also of psychological constraints. Actors who constantly orient their arguments towards the public interest cannot but be more deeply affected. In the long term, it is impossible to defend the common good 'du bout des lèvres' (Elster 1997: 12). Whereas they had first framed their arguments in the discourse of the common good for pragmatic reasons, or even out of hypocrisy, participants finally come to internalise these public-spirited positions. Their need to reduce cognitive dissonance might lead individuals to convince themselves of the soundness of the public interest argument. Civilising people's speech will eventually civilise their mind (Dryzek 2000: 47).

Elster's concept of the 'civilizing force of hypocrisy', therefore, enriches the interest hypothesis. If the driving force of civic virtue is self-interest, interests and motivations are nevertheless transformed in the process of deliberation. This theory therefore indicates that an empirical scrutiny of the emergence of civic virtue has to go further than a mere explanation in terms of interests. One cannot understand the educative virtues of participation unless the social norms regulating participation and deliberation in political contexts are studied. The main limit of the interest paradigm is that it reduces its analyses to the motivations of actors. Posing as an axiom – like in the case of Bourdieu or Elster – that no human action can be disinterested, and therefore that all altruistic, cooperative or public-spirited behaviour is interested, does not tell much about when and how this happens. What are the specificities of settings and institutions in which actors have to act virtuously? More precisely, what are the social mechanisms at work in these institutions leading individuals to play a disinterred role? What do they mean when these authors speak of shame, concern for reputation, esteem and distinction? Is interest a sufficient explanation of such feelings? Other factors, like the power of publicity, emotions created in face-to-face interactions, or the rationality of arguments in deliberative settings have also to be taken into account.

The publicity hypothesis: interacting under the scrutiny of others

While the interest hypothesis appears reductive, the introduction of ecological features might allow a better description of the process of personal change. Inspired by Kantian philosophy, the publicity hypothesis puts the emphasis on the power of publicity to filter people's selfish motives and to induce individuals to present themselves as oriented towards the common good. In certain public settings, it would pragmatically be impossible to state and justify selfish arguments (Benhabib 1996: 72–6; Gutmann and Thompson 1996: 126–7; Rawls 1997). The idea that people act differently (in a more civilised fashion) under the scrutiny of others has probably been best described by John Stuart Mill in his case for the public ballot, that appears already, back in mid-nineteenth century, extremely deliberative (Urbinati 2002: 104–22). Having to justify publicly one's vote – or at least to let people know your political choices – would curb voters from expressing morally unsustainable positions. Mill indeed foresaw the psychological consequences of publicity in terms of shame, esteem and honour. As people desire others' esteem and consideration, public interaction helps to shape social sentiments. Mill therefore saw the open ballot as transformative: people acquire a sense of responsibility towards their community by acting in public. Mill's argument on the virtue of publicity is all the more interesting in that he also supported direct political participation of lay citizens at the local level, participation fostering moral and intellectual development and creating a sense of responsibility vis-à-vis others that transforms the identity of the citizens in what he coins a 'sentiment of largeness' (Thompson 1976; Mansbridge 1999a).

Such arguments on the transformative power of acting under the eyes of others were central in British nineteenth century political thought, especially when it came to penal theory, as attested by Bentham's concept of 'Panopticon' (Foucault 1975). Lack of civility, moral deviance and unsocial behaviour could be curbed thanks to public scrutiny. Elias made of the emergence of a public space – the court – one of the driving forces of civilising human conduct, individuals internalising aggressive urges and desires (Elias 1939b). Public scrutiny can therefore work as a social control agent.

When proceduralised, deliberative democrats argue, public interaction can however have positive (and not domesticating) developmental effects on individuals. They thus offer different theoretical arguments to back up the publicity hypothesis. While Habermas insists on the presupposition of intersubjective communication, imposing actors to take distance with their own interests, and Elster stresses the need to adopt public-spirited positions to be convincing in a public assembly, Fearon (1998) argues that certain social norms ban appearing selfish in public. Infringing the norm of public-spiritedness is costly and, as people care about their reputation, they have to adopt public-spirited behaviour.

Strong theoretical arguments have, however, been made, contradicting the power of the publicity argument: indeed, publicity can have negative effects on both deliberation and public-spiritedness. First, the publicity of interactions could entrench individual positions and impede preference change. Once an argument has been voiced – especially a public-spirited one – it is extremely difficult for speakers to express publicly that they were wrong and that they have changed their mind, to avoid losing face. The difficulty of changing position in a public meeting can be a problem for deliberation for at least two reasons. First, if pre-defined positions do not change, consensus, or merely agreement, would be harder to reach in public than behind closed doors (Chambers 2005). Then, the pragmatic impossibility to change position might limit speakers' spontaneity. Deliberation might end up being a juxtaposition of prepared statements, no effective interactions taking place. This is problematic for the transformative power of deliberation, as publicity would, in this case, impede self-change.

This final argument can even be pushed further, following Eliasoph (1998), who challenges the assumption that actors necessarily endorse public-spirited discourses in public settings. Her conclusions are, indeed, the exact opposite. She convincingly demonstrates that participants, in the associations she studied, talked in more political and public-minded ways in private contexts than in public ones. Eliasoph depicts a culture of apathy, embedded in everyday life interactions, in which public contexts make political discussion impossible. What is expected of individuals in public settings is not that they talk about the common good, but about 'their kids', 'their interests' or 'their needs'. Citizens interacting in public have to appear – given the dominant cultural norms in American society – to some extent interested. In contrast, in face-to-face talks and private interactions, individuals felt they could freely express their personal feelings and opinions about politics. In opposition to Elster's thesis, public settings, by the type of interactions and expectations they create, make the expression of political and public-interested discourses impossible for ordinary citizens. Publicity does not exist in a social vacuum; it depends on the cultural context in which it is embedded. While deliberative democrats consider theoretically that publicity always pushes people to express concern for the common good, it might depend of the cultural context in which public interactions take place. What matters, therefore, is not publicity *per se* (as institutionalised in procedures) but the social and cultural norms regulating public interaction. Those norms have a powerful impact on the type of behaviour people are able to perform in public. The norms of civic life have therefore to be investigated further to understand when, where and how publicity confines politics and when, on the contrary, it lets it blossom.

The emotional hypothesis: the power of face-to-face interaction

The power of publicity to shape individual behaviour seems to be linked to the emotions felt under the scrutiny of others: shame, guilt and pride might have an important impact on the way citizens behave in the public sphere. Emotions conveyed by face-to-face interaction and mutual presence would be at the root of moral consciousness and civic virtue, as Adam Smith and Rousseau have already argued (Smith 1759; Boltanski 1993; Forman-Barzilai 2005). For Rousseau especially, reason led to self-love and vanity, while pity brought individuals – without reflection – into cooperation with others. Interestingly, contemporary critical and feminist theorists also understand the mobilisation of emotions as a means to undermine the inegalitarian assumptions at the basis of the rationalist conception of deliberation. Understanding deliberation as a process of rational argumentation ruled by the 'forceless force of the better argument' (Habermas 1984) is not neutral they argue; it excludes the most marginal actors from the discussion. Even if a formal equality is granted, some speak more than others, are more convincing, i.e., end up having more power over the group. These are very likely to be well-educated white males (Young 1996; Sanders 1997). They therefore, propose to enlarge the concept of deliberative discussion to emotional types of expression such as 'everyday talk' (Mansbridge 1999b), personal testimonies (Sanders 1997), and storytelling (Polletta 2005), which are supposed to be more inclusive. Emotions, mediated through discourses or felt through direct encounter with others, would shape people's behaviour and consciousness (Young 1990; Phillips 1995).

In some regards, social movements' scholarship offers interesting empirical insights on the transformative potential of emotions. Jasper (1997) stressed how 'moral shocks' – more than rational calculation – could be at the roots of engagement and participation in collective action. Then, such intense experiences might change people's lives. Participation in radical groups and high-cost activism – and the emotions associated with them – seem indeed capable of influencing the trajectories of individuals durably. McAdam shows that participation in the 1964 Mississippi Freedom Summer shaped and radicalised the political values and practices of individuals through what he calls 'a process of personal change and political re-socialisation' (McAdam 1989: 753). The shared emotions felt over a summer changed participants' lives, as they affected their professional, personal and political trajectories. Scholars who studied 'free spaces' (Evans and Boyte 1986; Polletta 1999), these small-scale settings removed from the direct control of dominant groups and organised along informal participatory rules, also defined them as 'schools in citizenship' or 'schools of pluralism' (Sirianni 1993), as individuals learn new civic skills and habits and learn to care about the common good.

The focus on collective action as a source of powerful transformative emotions can also be found in the social capital literature. The theory of social capital can indeed be summed up in a short formula: relationships matter. By making connections with one another, people are able to work together and achieve things that they could not achieve by themselves. Trust, reciprocity and solidarity are supposed to stem from face-to-face interaction (Putnam 1993; 1995). Internally, networks of civic engagement are believed to have positive effects on their members; they socialise them into democratic culture and teach them trust, cooperation and tolerance, making them better citizens. Externally, these networks lubricate institutional settings, making them more legitimate and efficient (Newton 1999; Selle and Stromsnes 1999; Warren 2001). As Robert Putnam puts it, social capital makes democracy work better, by increasing institutional performance. Putnam's central argument on the internal effects of social capital rests on the idea that direct face-to-face interactions are the most direct explanation of the socialising process at work in secondary associations. Norms of trust and reciprocity, co-operation and tolerance only come after a direct encounter with 'the other', i.e., the neighbour or the fellow citizen.[10]

The transformative power of face-to-face interaction has however been challenged from an empirical perspective, psycho-sociological experiments leading, for instance, to contradictory results (Hooghe 2003: 87). The emotional hypothesis is also criticised from a normative point of view. Trust created among a close circle has few chances of generalising to the rest of society. There is no evidence that repeated face-to-face interaction in small networks increases the level of trust in a society (Cohen 1999). It could, on the contrary, fragment it between different small high trusting groups within, while distrusting and fighting with outsiders and strangers. Far from promoting democracy and the common good, highly trusting groups – like the mafia for instance – can promote particularistic demands, driven by the self-interest of the local community (Levi 1996).

Research on civil society organisations tends to show that political participation affects their members. The question then centres on the type of 'good citizen' thus created. Is he a good taxpayer or a contentious and critical citizen marching for global justice (Polletta 1999)? The empirical doubts about Putnam's conclusions lead to some questioning of the assumptions of the emotional hypothesis. Are face-to-face interactions necessary for the development of empathy and reciprocity? Can social norms appearing at the local level be generalised outside the group where they were created? Are the face-to-face contacts taking place in participatory arenas, of the same nature as those happening in secondary associations?

The emotional hypothesis remains, nevertheless, useful for understanding self-change. It might even encompass some of the other approaches presented above. Especially, as we saw, the publicity hypothesis ends up, when fully developed, putting the emphasis on the civilising power of emotions like shame, self-esteem or honour. The emergence of such emotions – and therefore the power of publicity – is inconceivable without direct face-to-face interaction. It is therefore by articulating the publicity and the emotional hypothesis – made conceptually coherent through a pragmatist epistemology and concepts such as the 'grammars of public life' – that the process of self-change will be understood in this book.

Democracy, institutions and citizens' character

Even if offering different accounts of the emergence of civic virtue, these competing approaches share certain features. They are all, for instance, institutionalist perspectives. They consider institutions can shape actors' character and produce certain types of citizens. The focus on the role of institutions is not surprising, especially in the most recent theories, given the centrality of neo-institutionalism in political and social sciences in the last twenty years (Powell and DiMaggio 1991). These perspectives are not, however, merely institutionalist. Most of them try to enter the black box of institutions to describe and analyse the process of self-change. Interestingly, many emphasise the importance of the desire to get others' esteem, consideration and agreement, to avoid shame and get a good reputation, in shaping moral sentiments (Smith), public justifications (Elster), or disinterested behaviours (Bourdieu). Even if giving different explanation of the process going from institution, to shame and reputation (publicity, argumentation, emotions, or interests), the emphasis put on these powerful social mechanisms is notable. Many agree that what affects people's attitudes are the social norms defining what a proper or inappropriate behaviour is in certain public settings. Most of the research until now, however, remained pretty evasive on the production, diffusion and inculcation of these norms in the public sphere. How are the feelings of shame and the desire for reputation developed in public institutions? What does acting as a good citizen mean in public arenas? I argue that the connection between the emotional and publicity hypothesis can best be achieved through the concept of grammar, as it defines the rules of proper behaviour in certain situations, and emphasises the fluidity of actors' competences and identities depending on the setting in which they interact.

One of the main limits of the approaches presented here is indeed their uni-causal understanding of the phenomenon they aim at explaining. They all share a uni-dimensional theory of action – focusing on one factor driving human action, from the maximisation of individual interests, to the will to understand others through communication, or, on the contrary, the mere reproduction of social structures. We will, on the contrary, stress the power of situations – and especially institutional situations – in shaping actors' behaviour. People act differently given the context, the setting, the social field or the institution in which they are involved. Put it roughly, people have different hats. Rather than assuming a priori what people are – thus reifying human behaviour – it seems to fit empirical observations better to note that they partly act differently according to the setting. The focus should, therefore, be put on actions in context and on individuals' competence to act appropriately in certain settings, rather than on identities, preferences or inner selves.

By putting the emphasis on mutual interaction and the power of cultural norms ruling civic life rather than on the actor's motivations, the pragmatist approach appears the most suited for such an endeavour. To construct our own approach of self-change, inspired by the theories and empirical evidence presented previously, we need to investigate the (epistemological) origins of these different approaches of self-change, namely their underlying theories of action. The following part of this chapter offers firstly, a critique of the dominant epistemological paradigms grounding research on the construction of civic competence – and especially of the concept of preference – before presenting the added-value of a pragmatist perspective for the understanding of self-change.

Beyond the cognitive approach of the deliberative paradigm

While most scholars interested in the individual effects of political participation have emphasised that the experience of public engagement could change people, making them better citizens, they remained rather vague on the definition of how citizens were to change. A broad range of concepts has been used to define what should be affected and shaped by the participative process: preferences, interests, opinions, judgements, values, frames, identities, personality or character. By focusing on one of those terms, one takes both an epistemological and ontological position. The concept of 'preference' has however gained prevalence – especially in American political science scholarship – so well so that self-change is mostly understood as preference change. It is therefore necessary to understand the dominant conceptualisation of the process of preference formation at the core of the deliberative paradigm, before arguing for an enlarged approach of civic competence focusing on individuals' practices in the public sphere.

On the origins of political preferences

The dominant approach to citizens' political behaviour focuses on an inner conception of the self. What matters are people's heads, what they 'really' think and feel about politics. The democratic nature of a political regime would stem from the aggregation of individual opinions. The concept of 'preference', imported from rational choice economics, and especially Kenneth Arrow's social choice theory, is at the core of this subjectivist approach. A preference can be defined, following Druckman and Lupia (2000: 2), as 'a comparative evaluation of a set of objects'. Preferences are considered by social choice theorists 'exogenous' or 'given', as they are directly drawn from individuals' interests. More precisely, preferences are derived from a rational calculation that aims at the maximisation of the interests of individuals. As interests are deemed – by rational choice theorists – relatively stable, preferences are stable too.

Then, rational choice theory considers collective choices as a mere process of aggregation of individual pre-set preferences (Downs 1957; Riker 1982). This aggregative conception of collective choice formation was then translated in the field of democratic theory by the elitist school, which considers the aggregation of individual preferences through voting to be the ultimate criterion of a democratic regime (Schumpeter 1942; Lipset 1960; Sartori 1962). Democracy is thus understood as a mechanism to aggregate pre-political preferences. Following a purely liberal conception of democracy, aggregative theorists consider that individual preferences are sacred and beyond the reach of public intervention. Any intrusion of the government within the realm of individual preferences is, therefore, seen as a form of paternalism, illegitimate from a liberal perspective.

Theories of deliberative democracy emerged to answer this dominant paradigm. They generally hint at three illusions at the roots of the aggregative conception of collective choice. First, it is misleading believing preferences are autonomously and freely chosen by individuals. They are produced by a specific economic, social and cultural context. Liberal theorists of democracy are thus accused of being sociologically naive. Preferences are considered by most deliberative democrats to be 'caused' or 'endogenous' (Elster 1986; Sunstein 1991; Offe 1997). Then, as preferences are caused, they can change if the (cultural, political, social, institutional) context itself evolves. Generally, individuals only know partially what they want, and their desires are constantly changing. Information and learning processes can therefore take place and will have an influence on the preferences and desires of individuals. Preferences are thus not pre-political or fixed, but instead, the changing product of social interaction. The goal of deliberation is therefore precisely the formation or discovery of one's preferences (Manin 1987). Finally, the aggregation of pre-set preferences would hinder the promotion of social justice and the common good. With everyone voting according to his/her own preferences, determined by individual interests, collective decisions cannot be oriented towards the common good. As Elster argues (1997: 10–11): 'But the task of politics is not only to eliminate efficiency, but also to create justice – a goal to which the aggregation of pre-political preferences is a quite incongruous means.'

Deliberative theorists address, therefore, both formal and normative criticisms of the social choice paradigm. The way it conceptualises individual preferences is both sociologically reductive – preferences are not fixed in practice – and politically non-desirable, as it might be normatively suitable to question collectively individual opinions. But under which conditions is deliberative democracy more able to answer these shortcomings? Deliberative theorists propose an alternative conception of the formation of political preferences, in which the latter are understood as endogenous and malleable. As long as preferences are shaped by the context in which they are formed, the promotion of an alternative institutional framework – as well as a social and cultural one (Fung 2005) – could favour the promotion of more reflective preferences. Through a process of public discussion and mutual persuasion, individual and collective preferences would change, thus fostering the promotion of the common good. The locus of self-change for deliberative theorist is therefore at the articulation between the inside and the outside, in a neo-institutionalist, even if under-conceptualised, theory of action. Preferences being malleable, a favourable context should be offered to foster the formation of enlightened collective choices. Hence the conceptualisation of a new theory of democracy: the aggregation of pre-set preferences should be replaced by a public deliberation weighting alternative courses of action. In return, the development of deliberative institutions would affect individuals' inner selves, as their (caused or endogenous) preferences would be shaped in the process.

Moving from political preferences to public practices

The critique of social choice theories by deliberative democrats is, in many ways, right to the point. By focusing on the micro-level of preference formation, they allow a further understanding of citizens' political behaviour. The logical link between outcomes (votes and decisions) and institutional context is indeed overlooked by rational choice theorists. Taking preferences as a given – to impede an excessive paternalism – they cannot understand how preferences are produced nor how they can change depending on the institutional context. Assuming a form of reasonable and limited paternalism (Rostboll 2005), deliberative democrats insert the formation of preferences between institutions and outcomes. The logical link thus becomes more complex, as good procedures (deliberative ones) should foster the production of enlightened preferences that will, in return, produce fair decisions. In so doing, the deliberative paradigm embodies an important improvement with regards to the rational choice approach.

The critique of the concept of preference remains, however, incomplete. The logical chain going from institutions to citizens and democratic outcomes has to be elaborated further. I therefore argue for focusing on public practices rather than preferences, for three main reasons. First of all, what matters in a deliberative context are not preferences *per se*, but their public expression through argumentation. And it seems reductive, from a sociological point of view, to assimilate inner preferences with actually voiced arguments. Depending on the situation of interaction, not all preferences are always expressible. Given the social and cultural context, the degree of publicity of the interaction or the composition of the audience, speakers will voice different types of arguments. What remains in the dark – in the back of speakers' minds – has no direct influence on collective decisions. In a deliberative arena, outcomes depend on the arguments that are actually voiced along the debate, not on what people really think (Thompson 2008). Considering public justification as mere forms of hypocrisy or excuses (as Elster 1998), ignores their social efficiency in the given context. Independently of the intentions or motivations of the speakers – strategic use of argumentation or not – if they voice arguments (socially, culturally, etc.) acceptable to others, they will influence collective decisions. Hence the need to focus on arguments and language, expressed in interaction, rather than on preferences.

Then, second, it also seems ontologically flawed to distinguish 'what people really think' from what they say. Accordingly, the only way to scrutinise 'real opinions' would be either to conduct surveys or to use experimental methods, in the search for pure preferences unbiased by the specificity of a context. The recent success of political psychology and the cognitive sciences in deliberative studies directly stems from the ambition to evaluate social phenomena by getting rid of the context (Kuklinski 2001; Sunstein 2003a; Druckman *et al.* 2006). The main risk of experimental methods is that they grant the illusion of accessing pure social phenomena, whereas they just recreate new contexts for the expression of preferences, less public and more artificial than actual deliberative arenas. Answering a survey or participating in a social experiment is always being involved in a certain social transaction. No interaction is more 'real' than any other. It appears however more appealing to study genuine political contexts than artificial ones, as the transferability of the results to other contexts can more easily be controlled than from experimental to real-world settings. Experimental approaches forget deliberative democrats' arguments on the endogenous nature of political preferences. If preferences are caused, it seems indeed necessary to study their real (institutional, but also social and cultural) contexts of production, rather than artificial ones.

Finally, we also need to focus on public practices as civic competence cannot be reduced to holding reflexive preferences, expressed through voting. Due to certain recent political transformations linked to the 'deliberative turn' (Dryzek 2000) the conception of citizenship has evolved. In a word, what is expected from a 'good citizen' nowadays is different from fifty years ago, as voting is no longer the only way individuals can intervene in the public sphere. While voting is still the dominant form of participation in democracies, conventional political participation cannot be reduced to it, and civic competence can even less be counted down to mere knowledge of the political field. The participatory turn (see chapter two) pushes indeed for a greater involvement of citizens in the discussion of public policies. While voting imposed itself in the twentieth century as 'the legitimate if not exclusive form of civic participation' (Déloye and Ihl 2008: 361) – one of the justifications of universal suffrage being precisely the control of the political activities of the masses (Hirschman 1983) – we are now witnessing a re-enlargement of democratic practices, marked by a more direct link between the public sphere and the political system (Habermas 1996a). These different trends result in the multiplication of participation arenas, embodying various ways of expression for citizens. If voting is still the central mode for expressing one's political opinions, it is no longer the only one.

One of the consequences of this 'new spirit of public action' (Blondiaux 2008), is a transformation of what is required or expected from citizens in a democracy. A 'good citizen' should now not only vote in every election, but also participate in a certain number of public arenas.[11] Voting no longer being the only way in which citizens can express their political preferences, it appears necessary to scrutinise the (other) competences required to express oneself successfully in the public sphere. And it appears that public arenas – and especially participatory institutions at the core of this book – demand more competences than the mere knowledge of political programs, ideas and candidates that voting (and the traditional definition of political sophistication) required. In some regards, much more is expected from citizens today than in the past. The range of knowledge and know-how expected from citizens to intervene competently in the public sphere appears much wider than before: speaking in public, generalising one's discourses to target the common good, listening to others, facilitating a discussion, negotiating between conflicting positions, etc.

The recent transformations of democracies, therefore, require enlarging the understanding of civic competence, which can no longer be reduced to its sole cognitive aspect. Political sophistication is only one feature of civic competence, necessarily wider, encompassing all the skills and know-how that will be evoked in this book. By civic competence we shall therefore mean the capacity to master the norms to express oneself successfully in the public sphere. Civic competence is the whole range of cognitive, technical, political, emotional and practical resources held by individuals which allows them to intervene in the public sphere.

Opting for a process and long-term perspective on self-change

The capacity to express oneself – through vote, speech or protest – in the public sphere requires certain skills and competence that some citizen might possess – given their primary socialisation – but that they may also lack and need to acquire through a secondary socialisation process (in which participatory institutions and civil society organisations might play a crucial role). It appears therefore necessary to opt for a process perspective on the construction of civic competence, to understand how, through time, individuals manage (or not) to enlarge their skills and knowledge. Focusing on practices rather than on preferences – thus opting for an enlarged conception of civic competence – leads to scrutinising how interactions evolve through time, how actors learn the norms prevailing in certain public contexts, thus becoming competent enough to play the good citizen.

This approach embodies a radical departure from most empirical assessments of the self-change hypothesis, as they have mostly taken the form of an evaluation of preference change, before and after deliberation (see above). Opting for a process perspective requires scrutinising actors' political and civic behaviour before and after the participatory process as well, but it necessitates a wider perspective on the 'before and after' moments. It should no longer be understood as 'just before' and 'just after' the experience, but as the totality of the experiences lived by actors before the participation process and that might influence the way they live it and interact with others, and long after the experience, too. This perspective allows replacing the question of civic competence in its temporality and context of production, i.e., in the broader trajectory of individuals. The acquisition and mobilisation of new competences cannot be understood unless it is replaced in the broader trajectory of actors, comparing them to their previous experiences, which allows an understanding of how they are assimilated, incorporated or rejected. This has methodological consequences too, as it demands conducting life-history interviews, before and after the process. Such an approach has already received large attention in the field of social movements' scholarship, with the study of militant careers and the biographical consequences of activism (McAdam 1989; Fillieule 2001). It seems that importing such a perspective in the field of deliberative and participatory democracy, and more broadly in the study of the civic consequences of public participation, could be extremely fruitful and innovative. Self-change will therefore be assessed from a praxeologic and process perspective in this book.

How institutions shape practices: fluid identities and the grammars of public life

The move from a purely cognitive perspective – dominant in the empirical studies of deliberation – to a praxeologic one (centred on practices) can be enriched by adopting a pragmatist theory of action. The main contribution of pragmatist social theory lies indeed in the idea that actors and their environment are mutually shaped in interaction. Individual and collective action cannot only be explained by actors' intentions or structural processes; intentions, motives and goals emerge in situations depending on the context in which they are embedded. The focus put by Pragmatists on situations, and the opportunities and constraints they create for actors, indicates that unitarian theories of action miss the heterogeneity of actors' experiences and the conflicting impact they have on their identities.

A pragmatist theory of action: the co-construction of actors and their environment

Pragmatism is an action-centred philosophy that stemmed from a critique of Cartesianism, and more precisely, of the body/mind dualism (Peirce 1934; Joas 1987). The concept of experience – central in the philosophy of Dewey for instance – allows overcoming the distinction between subject and object, organism and environment, as it is along the experience that these two categories constitute themselves as two phases of a same process. Individuals and their environment have, therefore, to be understood as two phases of the same experience. Experiences emerge from the confrontation to a problem, a trouble coming from the environment, a breach in the routine, which can be an event, an object, but also a word, a text or an act. Encountering a problem, actors mobilise their memories of past experiences to solve it. If nothing they know fits, they have to improvise creatively to answer the challenge of the new experience. It is, therefore, by acting that actors become who they are. The experience modifies the organism by teaching it new skills and habits (developed to answer a new experience or challenge), and affects the objective conditions of future experiences by opening up a new environment (Dewey 1938).

The importance of such a conceptualisation for the understanding of collective action phenomena appears immediately, and was to be developed by Dewey in his famous volume of 1927, *The Public and Its Problems*. The major problem of the public that Dewey underlined is – already at the beginning of the twentieth century – its eclipse; what social scientists would probably label apathy today. The public is not considered as a given for Dewey, it has to emerge in the interactions between citizens and their political and social environment. The public, therefore, stems from the confrontation to a common problem or trouble, resulting from the consequences of some social activities (Quéré 2002). Then, it supposes a perception of these consequences and of their potential origins, to be able to formulate a common interest to regulate them. Dewey adds nevertheless a final condition for the emergence of the public – that was largely missing at his time, hence the eclipse – its organisation through (democratic) institutions. The best way the public can acquire the awareness of its common interests is through the direct public experience of local government. Democratic mores or a democratic self, for Dewey, are created in the public experience of self-government, which allows individuals participating in common affairs thus nurturing new skills and habits (Zask 2002).

The recent emergence of participatory institutions invites the investigation of their capacity to facilitate the emergence of a public, and more broadly, the consequences of these new potential experiences on actors. Evaluating how such experiences can shape actors' behaviour requires paying attention to the norms regulating interactions in such public settings.

The grammars of public life

The use of the concept of grammar can be confusing and even misleading. It appears however useful in understanding the way in which participatory experiences can shape citizens' character. In general, a grammar is the study of the use of the rules governing a language. The word 'grammar' has therefore two meanings in its traditional definition: the inner rules themselves (and their use) and our description and study of those rules. The use I make of the word grammar is somehow different from its ordinary meaning. Grammar is understood here as not merely syntactic – as in the ordinary use of the word – but as both syntactic and semantic, the distinction between the two disappearing, or being blurred, by the fact that the meaning of words and actions (their semantic) only appears within a certain set of grammatical syntactic rules. This broadening of the understanding of the word 'grammar' to include meaning mostly comes from Wittgenstein's second philosophy. The concept of grammar becomes with Wittgenstein, a wider and more elusive network of rules determining what linguistic moves are allowed as making sense in a certain community (or game), and what are not. The grammar defines the conditions of felicity of discursive interactions in a certain setting. They are merely discursive norms.

The rules of grammar are not mere technical instructions from on-high for correct usage however; rather, they express the norms for meaningful language. Wittgenstein identified grammar with the 'rules for use of a word' (Wittgenstein 1978: 133). Since he believed that a word's use may generally be equated with its meaning, he held that the rules for use of words which make up grammar 'determine meaning (constitute it)' (1978: 133), that 'the meaning of a sign lies [...] in the rules in accordance with which it is used/in the rules which prescribe its use' (Wittgenstein 2005: 84). The meaning and even the identity of a sign or an object lies in the grammatical rules of the game. As Forster argues:

Just as in a game such as chess the rules prescribe or permit certain moves and proscribe others for the pieces (for example, the bishop may move diagonally but not orthogonally), and thereby also constitute the identity of the pieces required for making particular moves within the game (for example, the bishop in essential part simply *is* the piece subject to the rule just mentioned), likewise grammar prescribes or permits certain linguistic moves and proscribes others [...] and thereby also constitutes the identity of the concepts.

(Forster 2004: 8)

The comparison with a chess game is illuminating, as Wittgenstein maintains, in an important and persistent analogy, that 'grammar [...] has somewhat the same relation to the language as [...] the rules of a game have to the game' (Wittgenstein 1978: 24). Often, I will therefore refer to the grammatical rules (of PB institutions) as the rules of the game (of these institutions); the two terms being used identically. Like the rules of game, grammatical rules are in some sense conventions. From this point on, by 'grammar' I shall mean: the set of rules required from individuals to act (and especially speak) meaningfully in a certain setting (or game). Thus, individuals' (linguistic) behaviours are moves in language games – even if done unintentionally – and get their meaning from the grammar of these games. The concept of grammar is therefore not logocentric, but praxeocentric, it focuses on uses and practices. The analysis starts from the moves – i.e., from uses and practices – to grasp their grammatical conditions of possibility. The investigation does not focus on phenomena, but rather on the (grammatical) conditions of possibility (and of felicity) of phenomena, and mostly of speech acts. In this sense, to paraphrase Wittgenstein, this investigation will be grammatical.

The use of the Wittgenstein concept of grammar can be confusing, but captures some fundamental sociological mechanisms. Especially, it allows understanding, in a linguistic fashion, why and how people follow the grammatical rules of the game (beyond the mere idea, evoked above, that it is a way to maximise self-interest). The grammar is derived from the observation of uses of language by actors in situation. From this perspective, it is the observation of the linguistic competence of actors – made explicit by the symbolic rewards and sanctions attributed by others – that draws the boundaries of the grammar, and in so doing, attributes meaning to individuals' behaviour. Grammars – they are more than one, according to the games, even if in a finite number – are therefore derived from the implicit or explicit consensus between actors on the right and wrong moves in certain situations. As David Bloor underlines:

In following a rule we move automatically from case to case, guided by our instinctive (but socially educated) sense of 'sameness'. Such a sense does not itself suffice to create a standard of right and wrong. It is necessary to introduce a sociological element into the account to explain normativity. Normative standards come from the consensus generated by a number of interactive rule followers, and it is maintained by collectively monitoring, controlling and sanctioning their individual tendencies. Consensus makes norms objective, that is, a source of external and impersonal constraint on the individual.

(Bloor 1997: 17)

In a word, the concept of grammar allows understanding why and how people do what they do. The relationship with pragmatist sociology (Lemieux 2009) – that imported the concept in this field – appears thereafter evident. The concept of grammar allows following the definition given by actors of what is a right or wrong behaviour in a certain situation. Rather than defining externally and theoretically what are the appropriate uses of language – like in the structuralist perspective with Chomsky's concept of generative grammar – the grammatical perspective adopted here allows following the actors in their own definition, as the meaning of their actions is derived from their practices in relation to the ruling grammar of the situation. This investigation is therefore inductive, moving from the observation of the practices to the understanding of their grammatical conditions of possibility. To better understand and specify the concept of grammar, other sociological concepts – from which it is partly inspired – need to be introduced however.

Conceptualising culture: vocabularies, codes and grammars

This grammatical perspective is inspired by, but also differs in some respects, from other major theories of culture, partly derived from a non-mentalist interpretation of Durkheim's concept of 'collective representations'. Culture is often conceptualised as a set of vocabularies and languages through which people explain their actions (Wuthnow 1992; 1998). Robert Bellah and his colleagues describe, for instance, different shared 'languages' of American moral thinking, not as static inner beliefs and values, but as accessible reference points on which people can lean to give meaning to their actions (Bellah *et al*. 1985). Without these shared languages, communication and understanding would merely be impossible they argue, as the meaning of what is said is understood by all the actors through the lenses of the same cultural tools.

As they focus on 'languages' and 'vocabularies', these approaches have mainly based their empirical research on interviews, to scrutinise how actors' discourses are constrained and framed by the cultural standards. This is however problematic for both methodological and theoretical reasons.[12] First, interviews are specific social situations, producing peculiar types of discourses, different from everyday life communicative practices. Interviews therefore cannot teach much on the mobilisation, use and constraining power of these vocabularies.[13] Then, from a theoretical perspective, the connection between discourse and action is under-conceptualised in these approaches. The gap between words and deeds and the creativity of actors in situations makes it problematic to reduce culture to vocabularies. In a word, these approaches overly focus on vocabularies and not enough on discursive and non-discursive practices actualising culture in interaction.

Culture is sometimes also conceptualised as shared codes, especially when dealing with public discourses (Alexander and Smith 1993). Alexander and Smith, reviewing 200 years of legislative crisis in the US, argue that such interactions are constantly ruled by binary civic codes, defining good and bad arguments. Good behaviour is thus defined as being active, critical, autonomous, open, trusting, realistic, altruistic, egalitarian, rational, etc. The codes are the bases on which speakers ground their arguments to justify their positions. The codes never determine a specific position or argument; on the contrary, people tend to share the same codes – even if using them creatively – while differing on opinions and ideologies. Alexander and Smith say little, however, about how codes are used differently across time, and more fundamentally, they offer a binary vision that is probably too reductive to map broader social and political realms than the US Congress. Even if there are dominant or hegemonic cultural codes, this does not mean they do not coexist with more subordinate ones, given the settings, the historical moments and the geographical spaces. A broader picture of the cultural codes or vocabularies is necessary to understand the versatility of actors in situations.

The concept of grammar appears from this perspective more satisfying (Céfaï 2002). Speech norms orienting actors' behaviour can be compared to the constraints grammar imposes on individuals willing to use a specific language. As Eliasoph and Lichterman (2003: 735) emphasised: 'A society's collectively held symbolic system is as binding and real as a language.' In a public setting, actors cannot say everything; or more precisely what is said is evaluated differently given the grammars of public life ruling the interaction. Grammatical rules impose norms of right and proper behaviour, with their specific symbolic sanctions in case of mistake. Grammars define the repertoires of concepts and arguments actors can use appropriately to justify their behaviour in a situation. Actors have to respect a certain number of rules, immanent to the game, to perform meaningful, communicable and accepted activities, allowing cooperation and coordination. Grammars are cultural standards, sedimented practices, discourses and customs, allowing people to interpret the world and make sense of their actions and those of others.

How constraining are grammars for actors however? Do actors just conform to the implicit social rules defining the situation or do they have a margin of interpretation? These questions – central for any theory of action – refer to the relative autonomy between grammars and social performances. They are, in part, answered empirically by the ethnographic research. Some theoretical grounding can nevertheless be drawn. These questions touch indeed on classical sociological debates about role and behaviour: is behaviour a mere alignment on the normative expectations of the role (due to social pressure, structural and cultural constraints)?

Roles are the normative expectations of situationally specific, meaningful behaviour. Grammars therefore define a set of specific roles, to which are attached certain normative expectations, that influence behaviour through sanction and reward mechanisms. As Turner underlined, actors strive to realise 'individual character' but they can only do it by taking:

> partly for granted the culturally defined roles supposedly played by that character: father, businessman, friend, lover, fiancé, trade union leader, farmer, poet, [and] these roles are made up of collective representations shared by actors and audience, who are usually members of the same culture.

> (Turner 1982: 94)

What Turner calls, in a Durkheimian prose 'collective representations' are normative expectations about what role to play, and can be compared to Goffman's concept of 'working consensus'. Participants must have a working consensus about each other's character to interact successfully. This working consensus specifies the qualities that each actor is expected to display (and be sanctioned for not displaying), and therefore, the qualities that each actor is entitled to treat others as having.

Individual and collective actions are not pure alignments on normative expectations however, as there can always be role deviation and role distance. The very fact that deviation is possible indicates that normative expectations do not 'cause' behaviour (Joas 1993: 226–7). Actors do not automatically internalise cultural values and normative expectations; they can always distance themselves from the expected partition, to keep face or to handle situations where conflicting roles are expected (Goffman 1961). Another sign of the autonomy between social performance and the grammatical rules is that actors sometimes fail to achieve what is expected from them (Lemieux 2009). Grammatical mistakes are always possible, and generally sanctioned.

The question the concept of grammar aims at answering is indeed why social performances are successful and why sometimes they fail. This question is at the centre of both Austin pragmatic linguistic and Goffman dramaturgic sociology (Austin 1975; Goffman 1981). Why are arguments sometimes accepted or rejected? In Austin's words, why speech acts succeed or fail? In a word, the concept of grammar allows understanding the conditions of felicity of the interactions. Austin's pragmatic linguistic answers that it all depends on the interactional context. The felicity of social performance would therefore be merely arbitrary. In so doing, Austin – but Goffman as well – cuts off the practice of language and social performance from their grammatical (or cultural) conditions of possibility. He cannot thereafter account for the regularity of interactions in situations. The conditions of felicity of the interactions do not depend only of the situation but on the broader grammatical framework in which they are embedded. It can indeed be considered, in a Wittgensteinian perspective, that a sign's meaning is derived from its relation to other signs in a system of signs relation, i.e., a language. The relation between signs is fixed by conventions – grammars – so that the study of the felicity's conditions must refer to the grammatical rules that render a performative, intelligible and meaningful. This is why Derrida criticised Austin for submerging the contribution of 'cultural scripts' or 'texts' into performative outcomes. Success (as a sign of competence) depends on a certain conventionality, the background grammatical rules from which speech acts derive their meaning (Derrida 1990).

The conditions of possibility and felicity of actions are therefore not arbitrary; they are conventional, being partly inherited from past social and cultural practices forming a grammar. Grammars of public life are embedded in certain historical traditions, constituting repertoires of arguments for the actors. Grammars have an historical trajectory and can therefore be localised in space and time; they do not exist in the air but are the product of past practices and sedimented meanings. These civic traditions are evoked in chapter three, to understand the contemporary ruling grammars of public life, and especially the recent emergence of a participatory grammar. As Alexander and Mast emphasised:

> An accounting of felicity's conditions must attend to the cultural structures that render a performative intelligible, meaningful, and capable of being interpreted as felicitous or infelicitous, in addition to the mode and context in which the performative is enacted.
>
> (Alexander and Mast 2006: 4)

I call these cultural structures, grammars.

Grammatical declinations: emerging group styles

To conclude this theoretical and epistemological map, it is necessary to introduce the concept of 'group style' proposed by Eliasoph and Lichterman, which appears as a declination of the grammatical rules of a certain setting. A group style is indeed: 'a recurrent pattern of interaction that arises from a group's shared assumptions about what constitutes good or adequate participation in the group setting' (Eliasoph and Lichterman 2003: 737). Introducing this concept allows avoiding taking an overly atomistic perspective on self-change, to concentrate on the collective definition of good membership and competent citizenship. If I followed and observed individuals acting together in public settings, their interactions made sense within the framework of certain groups. Studying participatory institutions, I observed their members forming groups, what I call 'groups of good citizens', who embody the good and integrated members – and therefore the leaders – of these institutions. The group style therefore corresponds to the local (successful) enactment and declination of the grammar of public life. Given the past local civic practices, the biographies of the initiators of the groups and the type of members interacting, the group is able to filter the grammar of public life, or more precisely, to give it a coherent and relevant meaning in this particular setting.[14] From this perspective, the concept of group style is proximate to that of 'sub-culture' (Fine and Kleinman 1979; Hedbige 1979), 'idioculture' (Fine 1979) or 'local political culture'. Three dimensions appear crucial in determining the group styles that each institutional setting developed: (1) the symbolic boundaries of the group (Lamont and Fournier 1992), i.e., the way it relates to the wider world, thus defining an 'us' and a 'them'; (2) the speech norms, defining what proper arguments and behaviours are, thus defining the role of 'good citizen'; (3) the bonds among the members of the group (are they more or less cooperative or contentious, hierarchical or horizontal, etc.), i.e., the mutual obligations actors give to one another.

A limit of the overall brilliant theoretical framework presented by Eliasoph and Lichterman is that they do not analyse explicitly how people get to know the style and the rules of the game. As an implicit cultural code, the style should naturally be recognised as such by the actors, who could therefore automatically adopt the appropriate behaviour. It appears however, that actors do not necessarily fit with the style; they have to learn it, to adapt and eventually to change, i.e., to negotiate their position in the group. While Eliasoph and Lichterman reject a consensual conception of cultural structures, they overlook the process of construction of the groups they study, while it might be of interest understanding where the style comes from and how people learn to respect it (especially when it comes to speech norms). The study of the construction of the group of good citizens, of how new-comers are integrated, through trial and errors, grammatical mistakes, sanctions or symbolic rewards, but also of how participants might get (self-)excluded, should be the first object of attention for sociologists interested in the meaning and sustaining of civic life. Opting for a process analysis, seeing how groups are formed, members integrated or rejected, allows for a better understanding of the rules of game, as well as assessing the consequences of civic engagement on participants. The process of self-change will therefore be understood as the progressive integration into the group of good citizens and the learning of the grammatical rules of the institutions studied. Opting for a process perspective on the construction of the groups (of good citizens) – and their styles – allows an understanding of the power and domination mechanisms at stake within groups as well. Some members might be more integrated than others, some become leaders and have the power to recall the rules and sanction the deviations; others, on the contrary, remain outsiders or are even expelled. By replacing the grammatical approach – and its group style declination – in a process perspective, one is, therefore, better equipped to both understand self-change and the domination mechanisms at works.

A methodological consequence: the necessity of political ethnography

The direct consequence of the theoretical and epistemological arguments present-ed here is reflected in the methodological choice to opt for ethnographic research, mostly based on the observation of the interactions among citizens within partici-patory institutions. The ways in which the grammatical rules of the game appear to the researcher are indeed double: they are either explicitly voiced by the actors, as positive rules, or they are recalled and redefined in situations of crisis, when actors disagree on the rules or when some of them do not respect them (Lemieux 2009). Direct observation within the institutions over a long period of time was therefore indispensable. It was complemented with life-history interviews with participants to understand how their participatory experience took place in their broader civic and personal trajectory, and potentially affected them (see Appendix). Before un-derstanding who these characters are, a look at the central setting of this investiga-tion – participatory budgeting institutions – is necessary, and follows in chapter two.

NOTES

1   Arendt 1995: 146. Author's translation.

2   More broadly, four justifications of citizen participation can be severed out in the literature. (1) An educative justification – mostly developed by civic humanist and neo-aristotelian philosophers like Pateman (1970) or Barber (1984) – makes of participation an end in itself, its aim being the nurturing of good citizens and the accomplishment of human nature; (2) A functional justification put the emphasis on the increased rationality of the decisions arrived at after a large process of civic engagement; (3) An equalitarian frame, inspired by critical theory, asserts that the involvement of actors, generally excluded from public decision-making, should foster social justice by promoting different decisions than those generally enacted by political elites; (4) Finally, a symbolic justification – directly linked to the deliberative democracy paradigm – stresses that civic engagement increases the legitimacy of public decisions.

3   A deliberative poll is a social-scientific experiment, gathering a representative sample of a few hundred people over a weekend, during which participants are offered information before discussing a particular policy issue. The goal of this experimental method is: 'to make the participants more like ideal citizens, at least with respect to the topics under discussion'. (Fishkin, Luskin and Jowell 2002: 460)

4   For other empirical evidence on preference change from deliberation, see Mayer, de Vries and Geurts 1995; Joss 1995; Pelletier et al. 1999; Jacobs et al. 2009.

5   Rawls makes a similar argument (1971: 358–9): 'We normally assume that an ideally conducted discussion among many persons is more likely to arrive at the correct conclusion than the deliberations of any one of them by himself. [...] No one of them knows everything the others know, or can make all the same inferences that they can draw in concert. Discussion is a way of combining information and enlarging the range of arguments.'

6   Even if it is not directly linked to political participation phenomena, public opinion research has proved quite convincingly that information input has considerable effect on policy preferences and fosters better-considered opinions. For instance, as Lindeman argues (2002: 203): 'In a 1995 survey, the average respondent overestimated the proportion of the U.S. budget devoted to foreign aid by 15 percent, once they were supplied with the correct proportion (1% of the federal budget) the percentage who agreed that "too much is spent on foreign aid" dropped from 75% to 18%.'

7   As Claus Offe underlines, Tocqueville had an implicit institutionalist perspective, in which democratic institutions were to shape citizens' democratic character (Offe 2006). Tocqueville probably romanticised and idealised the aims and practices of the American townships however (Gannette 2003).

8   For an interesting analysis of Bourdieu's concept of 'corporatism of universality' in relation to the notion of public space see Sintomer 1996; 1998.

9   This question is pivotal, as Elster demonstrates that the distinction between communicative and strategic actions built by Habermas does not stand, since communication can, under the appearances of a discourse of the common good, aim at the maximisation of private interests. For further developments on this question see Austin Smith, 1990.

10 This is why Putnam excludes many political organisations, tertiary associations and new social movements from his study, considering them as mere 'cheque-book organisations' in which membership amounts to financial contribution and not to direct physical interactions among the participants. This type of membership could not have any internal effects on participants according to him. Putnam's argument, that non-political associations (such as football clubs or choirs) would create 'better citizens' than political and contentious ones, was however widely discussed (Foley, Edwards and Diani 2001).

11 This transformation is part of the move from a 'dutiful citizenship', requiring obeying the law, not evading taxes and voting in elections, to an 'engaged citizenship' implying a more active participation of the citizenry in the public sphere. See Dalton 2008.

12 These criticisms are mostly inspired by Eliasoph and Lichterman 2003: 742–744.

13 While interviews were conducted in this research, they focus on the trajectory and past civic practices of actors, not on their opinions and values. The analysis of discursive interactions and grammars of public life is in contrast derived from the direct observation of public assemblies.

14 From this perspective, each case-study of this research has its own style (see chapters two and three), respecting the participatory grammar, but adapting it to the local configuration of the city. From now on, I will use the terms 'group style' and 'participatory budget (PB) style' as synonymous, as the groups dealt with in the research are PB groups. In general, PBs are constituted of different neighbourhood assemblies, in which groups of good citizens emerge. It is considered however that within the same city, given the relative cultural homogeneity among the zones, all neighbourhood assemblies (and groups of good citizens) share the same style, with minor variations however.

chapter two | power to the people? three participatory budget experiences in europe

...the expectation deriving from a discourse-centred theoretical approach, that rational results will obtain, is based on the interplay between a constitutionally instituted formation of the political will and the spontaneous flow of communication unsubverted by power, within a public sphere that is not geared toward decision making but toward discovery and problem resolution and that in this sense is *nonorganized*. If there still is to be a realistic application of the idea of sovereignty of the people to highly complex societies, it must be uncoupled from the concrete understanding of its embodiment in physically present, participating, and jointly deciding members of a collectivity. There may actually be circumstances under which a direct widening of the formal opportunities for participation and involvement in decision making only intensifies 'generalized particularism'...

(Habermas 1992: 451)

Is participatory democracy a fraud? While its promoters constantly refer to Jürgen Habermas' democratic theory, it seems that the latter explicitly rejects the insti-tutionalisation of his communicational theory in organised public bodies open to the participation of all. According to Habermas, participatory democracy could only foster the development of a 'generalised particularism'. Is the German social theorist right and participatory democracy doomed to fail? Despite these theoreti-cal doubts, participatory democracy has mushroomed in the last two decades in Europe and the rest the world. Why did this happen despite the risks of the de-velopment of parochialism it might imply? Why are such hopes expressed in the capacity of such institutionalised forms of participation to deepen democracy? Conversely, how can civic competence be nurtured if citizens are not given the opportunity to participate? If participation is not organised and is disconnected from administrative power, who will be ready to commit his/her time and energy to exchange mere words?

Contrary to Habermas' arguments evoked above – and in keeping with many social theorists from Jane Mansbridge to Archon Fung and Iris Marion Young – I consider that participatory democractic institutions, embodying organised forms of popular sovereignty, could potentially be good training grounds for citizens. The 'school of democracy' discourse is indeed granted specific value among the justifications of participatory democracy. Both official reports and political dis-courses repeatedly praise the virtues of public participation and its ability to nur-ture a more competent, public-spirited and active citizenship. This chapter aims at offering a synthetic panorama of the width and depth of the participatory democracy phenomenon in Europe. A special emphasis is put on municipal participatory budgeting institutions, as they constitute the main object of study of this research.

Participatory democracy owes indeed a lot to participatory budgeting. It developed and became popular largely due to the audience given to the Porto Alegre experience, since the end of the 1990s. Labelled 'good governance practice' by the World Bank, citizen participation in budgetary decision-making processes has, since then, spread throughout the world. In Brazil, about 200 experiences at communal or regional level are nowadays defined as 'participatory budgets'. In the rest of Latin America, from Argentina to Ecuador and Peru, hundreds of municipalities have introduced citizen participation mechanisms in their budget decision-making processes (Allegretti 2010). Popularised by the 'No Global movement', and especially by the influential leftist magazine *Le Monde Diplomatique,* participatory budgets have been imported into Europe by a few adventurous political and civil society actors, in an uncommon 'return of the Caravels' (Allegretti and Herzberg 2005), in which Latin America advises Europe on how to renovate its democracies.

Due to its popularity and rapid development, the term 'participatory budget' covers a variety of procedural designs and civic practices. If one follows actors' definitions, a participatory budget can be either a mere system of neighbourhood funds, implying the discussion of a few thousands Euros, or in contrast, a very ambitious and sophisticated procedural design based on the city-wide discussion of budget priorities. It is, therefore, difficult to define participatory budget objectively – following a set of criteria – as many of the experiences labelled as such by the actors would thus be excluded from the picture. A participatory budget is therefore defined *a minima*, as the involvement of citizens in the budgetary decisions of a public body and labelled as such by the actors. The aim of this chapter is to offer a synthetic presentation and analysis of the development of municipal participatory budgets in Europe.

Explaining the Deliberative Turn in Public Policies

Contemporary democracies are at a turning point: facing a tremendous challenge in terms of legitimacy with the growing indifference, or worst, hostility of the citizenry. They have been implementing a large range of democratic innovations in the last twenty years, all aimed at involving citizens more directly in the discussion of public policies. Public engagement seems indeed to be on everyone's lips; politicians, public officials, association leaders are all constantly praising and pushing forward the increasing implications of 'lay citizens' in the discussion of public policies. While representative government is based, on the contrary, on the domestication of the masses (Manin 1997), they are now required to participate more actively than just casting a ballot every five years. Has the spirit of representative government changed (Blondiaux 2008)? Have we entered a 'democracy of the public' (Manin 1997)? More precisely, why has participatory democracy and deliberative devices developed so widely, in Europe and beyond, in the last twenty years?

It seems that public participation can grant a new legitimacy to public policies. The direct involvement of civil society and non-professional actors could impede protest and create consensual and efficient public decisions. But is this all? Is the instrumental interpretation – the legitimation of public policies – enough to understand the spread of participatory democracy? Four reasons explaining the recent development of participatory democracy are emphasised below. First, some structural transformations of democracy can be observed, marked by a crisis of expertise and a call for the growing inclusion of the public in decision-making processes. Second, these transformations create new political opportunities, especially for marginalised political actors, who therefore invest in participatory democracy. Third the role of social movements, pressuring for greater democracy and transparency should also be highlighted. Finally, the role of actor networks and transfers of experience, that appeared particularly important in the spread of participatory budgeting, is stressed.

The participatory requirement: a new dominant narrative

Laws and official reports related to urban policies and devolution are full of references to public participation. The increased powers of local institutions have to go along with the involvement of both associations and lay citizens in the making of public policies. Words such as 'participation', 'dialogue', 'consultation', and 'partnership' are mushrooming across official documents. All these concepts, even though ambiguous and unclear, are indeed granted strong symbolic power (Blondiaux 2008). The World Bank, the OECD, the Council of Europe and most international organisations are therefore constantly praising the involvement of citizens in local decision-making processes (Narayan 1999; OECD 2001; Schmitter and Trechsel 2004; Caddy and Peixoto 2006).

From the analysis of official reports and of the discursive formulation of public laws, three justifications of citizen participation have been distinguished, differently mobilised in all European countries (Bacqué and Sintomer 1999; Blondiaux 2005; Sintomer and Maillard 2007): (1) functional or managerial objectives – stressing the idea that public participation could improve public management; (2) a social justification, arguing that public participation could help to reconstruct trust and social bonds among neighbours, and between politicians and citizens; and (3) a political ambition, emphasising that public participation can help to solve the crisis of representative government and potentially deepen democracy (Fung and Wright 2003).

These justifications, and more broadly the development of participatory democracy in the last decade, can be attributed to a radical transformation of the modes of legitimating public-policy decisions in western democracies. Scientific expertise, that used to be the basis of decision-makers, has been criticised for being unable to offer more than uncertain answers to crucial technical problems, and more radically, the faith in science and progress has largely declined (Latour 1993). We have, therefore, moved from a paradigm of rationality to a model of reflexivity, where reason is seen as provisional and unstable (Habermas 1971; Goodin 2003). Public decisions in a context of uncertainty are necessarily iterative – i.e., never definitive – understood as a process of discussion implying a variety of actors, whose rationality is in conflict or debate (Callon, Lascoumes and Barthe 2009; Cantelli *et al.* 2006). Reflexive public action therefore takes for granted the end of the 'monopole of reason' held by scientists and official experts. A variety of actors can therefore claim to have their say in public decision-making processes in the name of their lay knowledge or counter-expertise (Fischer 2000).

Excluded for a long time from decision centres for being widely ignorant, citizens are now encouraged to participate. To reach both rational and legitimate decisions the inclusion of a variety of perspectives and potential expertises appears necessary. With the emergence of a risk society, the borders between science and politics have therefore become more porous, traditional and new forms of expertise appear as complementary and potentially able of mutual hybridisation (Beck 1992). This has opened the door to a more participatory conception of the decision-making processes.

Social movements fighting for democracy

The questioning of rationality and expertise has resulted in a growing fragmentation of public decision processes, given the range of actors to be included and the diversity of information to be discussed (Fisher 2000). This increased complexity translated in a lack of transparency: decisions no longer being taken by the one and sole actor; accountability became more blurred. This lack of transparency and accountability – at all levels of government – has been criticised by a wide range of social movements and civil society actors. This criticism has, for instance, been one of the driving forces of the anti-globalisation movements that spread at the end of the 1990s (Sommier 2001; Norris 2002; Polletta 2002; Della Porta *et al.* 2006).

One of the common hypotheses about the development of participatory democracy in Europe, therefore, stresses the role of the claims and criticisms of social movements. In this regard, the role of urban social movements seems to have been decisive in the development of participatory democracy in the last thirty years (Castells 1983). In the US, the theme of participatory democracy had already been fashionable from the beginning of the 1960s on American campuses (Polletta 2002). In contrast, in Europe, it mainly developed after 1968 (Blatrix 2000), the first experiences of urban democracy being pushed forward by urban social movements, and some reformist political circles (for instance, around the PSU and the CFDT in France) (Bacqué and Sintomer 2011; Lefebvre 2011). This gave rise to a wealth of participatory experiences in the 1970s (Hazfeld 2006), that influenced French urban policies (the *Politique de la ville* especially) and that put forward the need for increased participation.

In many ways, participatory democracy was put back on the agenda at the end of the Millennium by personalities and association leaders who were already active in the urban social movements of the 1970s. The re-emergence of democracy as a central claim of the social movements at the end of the 1990s, cannot be understood without taking into account the ideological revolution created by the fall of the Berlin Wall and the loss of legitimacy of the communist critique, which was dominant at the time. The relegation of the 'materialist' – or socio-economic –

critique, which had lost its legitimacy with the failure of real socialism and the absence of a clear economic alternative, opened the door to more qualitative claims linked to participation. New social movements focused on 'the failures' of representative government, and the will to deepen democracy. In a word, they moved from a critique of capitalism to a critique of democracy. The anti-globalisation movement made of Porto Alegre one of the symbols of the possible alternatives to representative government. The Brazilian city was chosen as the host of the World Social Forum, from 2001 onwards, and labelled 'the capital of democracy'. Thus, the participatory budgeting of Porto Alegre gained worldwide publicity and was understood by many European activists as a radical and constructive alternative to be experimented elsewhere.

A political opportunity for marginalised political actors

The development of participatory democracy, and especially of PB, in Europe cannot be understood however as a bottom-up process, stemming from social movements and ratified by local politicians. Participatory democracy has indeed been mostly a top-down process in Europe, coming from elected officials. As with the Porto Alegre PB, created by the Workers Party (PT) in close co-operation with community organisations, most cases of participatory budgeting in Europe have been incepted by political parties, mostly from the left (Sintomer, Herzberg and Röcke 2008b).

The main reason why leftist political parties – and especially Communist or former Communist parties that are over-represented in this process – focused on participatory democracy in Europe stems from the political opportunity structure they faced at the time. Communist parties underwent an important ideological and political crisis in the 1990s (decline of electoral results and of the number of militants); participatory democracy was thus seen as an opportunity to rebuild a positive and valued identity, far from the archaic image often ascribed to them (Font 2001; Nez and Talpin 2010). Participatory democracy appeared both modern and innovative. It also allowed the Communists to (re)build political alliances with the social movements. By integrating some of their claims, and sometimes even some of their members, they tried to find a new political dynamic.

Finally, participatory democracy has also been part of the urban renewal programmes born at the end of the 1980s that, from the beginning, had the ambition to solve the social problems that deprived peripheral neighbourhoods faced. Communist parties saw in participatory budgets a way of stopping the decline of municipal communism (Bacqué and Sintomer 2001) and of renewing contacts with the popular classes by proposing alternative modes of political and social integration. Beyond Communist parties, it can be noticed that participatory democracy has been put forward by politicians at the margins of their own organisations, looking for new ways of distinguishing themselves, like Ségolène Royal in France (Talpin and Sintomer, 2011).

The emergence of participatory discourses and institutions was thus made possible by the evolution of the political opportunity structure in the 1990s. More than just an answer to 'the crisis of representative government', citizen participation was a new political product, from which political gains were extractable.

Transfers of experiences and networks of actors

Finally, transfers of experiences and networks of actors played a crucial role in the development of participatory democracy and especially of PBs in Europe. The number of PBs has, for instance, largely been boosted after the first World Social Forum held in Porto Alegre in 2001 (Sintomer, Herzberg and Röcke 2008a). The PB experience was publicised, and many actors (local politicians, civil servants or social movement activists) who had made the trip to Brazil came back to Europe with the idea to implement such institutions in their own territories. Politicians from Seville and Rome travelled to Porto Alegre, just like Ségolène Royal and her advisors (Sintomer, Herzberg and Röcke 2008b). In Europe itself, networks of PB activists and experts emerged, and have played an important role in both replicating the Porto Alegre model and adapting it to national and local contexts. In France, associations like 'Démocratiser Radicalement la Démocratie' [Democratising radically democracy], 'Adels', 'Capacitation' or ATTAC around *Le Monde Diplomatique*, played a crucial role in the popularisation of the PB model, at least among the left. Similarly, in Italy, a magazine like *Carta*, or associations like the 'Nuovo Municipio', in close cooperation with committed scholars like Giovanni Allegretti, played an important role in the recent spread of PBs at the local level (Sintomer and Allegretti 2009). In Spain, associations like ATTAC, and intellectuals like Tomas Villasante, and his method, 'social participatory investigation', played a pivotal role in the creation and reproduction of many PBs, like in Cordoba, Rubi or Seville.

At the end of the 1990s there were therefore favourable structural conditions in Europe for the development of participatory institutions, such as the crisis of science and rationality that opened up to a pluralisation of expertise, as well as the growing defiance towards distant politicians. From this favourable ground, participatory budgets emerged as the result of both the endogeneisation of social movement critiques by the political system and the import and transfers of experiences allowed by some highly connected actors. This has also given rise to important legislative evolutions, from which a wide range of local democratic innovative institutions have stemmed.

Innovative democratic institutions in Europe

Even if new laws have been passed to foster citizen participation since the beginning of the 1990s, it has often been at the margins of the law that innovative democratic institutions developed in Europe. A special focus is put on the French, Spanish and Italian cases, i.e., the three countries at the centre of this book, in which avant-garde politicians have often spurred the development of participatory democracy.

Participatory democracy emerging at the margins of the law

Most participatory experiences have emerged at the margins of the law, from the political will of committed elected officials and social scientists. Participatory democracy is the answer offered by some adventurous politicians to the critique of expertise and technocratic policy-making, as well as the crisis of legitimacy of representative government. Innovative institutions were set up to increase public policy efficiency, to reinforce social cohesion and to deepen democracy, but also to gain legitimacy – and thus be re-elected. From this perspective, political will, more than a constraining legal framework, explains the development of participatory democracy. The emergence of innovative democratic institutions did not occur in a legal vacuum however. The bills and laws relating to citizen participation, passed in a large range of European countries, also played an important role in stimulating the development of citizen participation. As participatory democracy developed above all at the local level, a special emphasis is put on the legal and administrative framework of local government in Europe, whose increased autonomy created renewed opportunities for citizen participation.

'Politique de la ville' and 'proximity democracy' in France

France relied a lot on legislation to foster public participation, embodied especially in the 'Proximity Democracy' bill, passed in 2002. The first direct reference to citizen participation in French law appeared in 1977, however, with the 'Housing and Social Life' (*Habitat et Vie Sociale*) programme, emphasising the necessity to support urban projects promoting citizen participation.[1] Participation was also encouraged in the first programmes of the 'Politique de la ville', like the 'Social Development of Neighbourhoods', stressing the role of civic engagement in the improvement of the quality of life in deprived suburbs. The spirit of French urban rehabilitation policies is thus full of references to public participation. After ten years of experiments, the City Orientation Act (13.07.1991) stated the necessity to involve citizen voices before any public action at local level, that substantially affects their lives, was taken. Laws related to decentralisation and local democracy all stress, as well, the need to inform and consult citizens on the decisions of the communes (Marcou 1999: 21–2).[2] This legal framework did not result in many institutional or legislative innovations however, apart from the possibility for mayors to organise consultative local referendums (Paoletti 2007).

An innovation appeared in 1995, namely 'public debates', created by the Barnier Law related to environmental planning. The consultation of all relevant actors thus became compulsory before any decision on important planning projects with potential impact on the environment. Public debates have been organised on a variety of issues such as high-speed train lines, new highways or nuclear power plants. An independent administrative body, the 'National Commission of Public Debate' (CNDP) has also been created to organise and coordinate public debates on large planning projects. Public debates appeared as a way to avoid the frequent conflicts arising with planning projects, and to convert tensions into constructive collective discussions.

A new innovation appeared in 2002, with the Law on 'Proximity Democracy', which made the creation of neighbourhood councils compulsory for cities over 80,000 inhabitants and reinforced the powers and independence of the CNDP. Neighbourhood councils already existed in dozens of cities before 2002 however, created at the margins of the law by innovative mayors (Bacqué and Sintomer 1999; Blondiaux and Lévêque 1999). Similarly, the French cases of participatory budgeting, that started to emerge at the end of the 1990s, were set up due to political will much more than legislation, as no bill or law evoked the involvement of citizens in the financial decisions of public administration.

Finally, participatory democracy has also reached the centre stage of French political debate during the 2007 presidential campaign. After having implemented participatory budgeting in high-schools and other deliberative devices in her Region (Sintomer, Röcke and Talpin 2009; Talpin and Sintomer 2011) – without any legal incentive to do so – the Socialist candidate, Segolène Royal put 'participatory democracy' at the centre of her campaign. She organised hundreds of 'participatory debates', supposedly to draft her programme, and put forward the idea of developing citizen juries, which created a national controversy at the time (Sintomer 2007). She also proposed to pass a law generalising PBs in cities. Her loss in the presidential run marked, however, a pause in the development of participatory democracy in France.

Italy: Modernising the administration through citizen participation

The legislative framework in France had, therefore, to evolve a great deal in the past fifteen years to allow for the emergence of participatory institutions, even if the most innovative ones appeared at the margins of the law. The situation is somewhat similar in Italy, as the main references to civic engagement only appeared at the beginning of the 1990s. From the 1960s onwards, however, experiences of resident participation at local level mushroomed in the newly created circumscriptions and neighbourhoods. These informal experiences were institutionalised in the 1970s with the creation of neighbourhood councils, in the framework of the Decentralisation Law No. 278 of 1976, which also brought the regionalisation of the country. The right to popular initiative was then introduced, but the quorum of signatures to be collected was so high that, in the end, few grassroot law initiatives were presented.[3] Despite this first wave of decentralisation in the 1970s, Italian local government remained weak in the main (Gelli and Pinson 2001; Laughlin 2004) being firstly understood – until the 1990s – as juridical bodies in charge of the decentralised administrative functions of the state. Article 6 of Law n.142 of 1990, emphasised in its first paragraph that 'municipalities should promote institutions which allow the *participation of citizens* to local administration' (Pasquier and Pinson 2004). This law emphasised the involvement of citizens in local administrations and allowed further co-operation between neighbourhood councils, committees and local administrations (Sabbioni 1999). The Consolidated Act for Local Authorities, voted in 2000, and the reform of the Title V of the Constitution in 2001 restated the autonomy of local government and insisted on the necessary 'communication' between citizens and administration and on the development of 'co-decision' mechanisms. The Italian government also implemented an important urban renewal policy, comparable in its scope to those of France and the UK, involving some participation of residents. Neighbourhood contracts (*Contratti di Quartiere*) are aimed in particular at involving residents in the design of deprived neighbourhood renewal programmes (Pasquier and Pinson 2004).

Spain: Public participation in the wake of the country's democratisation

The development of Spanish experiences of public participation occurred mostly at the margins of the law. Apart from Article 69.1 of the 1985 LRBRL – the basic law regulating Spanish communes' competences – that formally encouraged local governments to develop citizen participation mechanisms, there was no legal framework for the development of citizen participation until the turn of the millennium. At the end of the 1980s (especially between 1987 and 1991), seventy per cent of municipalities with over 100,000 inhabitants had adopted 'Charters of Citizen Participation' (Font 2001). Many thus created 'Consultative or Thematic Councils', understood as discussion platforms between the municipality and local associations. Citizen participation mostly developed in Spain in the form of associative democracy; hence the conflicts that emerged when some cities started to create participatory budgets at the turn of the Millennium, directly oriented towards lay citizens. Before that, some cities had created neighbourhood or district councils, even though territorial assemblies remained less developed than thematic ones.

A decisive step was taken in 2003, with Law 57/2003 for the modernisation of local government (LMMGL), which updated and gave legal existence to many of the Spanish participative mechanisms.[4] The two main results of this law were the reinforcement of municipal executive power (the mayor and the municipal council) and the institutionalisation of participatory mechanisms. The LMMGL restated the participatory requirement for local governments, emphasising information of the citizenry through new information and communication technologies and creating local popular initiative referendums.[5] Finally, like in France, this law encouraged citizen participation in urban and strategic planning projects, with the creation of a 'social council of the city' with consultative powers on strategic projects and open to civil society actors. The innovations brought by the LMMGL were considered by some as 'revolutionary', implying a large reorganisation of Spanish local governments and fostering citizen participation (Rodriguez Alvarez 2005). It has to be stressed, nevertheless, that the most innovative participatory experiences – citizen juries (Font and Blanco 2007), community planning and participatory budgets – were not encouraged or regulated by the law, they emerged in its margins, stemming from the political will of committed local representatives.

Even if most European countries passed laws promoting citizen participation in local government and urban planning projects, this legal framework mostly created guidelines, few compulsory participatory mechanisms being created apart from neighbourhood councils and public debates in France and popular initiative referendums in Spain. The most innovative and empowered cases of participatory democracy emerged at the margins of law, in the space of some autonomy allowed for mayors or regional councillors. Truly convinced of the virtues of participatory democracy or in search of an increased legitimacy through a new form of local governance, many politicians decided to set up innovative democratic institutions aimed at including the public in the construction of public policy. Despite heterogeneous legislative dispositions across European countries, most of them developed rather similar innovative democratic institutions, which constitute the core of participatory democracy.

A diversity of participatory institutions across Europe

The transformation of public governance in the last decades led politicians and public officials to innovate by creating new bodies aimed at including the public. A wide of range of innovative democratic institutions have therefore mushroomed all over Europe. The cases presented here are top-down ones, institutions created by the state to involve citizens more directly in the policy process. Bottom-up experiences are, in some regards, more radical than the urban democratic cases studied here, but also, being less institutionalised, they are less empowered. The cases of participatory democracy analysed here are therefore, mostly experiences in which citizens have their say – from mere consultation to co-decision – in the policy process.[6]

Public hearings and inquiries

Public hearings and inquiries aim at including the public in important development plans such as pigsties, town planning documents, highways, nuclear plants or airport building. They can be considered as the first institutionalised participatory technique, as public inquiries were created in France in 1810 by Napoleon, developed after 1834 under the Monarchy of July, and were democratised after 1983, when the Bouchardeau Law increased the inclusiveness of the procedure, and included environmental concerns in the evaluation of the social desirability of public planning projects (Blatrix 1998). Each year, from 10,000 to 20,000 public inquiries and debates are, for instance, conducted in France. They are also very common in the US, with tens of thousands running every year (Cole and Caputo 1984; Checkoway 1986). They are consultative processes, having in general a limited impact. Piechaczyk shows for instance that in the French case, out of 9,241 inquiries, the secretaries have only given negative recommendations – impeding the realisation of a project – in 5.1 per cent of the cases (Piechaczyk 1997). These negative recommendations generally stem from technical, rather than political, concerns (Fiorino 1990: 230; Callon, Lascoumes and Barthe 2009). Public inquiries are scheduled too late in the decision-making process to stop the projects, even when the public mobilise for it (Blatrix 1998; 2003). In the end, the few empirical analyses on public hearings conclude they have little impact on decisions and that participants' policy choices are hardly affected and little enlightened, given the strength of their initial preferences (Cole and Caputo 1984; Blondiaux and Michel 2007).

Citizen juries, consensus conferences and planning cells: the rise of mini-publics

Citizen juries, consensus conferences and planning cells gather randomly selected citizens to recommend a set of solutions on a technical policy-issue after receiving information from experts. Citizen juries appeared in the midst of the 1970s in the United States, based on an idea of Ned Crosby, and sponsored by the Jefferson Centre. In Europe, the model of the citizen jury has also been highly influenced by the German experiment of the 'Planning Cell', which appeared in 1969, from an idea of Peter Dienel (Dienel 1997). Consensus conferences appeared in Denmark at the end of the 1980s, from an initiative of the Danish Board of Technology, and then spread all over Europe.[7] Their procedural organisation is broadly the same, except that Planning Cells assemble from twenty-five to fifty members, who are then subdivided into groups of five, whereas citizen juries are composed of only one discussion group of about twelve people. Mini-publics are generally organised by public institutions (municipal or regional councils, but sometimes central governments as well) trying to solve technical policy issues such as health policies, GMOs (Boy, Donnet Kamel and Roqueplo 2000), environmental problems or urban planning (Crosby 1995; Coote and Lenaghan 1997; Blanco 2001; Delap 2001; Koehl and Sintomer 2002; Goodin and Niemeyer 2003; Font and Blanco 2007).

The main innovation of mini-publics comes from the use of random selection in the public sphere; the panel thus created, supposedly mirroring the diversity of the wider population. The aim is not to create a statistically representative sample, but to ensure that all viewpoints on an issue are represented given the diversity of the jury (Sintomer 2007). This especially allows the participation of citizens traditionally excluded from public arenas. Citizen juries are also praised for the quality of the deliberative sequences they allow. The small size of the jury should favour listening, mutual respect and understanding (Smith and Wales 2002: 164–6). Citizen juries and consensus conferences are generally divided into an information phase, in which citizens receive arguments and data from a plurality of experts, and a discussion phase, in which the panel deliberate to reach a consensus on a recommendation. Even if they make non-binding recommendations, there is a strong incentive for the representatives to follow the jury's advice, or at least to justify their refusal, given the publicity of the process. Some citizens' juries have been, however, more empowered than others. In Berlin for instance, each jury was provided with a 500,000 Euros budget to finance local social, cultural or development projects. They had, therefore, direct decision-making power, much more than common citizen juries (Koehl and Sintomer 2002).

Quantitative analyses of preference changes in mini-publics show that participation in this type of institution makes citizens change their minds (Mayer, de Vries and Geurts 1995; Button and Mattson 1999; Pelletier *et al.* 1999; Goodin and Niemeyer 2003). Not only do preferences change during the process, but the long-term behaviour can also evolve, several jurors expressing an interest in getting involved in other community related activities after their jury experience (Coote and Lenaghan 1997). There is however no evidence so far of the long-term civic trajectory of citizen jury participants.

The British Columbia Citizen Assembly (BCCA): articulating mini-publics and direct democracy

While a unique experiment, the BCCA deserves being evoked given its radical enactment of some of the central principles of participatory democracy (Lang 2007; Warren and Pearse 2008). Going further than deliberative polls in terms of empowerment, it can be argued that never before in a representative democracy has a randomly selected group of citizens been granted such a responsibility (Sintomer 2007: 126–8). From January to November 2004, 160 randomly selected Canadian citizens met regularly to propose an electoral reform for the province of British Columbia. The citizen assembly was organised along three phases, spread out over a year: a learning phase, a public hearing phase and a deliberation phase. Citizens therefore learned about the variety of voting procedures around the world. They then had the possibility to invite experts and supporters of specific procedures to make a case. The information phase was mixed with small group discussions. Finally, citizens had to deliberate collectively about which electoral system they preferred. Their agreed position was then proposed by referendum to all the citizens of the state. The proposal did not pass however, failing to reach the quorum of 60 per cent of the electorate. Despite this final failure, this participatory experience appears appealing as it combines random selection, information and deliberation phases, and has been granted high autonomy and empowerment. The citizen assembly is also one of the rare cases (with Berlin citizen juries) where random selection has not been restricted to a one-shot event, and allowed lay citizens getting involved in a one year participatory process.

Neighbourhood councils

Neighbourhood councils appear as the embodiment of urban democracy, inspired in their mythology by town meetings or the Greek *polis*. The French case is probably the most developed, as the 2002 law on 'Proximity Democracy' made them compulsory for every city with over 80,000 inhabitants. While varying from city to city, the council board is composed of different actors, half of them being, in general, lay citizens randomly selected from a list of voluntary candidates, the other half local notables (political representatives, stakeholders, members of associations). Neighbourhood councils' meetings are public and take place in front of an audience of 50 to 100 people, free to speak up at the end of the meeting. The self-selection bias is evident in both the board and the audience, as most scholars underline the under-representation of young, low-income and foreign participants (Bacqué and Sintomer 1999; Blondiaux and Levêque 1999). Neighbourhood councils are little empowered, but can give one 'recommendation' to the mayor per year. Recommendations are not binding, even if mayors generally respect them to maintain their legitimacy.

Neighbourhood councils have also been incepted in many American cities (Berry, Portney, and Thomson 1993). While most of them are consultative, some experiments are more empowered, allowing the co-governance of neighbourhood development plans, like in Minneapolis, where $400 million has been granted to develop local project plans (Fagotto and Fung 2006).

Participatory Budgeting: beyond consultation

Since 1989, the city of Porto Alegre, Brazil, has implemented a very ambitious mechanism of participatory budgeting. The concept is simple: making citizens participate in a central public decision, namely the definition of the municipal budget. Procedurally, the PB process is divided among different institutions at different territorial levels: the neighbourhood, the district, and municipal levels, each one organising its own assemblies, composed of lay citizens at the neighbourhood level and delegates at the higher ones (Sintomer and Gret 2005; Baiocchi 2005). In PBs, discussions are generally aimed at taking decisions, related to the ranking of the priorities of the district or the neighbourhood. PBs appear as paradigmatic empowered participatory bodies, as citizens are asked to take financial decisions concerning the budget of the city. The effects of the PB in Porto Alegre in the last fifteen years have therefore been tremendous, allowing an incredible boost in the social development of the city.[8] These results are all the more notable that PB fosters the participation of poor people, generally excluded from public participation arenas (Baiocchi 2001: 49; Smith 2005: 64).

It has had, since then, a great deal of success first in Brazil, then in Latin America, and more recently in Europe. In 2008, about 1,000 cities in the world had adopted it, in one way or another (Sintomer, Herzberg and Röcke 2008a). Apart from Porto Alegre, Sao Paolo, Buenos Aires, Mexico DF, and Montevideo in Latin America, more than 200 PB experiments have developed in the last years in Europe (Sintomer, Herzberg and Röcke 2008b). PB is relatively widespread in Germany, with about twenty cases, its recent development being closely linked to the effort to modernise public administration. While there have been some previous experiments of consultative referendums on public finances – like in Mons-en-Bareuil, in the North of the country – at the end of the 1970s, French PB experiments mostly developed in relation to the emergence of proximity democracy and the generalisation of neighbourhood councils. PB has been mostly implemented in historical Communist cities (such as Saint-Denis, Bobigny and Morsang-sur-Orge) and has been framed in a political manner, as both answering the crisis of representative government and reconstructing social bonds. The recent experience of Regional PB led in Poitou-Charentes has also gained large attention due to the personality of the president of the Region, the Socialist Ségolène Royal, and the important decision-making power granted to participants (Talpin and Sintomer 2011).

PB has also known a recent development in Italy, in cities such as Rome Municipio XI, Grottamare, Pieve Emmanuele and Venezia, most experiences being led by post-communist mayors. Spanish PBs are somehow more directly related to the Latin American experiences, and connected to the will to 'invert priorities', 'deepen democracy' and 'foster social justice'. PSOE sponsored experiences, like in Albacete, have put the emphasis on civil society and associational democracy, while Post-Communists led PBs, like in Cordoba and Seville, have a more grassroots style, aiming at involving lay citizens in the policy process. PB in Portugese cities has also grown tremendously in recent years. Isolated experiences have also been launched in other countries, like Salford in the UK, Mons in Belgium, Utrecht in the Netherlands and Hämeenlinna in Finland.

Given its degree of empowerment and the intensity of the participation it requires, PB should have an important impact on participants. It has even been indeed qualified a 'school of democracy' by some of its most prominent specialists (Baiocchi 2001: 55; Sintomer and Gret 2005: 132). These results have been contested however, some refuting the empowerment thesis, as most PB participants would be already active and politicised (Nylen 2002). These contested conclusions need therefore to be evaluated further. If such an ambitious institution cannot work as a 'school of democracy', then few participatory devices will. In particular, newer and less empowered European PB experiments might have even less effect on their members than Porto Alegre's.

Why participatory budgets in Morsang, Rome and Seville?

From the diversity of democratic innovations in Europe, this study focuses on participatory budgets. This choice is guided by two main reasons. First, PBs (like neighbourhood councils) provide a participation opportunity that is spread over time, with meetings organised regularly throughout the year. In this regard, they seem to fit more adequately with the questioning on the potential bifurcation of the participants' trajectory, than the 'one shot' method of mini-publics, organised over a couple of weekends only. Time and repeated participation might indeed be hypothesised as an important factor for citizens to be significantly affected by their engagement. Then, being more empowered than neighbourhood councils, PBs appear more accurate to evaluate the impact of institutional empowerment on individuals.

This book focuses on three cases, Morsang-sur-Orge in France, Rome Municipio XI in Italy and Seville in Spain. These cases have been selected in the countries where participatory budgets are most developed in Europe: France, Italy and Spain. Focusing on these countries also makes the comparison easier, as local governments share relatively similar levels of competence and administrative attributions. The three cases belong to what has been defined as 'the southern systems of local governments' (Page and Goldsmith 1987; Reynaert et al. 2007), characterised by a rather low functional capacity due to the historical trajectories of these countries, marked by a Napoleonic centralising tradition. Despite their history of centralisation, the three countries have been marked by important decentralisation laws at the end of the 1970s and at the beginning of the 1980s, which increased local government autonomy and competences.

These countries do not embody the ideal conditions for the emergence of empowered participatory institutions however. Local governments in the three countries are indeed rather weak, especially lacking in financial autonomy. The resources to be discussed in the PB meetings were, therefore, very often scarce, as the investment budgets of French, Italian and Spanish communes are limited. The strength of local executives – and especially of the mayor – leaves, nevertheless, some room for political voluntarism. It is indeed mostly from strong political wills, of some decisive actors committed to participatory democracy, that PBs emerged. The case selected in each country appears, therefore, as one of the most emblematic or empowered.

The presentation of the case-studies follows a set of criteria. Inspired partly by the deliberative democracy literature (Cohen 1989; Dryzek and List 2003: 8–9; Fung and Wright 2003), these criteria focus on the decision-making process and the procedures guiding participation:

Inclusiveness: Who is allowed to participate in the institution? Are invitations or membership cards necessary or is participation open to anyone? Then, how much publicity is given to the process (through various information means, such as the internet, newspapers, grassroots mobilisation, etc.) to boost participation?

Discussion: To what extent does the decision-making process allow a collective discussion on the common good to happen? How far is the discussion proceduralised?

Decision-rule: How are decisions enacted? Through consensus or vote? Is the vote secret or public?

Empowerment: What do collective decisions become? Are they purely consultative or can they translate in binding public-policies?

Autonomy: Is the process autonomous from the institution – in this case the municipal administration – that created them? To what extent do elected officials participate in the process and enact collective decisions?

Given how institutions 'score' on these different criteria they will be considered more or less deliberative. A final criterion is added, namely the *intensity* of the participatory process. It is indeed hypothesised that the higher the intensity of the interactions allowed by the institution – measured especially through the number of meetings people can attend and the level of turn-over from one assembly to the other – the higher its self-change potential. These different criteria guide the presentation of the three case-studies.

Morsang-sur-Orge: participatory budgeting in the suburb

Morsang-sur-Orge is a 21,800 inhabitant city, situated about twenty kilometres south of Paris. It is a typical middle-class suburban city with 55 per cent of the population living in private houses and 25 per cent in social housing. Morsang-sur-Orge is not made up of a rich economic terrain, and 80 per cent of the employed active population work outside of the city; the city being often considered a 'dormitory town'. The unemployment rate has been rather stable at about ten per cent in the last ten years, similar to the situation at national level. The municipality has been ruled since 1945 by three successive female mayors, all members of the Communist party.

Participatory democracy as an answer to the crisis of representative government

Despite this historical embeddedness in Morsang-sur-Orge, the Communist Party almost lost the municipal elections in 1995. The closeness of the ballot (a difference of eighteen votes between the first two lists) led the opposition to the courts to claim a new election. After two years of juridical imbroglio, a new partial municipal election was organised at the beginning of 1997, where the left won more easily. While the difficulties to get re-elected in 1995 could be attributed to the crisis the Communist Party faced at the time, and to the national political context of a wide domination of the right, the municipal majority tried to reach a deeper understanding of the phenomenon. The development of participatory democracy in Morsang-sur-Orge was framed as a way of countering the 'crisis of representative government' and of encouraging proximity between elected officials and citizens:

> The goal was to achieve proximity. [...] We have a political responsibility on the questions of disinterest from politics, on abstention. And the commune is the best place to help things to be done differently. [...] It is here that we have to make original experiments, to innovate.
>
> (Participatory Democracy Deputy Mayor, 14th January 2005)

The local left thus decided to propose a large renewal of the municipal majority for the partial election of 1997. A new candidate was presented, Marjolaine Rauze, a reformist member of the Communist Party in her 30s. Active citizens coming from 'civil society', i.e., mainly from local associational life, were also included. The mayor was then re-elected in the municipal elections of 2001. After the victorious election of 1997, a new spirit floated on the municipal majority. In this context, rapidly after the election, the first participatory mechanisms were set up. At first, residents were mainly involved in the management of municipal sport and music facilities. A consultative youth council was also created to involve residents under 18 years old. The desire to increase proximity between elected officials and citizens was embodied in the creation of the *House of Citizenry* in 1999, a new municipal administration in charge of the co-ordination of all the participatory activities of the city. With four permanent employees organising the civic life of the city, the *House of Citizenry* also played an important role in structuring the participatory process, as its employees welcomed the participants, wrote the minutes of the meetings and coordinated the publicity of the PB.

The municipal majority then decided to create eight 'neighbourhood councils' (*Comités de Quartier*), an unusual practice in a city of this size with no legal obligation to do so. It allowed an institutionalisation of participation, with local meetings organised almost every month. The main innovation was to grant a financial portfolio of about 60,000 Euros to each neighbourhood council (NC), to finance local projects. Allocated 480,000 Euros per year, NCs decide on about eighteen per cent of the investment budget of the city (2.7 million Euros in 2004). After its re-election, the municipality decided, in 2002, to go one step further with the creation of city-wide budget workshops, aimed at countering some forms of parochialism stemming from the micro-local basis of NCs: 'We told ourselves [the municipal majority] that people shouldn't only focus on their little problems within the neighbourhood councils, but had the right to know about the communal budget as a whole.'[9]

Five thematic budget workshops were therefore created, to discuss and propose investment priorities to the municipal council. The decisions of the Municipal Council were also assessed by a Citizen Monitoring Board – *'L'observatoire des engagements'* – in charge of evaluating the conformity between budget workshop investment priorities and the actual decisions of the municipality. From 2004 onwards, however, the municipality decided to move from a financial to a project perspective. Discussions moved from which investments were to be made at city level, to which orientations and priorities should be adopted by the municipal council. With the end of the financial approach at city-wide level, the Citizen Monitoring Board also lost its *raison d'être*, and was dismantled.

At the beginning of 2005, when I arrived on the field, participatory democracy in Morsang-sur-Orge was therefore composed of a two-level structure. At the district level, eight neighbourhood councils are organised every other month. They are granted a financial budget of about 60,000 Euros, which they can allocate at their discretion. Then, at city-level, seven thematic workshops are organised three to four times a year on issues of: (1) pedestrians, bikes and cars; (2) the municipal budget; (3) the municipal theatre; (4) the environment; (5) tranquillity; (6) housing projects; and (7) the Agglomeration Community.

The PB procedural design

Neighbourhood councils and thematic workshops meetings are *public*. They are organised in public places, primary schools for the former and the House of the Citizenry for the latter. The publicity of the process is ensured by the bi-monthly circulation of a free local newspaper, the *FlashInfo*, in which information is provided about the date and location of future meetings. The newspaper also offers short articles about past participatory activities, as well as other public meetings organised by the municipality. Participants can also receive the minutes of the previous meetings by mail. In comparison with other European experiences of participatory budgets, as in Rome for instance, the internet is almost never used as a source of information or for the mobilisation of the population in Morsang-sur-Orge. Neighbourhood Councils and thematic workshops are also *formally inclusive*, as they are open to all neighbourhood or city inhabitants. It has to be stressed, however, that formal inclusiveness does not seem to provide solid grounds against the exclusion of marginalised residents such as ethnic minorities, unemployed workers, and, more generally, individuals with low social backgrounds.[10]

A second procedural criterion to take into account is the centrality of *discussion* in the decision-making processes of the Morsang-sur-Orge assemblies. The first aim of the NCs and thematic workshops is to allow individuals to express their views and judgements. A formal equality is granted to all the participants, as anyone is allowed to speak and give his or her say during the meetings. The discussion is ruled by few formal procedures, however. There are generally no time limits and no speakers lists; PB discussions are therefore often disorganised because of this *laissez-faire* behaviour of the moderators. The moderator is usually a member of the municipal majority who lives in the neighbourhood (in the case of neighbourhood councils) or is specialised in the issue at stake (in the case of thematic workshops). The moderator establishes an agenda, which remains very flexible as any topic can be brought into the discussion by the participants. The substance and quality of the discussions thus vary a lot from one meeting to another (see chapter five).

Discussions are, in general, aimed at taking *decisions*. Different types of decisions have to be distinguished however. The main decisions taken by NCs deal with the financial portfolios. Every year, generally at the end of March, NCs have to agree on the projects in which they wish to invest their funds. But NCs also take non-financial decisions. The organisation of neighbourhood events and parties is indeed also a central part in their activities. Convivial initiatives like 'Hello Neighbour!'[11] or 'Courtyards and Gardens'[12] are organised by the neighbourhood councils.

Discussions in thematic workshops also lead to decisions. Until 2004, as the discussions regarded the financial orientations and priorities of the municipality, clear and important decisions had to be made. From then on, the decision-making power of the assemblies was reduced. The 'pedestrians, bikes and cars' workshop, for instance, takes binding decisions, as it has to decide on most of the urban planning and road management projects of the city. Other workshops, such as the one dealing with environmental issues or with the Agglomeration Community, have fewer decisions to take, as these issues remain mostly outside of the city's competences.

Sometimes, however, innovative methods are used to take important city-wide decisions. An interesting example came from the 'tranquillity workshop' in 2004. As the issue of security and delinquency had become a 'hot potato' in the French political debate, as well as locally in Morsang-sur-Orge, the municipal opposition – mainly composed of members of the right wing political party, UMP – proposed the creation of a municipal police force. The initiative did not pass, but the municipal majority decided to raise this question at the thematic workshop on tranquillity. Given the highly contentious nature of the issue, the workshop decided, with the support of the municipal majority, to organise a city-wide referendum of the inhabitants on the eventual creation of a municipal police force. Although this referendum had no legal authority, the municipal majority committed to follow the opinions expressed by the citizens. The ballot was sent by mail to all the citizens enrolled on the city electoral roll. In the end, out of 12,600 potential voters, 3,000 took part in the consultation, i.e., a participation rate of about twenty five per cent, who rejected the creation of a municipal police force.

Interestingly, in contrast with the participatory budgets of Rome or Seville, there is no written convention defining the way decisions have to be taken in Morsang PB. In both neighbourhood councils and thematic workshops, decisions are indeed taken through discussion, and are generally considered by the actors to be taken 'by consensus'. During the eighteen months spent on the field, no vote has ever been observed in a Morsang participatory assembly. Consensus does not appear magically however. It has to be created and constructed through discussion and often implies power relationships in the framing of the debate. Mansbridge offers enlightening empirical insights on the power relationships underlying the practice of consensus:

> In a consensual system, the minority is, in a sense, eliminated. After it agrees to go along, it leaves no trace. Its objections go unrecorded. Indeed, if those in the minority are intimidated, cannot give their reasons convincingly, or do not care enough to make a scene, they may never voice their objections.

> (Mansbridge 1980: 170)

This point is tackled more systematically in chapter five.

Formal empowerment and lack of autonomy: the power of elected officials

To what extent are the decisions taken in these local assemblies binding for the municipality? Following Fung (2006), levels of power can be represented on a zero to one axis, from purely communicative influence to consultation, co-governance and direct authority. The different decision-making processes of Morsang-sur-Orge can, therefore, be evaluated following this empowerment scale. First, decisions taken by neighbourhood councils concerning their financial portfolios are automatically integrated in the municipal budget, through a decision taken by the municipal council. The latter has no juridical obligation to do so, but as the main promoter of participatory democracy in Morsang-sur-Orge, the municipal majority is supposed to respect the decisions coming from the NCs. Since their creation in 1998, it does not seem that any decision taken by NCs has ever been rejected. Decisions on the financial portfolios are therefore co-decisions between NCs and the Municipal Council. In this regard, about 18 per cent of the investment budget of the Municipality is co-decided by citizens in these local participatory institutions, which makes of Morsang-sur-Orge one of most empowered examples of municipal participatory budgets in Europe.

It is however necessary go further in the understanding of the concept of empowerment, which cannot be reduced to the amount of public money made available to the participatory bodies. The degree of *autonomy* of the institution, with regard to the municipality, is also an important criterion of empowerment. The presence or absence of the members of the municipal majority at the public meetings, the degree of contention between the participatory institutions and the municipality, and the framing of the debate by city officials are important factors too.

In Morsang-sur-Orge, debates are indeed moderated by members of the municipal majority, there are few conflicts and the discussions seem to be largely framed by elected officials. If participatory institutions are indirectly controlled by the municipality, they could embody legitimising window-dressing institutions, allowing similar decisions to be taken through other channels. In this sense, the remark by the 'Participatory Democracy Deputy Mayor', Francis Diener, is telling: 'We realised, after one or two years, that the choices made by the citizens were, more or less, pretty much those that the elected officials would have made. It was really reconfirming for us.'[13]

The most powerful actors in Morsang-sur-Orge participatory assemblies are elected officials, as they have the information, the skills and the legitimacy to influence and frame the debates. In this regard, they play a crucial role in orienting the discussions about the allocation of the neighbourhood council financial portfolios. An example from the discussions of one of the neighbourhood councils held in January 2005 is very telling from this perspective. The debate about the allocation of the neighbourhood budget had started at the beginning of the meeting, when the participatory democracy Deputy Mayor referred to the activities of the 'urban planning workshop':

> ...last year, fifty per cent of the municipal budget has been used to improve safety (through road signals, speed bumps, etc.), but not to improve the quality of the roads and pavements […] It was a choice, a question of priority. But we have to decide what we would like to do this year. We have to talk about it.

His framing of the debate was even clearer, when he then said:

> Given the traffic circulation plan of the Agglomeration Community, we have to make certain choices […] it is a matter of coherence. We have to make pavements, roads, or a mixture of both.[14]

He therefore largely framed and oriented the choices of the inhabitants, implying that there were no alternatives for the allocation of the financial share. Later on, Françoise, member of the Municipal majority and usual moderator of the group, spoke on behalf of the organising board of the neighbourhood council and explained that there were some 'objective needs' in the neighbourhood; these needs being essentially seen in terms of roads and pavements. The debate on the allocation of the budget remained thereafter within the limits defined by the moderator and the members of the municipality. The only alternative proposals that were voiced were about which street, or which part of the pavement, to renovate. At some point, an elderly woman, Louise, who seemed to disagree, said *sotto voce* to her neighbour: 'That ought to come under the municipality's budget' (i.e., not the neighbourhood council budget). Although she disagreed with the use of the neighbourhood budget for pavements, she did not voice her opposition publicly. At some point, Françoise realised that the organising board had perhaps over-influenced the decision about the financial allocation, and expressed some kind of remorse: 'This [the idea of the pavement] was just an idea we had. But maybe you have other ideas, other wishes. This is a discussion.' Nobody answered and a long silence followed. After a few minutes of confusion, Françoise said: 'So, what shall we do about the neighbourhood budget?' Louise answered: 'Exactly like you said!' The moderator appeared embarrassed, realising how she had influenced the debate and therefore the decision. After a few minutes of confusion, Isabelle, a woman in her late 30s, a member of a PTA in the local school, made a proposal: 'what about the kindergarten?' (i.e., what about improving it?). The moderator answered immediately: 'We shouldn't have eyes bigger than our stomachs.' (i.e., it is too expensive; we cannot afford that, etc.). The only alternative proposal was thus rejected, *a priori*, not after a collective discussion of the assembly, but arbitrarily by the moderator, who considered it too ambitious. A little later, once the decision about the use of the financial allocation had already been made, a man said: 'It is pity that all the money from the council always goes to pavements.' He did not seem to agree with the choice made for the use of the budget, but did not voice his disagreement publicly.[15]

This scene, far from being idiosyncratic, shows how consensus can be constructed in Morsang-sur-Orge. It is created by excluding all alternative proposals and by framing the debate in such a way that only a minimalist solution, decided beforehand by the organising board, could be agreed upon. By defining what is doable or not, what it is possible to suggest, the members of the municipality considerably reduce the autonomy, and therefore the empowerment, of Morsang-sur-Orge participatory institutions. It comes as no surprise then that, in the first seven years of their existence, most neighbourhood councils funds have been directed towards the repair of the pavements, rather than to more innovative projects. We will see however later on how, in some cases, inhabitants managed to gain an increased autonomy, thanks to the support of public functionaries.

Thematic workshops appear even less empowered, depending on the issue at stake. Decisions of the 'pedestrians, bikes and cars' workshop, dealing with a direct competence of the municipality, are directly accepted by the municipal council. There is therefore a co-decision at city-level concerning urban planning issues, one of the main competences of French cities. Decisions concerning the communal theatre, as they depend on the city, result as well from a co-decision process between citizens and the municipality. On the other hand, other workshops have a purely consultative or even informative power, such as the workshop on environmental issues or the one on the agglomeration community, which do not depend directly on the municipality.

In between, there are a lot of public services, partially managed by the municipality, where citizens are included in the decision-making processes. Among these services, those related to youth policies – such as nurseries, kindergartens and primary schools – are municipal competences and can be discussed in thematic workshops. The thematic workshops on 'housing projects', do not take decisions directly, as the social housing facilities are managed by semi-public agencies, not by the municipality directly. This thematic workshop, therefore, has a more informative function, with citizens coming to give testimony on the different problems faced by the residents of these neighbourhoods. However, this workshop also has a power of mobilisation, as it is often used to organise *ad hoc* meetings between residents and the renting companies to solve specific problems. The degree of empowerment therefore varies from one thematic workshop to another, given the competences of the city. In all the cases, however, the degree of autonomy of the workshops is low, as the discussions are generally moderated and framed by the elected officials of the municipality.

An intensive participatory process

From a procedural perspective, the Morsang-sur-Orge participatory process creates the conditions for intensive civic engagement. Between neighbourhood councils, thematic workshops, and the preparation meetings, regular participants can attend almost a public assembly every a week in. Apart from PB meetings, a lot of other informal initiatives are organised throughout the year (neighbourhood and school parties, public debates, thematic weeks, 'hello neighbour!', 'Courtyards & Gardens', etc.). All this creates a very intensive participatory atmosphere. However, apart from a few really committed participants, few people attend all these assemblies; there is indeed a high turnover from one meeting to another (see chapter four).

Rome's Municipio XI: participatory budgeting in a metropolitan city district

Rome is a 2.8 million inhabitant city, divided into 19 districts since 2001, in the framework of Italian administrative decentralisation. The 11th district of the city, '*Municipio XI*', has developed a participatory budget since 2003. Municipio XI represents an area of about 4,700 hectares (3.7 per cent of the total surface of the city), in the south of the Italian capital. It is composed of a little more than 139,000 inhabitants, about five per cent of the total population of Rome, and its unemployment rate is lower than the Roman average, at about 16 per cent (against 18.9 per cent in Rome), with 10,000 of its residents being unemployed.

Unlike Morsang-sur-Orge and Seville, Rome's Municipio XI does not have a long administrative history. Even though it exists administratively since the 1970s, called 'circumscription' at the time, it did not have high autonomy. It took about ten years of administrative decentralisation, from the beginning of the 1990s to 2001, to reach the actual status of Rome's districts (Loughlin 2004: 211–28). In August 2000, law no. 267/00, stated that portions of metropolitan city territory – therefore 'Municipi' – could be structured as normal communes. The main difference, however, between a *Municipio*, and other Italian communes, is their lack of budget autonomy (Minaldi and Riolo 2005; Gelli and Pinson 2001). The budget of the districts depends on financial transfers decided by the municipal council. Districts can only propose (to the commune of Rome) a provisional budget, i.e., a financial evaluation of the planned spending of the district for the upcoming year.

The first elections of Rome's Municipi took place in 2001. In the *Municipio XI*, the left, from the centre-left (*Margherita* and DS) to the more radical *Rifondazione Communista (RC)*, won with 53.4 per cent of the votes, with Massimiliano

Smeriglio (RC) at its head. It was not a complete surprise however, as the territory has traditionally been considered a liberal territory. Interestingly, as in Morsang-sur-Orge and Seville, the municipal majority is not only composed of members of political parties in the Municipio XI, but also of non-professional politicians, coming from 'civil society'.

The 'Participatory Budget Councillor', Luciano Ummarino, is probably the best example of this opening to civil society. Asked about his previous political experiences in an interview, he answered:

> I have been involved in politics since I was 13. In the student movements at university, and then, in the Social Centre Movements, occupying a social centre in Garbatella[16] ['La Strada', one of Rome's main social centres], blocking the street. This was the beginning of everything. [...] Then, I was with the Desobbedienti, and there was also Genoa [in July 2001].[17]

The very setting of the interview he gave me was, from the beginning, very telling about the style of this administration. I arrived at the town hall rather formally dressed for the appointment, expecting to meet an old classy Italian politician. I was greatly surprised then to see this 32-year-old man, dressed casually, with a rather untidy beard, who smoked half a packet of cigarettes in his office during the two hour long interview. Luciano Ummarino has been one of the prominent figures of the local social movement scene since the beginning of the 1990s. He has met Massimiliano Smeriglio, the Mayor of the Municipio, in the mist of their common struggle to take over this empty building that was to become La Stada.

Participatory budgeting as a means to deepening democracy

As in other Italian cases, the introduction of this citizen participation design in Rome's Municipio XI was due to the commitment of leftist activists to the 'deepening of democracy'. The development of a PB in Municipio XI is seen by Luciano Ummarino, and by the Mayor himself, as an enactment of the criticisms addressed to representative government by the anti-globalisation movement. Luciano Ummarino's regular references to the Zapatist Movement, and especially to Sub-comandante Marcos, are clear signs of this rather uncommon political orientation at municipal level. The main motivation for the municipal majority to initiate such a project was:

> ...above all, to put into discussion the fact that, if there is something in crisis in today's world, it is democracy itself. We believe that, starting from the territory, from the local community, from the proximity with the citizens, it is important to build a welcoming, substantial and constituent democracy with local communities.[18]

The aim of this democratic project has not remained, however, at a macro-political level; it is also aimed at creating active and competent citizens. The first article of the participatory budget constitution thus clearly states: 'Participatory budgeting is an experiment in participatory democracy which aims at the promotion of active citizenship.' The 'school of democracy' frame is thus central to the justification of the participatory budget in the Municipio XI.

Formal and informal processes of participation

Municipio XI PB experiment started in May 2003, with a general assembly organised at the town hall to launch the process and publicise it. At odds with Morsang-sur-Orge, the experience has been framed from the beginning as a 'participatory budget', in direct reference to the Porto Alegre model. The main principles, which remained for the most part stable afterwards, were settled from the beginning. First, the Municipio was divided into eight neighbourhoods, that claimed to have historical roots in the territory.

Public assemblies are organised in each neighbourhood to decide on local projects to be financed by the district's budget. Projects can be presented in four thematic areas, corresponding to the main competences of the Municipio: (1) public works; (2) mobility and viability; (3) local green spaces; and (4) cultural activities. A fifth thematic area was added in 2005, namely, sport and youth policies.[19] The PB then follows a yearly cycle. At the beginning of the cycle, generally in January or February, 'territorial assemblies' (TA) are organised in each neighbourhood, in which people over 14, living, working or studying in the zone, can vote for 'delegates'. The number of delegates elected in each TA depends on the number of voters; one delegate is elected for every fifteen voters. The proportionality between the number of participants and the number of delegates – imported from Porto Alegre – is aimed at spurring participation. During this first two hour assembly, candidates introduce themselves briefly, the rest of the session being devoted to a vote by secret ballot. Delegates are elected for one year, and cannot run for more than two years consecutively. The delegates' main function is to serve as a formal link between the neighbourhood and the municipal majority. They are supposed to inform and mobilise local residents. They are not the representatives of the citizens who elected them, but delegates of their TA before the Municipio.

During the second phase, generally between February and May, working groups (WG) meet regularly in each neighbourhood to elaborate projects and proposals in the different thematic areas. The discussions are facilitated by members of a non-profit association, *Progetto Sensibilizzando,* as members of the Municipality and even public officials prefer not to participate in the assemblies. Facilitators allow a non-political co-ordination of the experiment, which differs largely from the practices of Morsang-sur-Orge elected officials, for instance. They thus foster the quality of the communication in the assembly. One of their central principles is to 'help citizens in their move from an emotional to a rational voice, facilitating the transfer from the private to the public sphere, from a physical and also mental perspective' (Associazione Progetto Laboratorio Onlus 2005: 160). Their explicit aim is therefore to orient the discussions towards the common good. Facilitators thus see participation in the PB process as a school of democracy; the aim of this experience being to 'increase and interiorise a sense of active participation' and also to 'offer an opportunity of personal development to the citizens by making individual knowledge common to all citizens' (Associazione Progetto Laboratorio Onlus 2005: 160).

During the second phase, proposals are made by the citizens, progressively refined and operationalised to make them applicable, and then analysed by the technical services of the Municipality, who evaluate whether they enter within the district's competences and financial capacities. The aim is to arrive, at the end of the working group phase, at a list of possible priorities in each thematic area, which will then be voted in the successive stage of the process.

The third phase generally takes place in June. TAs meet again in each neighbourhood for a final assembly to vote on the priorities. Proposals for each thematic area are presented by the delegates, and the rest of the assembly is devoted to the actual voting procedure. Each participant can vote for one priority in each thematic area. The proposals receiving more votes become the priorities of the TA, and are then transmitted to the administration. The fourth stage only concerns the delegates and was supposed to take place in September. The Participatory Budget Forum (PBF), assembling all the delegates of all the neighbourhoods of the Municipio and the Mayor, was aimed at evaluating all the priorities that have emerged from the TAs and to rank them, for each thematic area. The PBF has never been organised so far however, it could have allowed the process in Municipio XI to be more than mere neighbourhood funds.

The final document of the ranking of the priorities at district-level is then transmitted to the Budget Office of the Municipio; this is the fifth phase. The priorities are therefore included in the provisional budget of the Municipio, which then have to be voted by the Municipal Council. Between October and November, the TAs meet again in each neighbourhood to account for the priorities approved by the Municipal Council. The last phase takes place at the beginning of the following year, when the Municipal budget is integrated (more or less completely) in the whole Commune's budget; the approved priorities thus obtain their financing. The participatory budget cycle of Rome Municipio XI is summed up in Figure 2.1.

Decision-making process: aggregation vs. deliberation?

From a procedural point of view, the Municipio XI participatory budget decision-making process respects the criteria of fair deliberation. First, PB meetings are public and inclusive. In each neighbourhood, TA and WG meetings are organised in public places, such as state schools, municipal buildings and public libraries. Then, the municipality and, in particular, the participatory budget office are aware of the importance of information and communication for the success of the experience. From the second year onwards a letter was sent to all the inhabitants of the Municipio, posters were put all over the walls of the district, and SMS messages were sent to the participants of the neighbourhood assemblies to remind them of the dates of the meetings. The PB office was also created to give more institutional visibility to the process.

In 2005, a website was launched,[20] providing a great deal of information: presentation of the process, information about when and where the assemblies are organised, minutes of the meetings, information about the delegates, news about the civic and political activities of the Municipio, bibliographical references about participatory democracy, etc. In 2005, the Municipio received special funds – 30,000 Euros – from the commune of Rome to finance communication material.

The participatory process of Municipio XI is also formally inclusive. It goes further than Morsang-sur-Orge from this perspective, as it clearly establishes formal participation criteria. Not only are residents allowed to participate, but also non-residents working or studying in the Municipio, who are over 14 years old. These criteria formally allow the participation of foreign residents, workers or students, as well as the inclusion of under 18-year-old citizens. The decision to open the process to individuals generally excluded from political participation arenas, is clearly understood by the Municipality as a political stance on the necessary inclusion of all the traditionally marginalised fringes of the population.

Then, discussion plays an important, albeit secondary, role in the Municipio XI PB design. The main discursive phase takes place in the working groups, when the participants discuss the different proposals. In these discussions, a formal equality

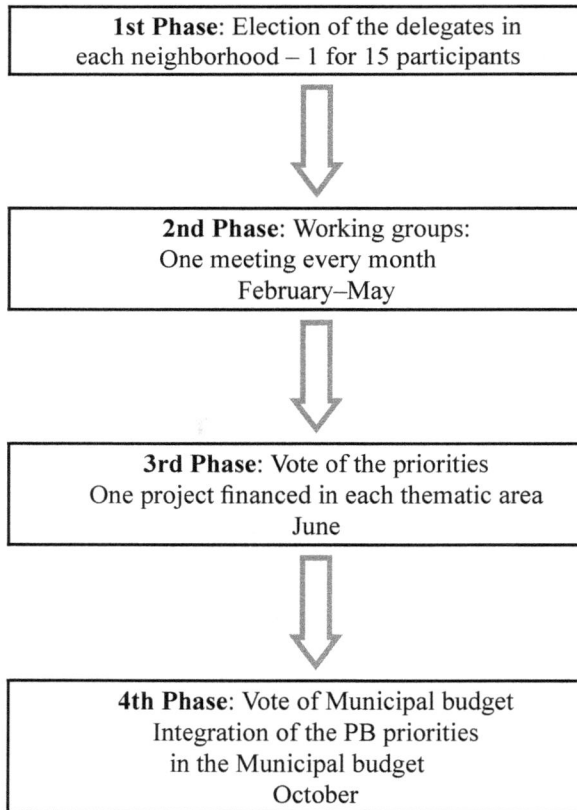

1st Phase: Election of the delegates in each neighborhood – 1 for 15 participants

2nd Phase: Working groups:
One meeting every month
February–May

3rd Phase: Vote of the priorities
One project financed in each thematic area
June

4th Phase: Vote of Municipal budget
Integration of the PB priorities
in the Municipal budget
October

Figure 2.1: Roma Municipio XI PB cycle

is granted to all the participants, as anyone can speak up and give his/her opinions and proposals. The discussions are governed by a few informal rules that the facilitators generally remind the participants of at the beginning of the meeting: not speaking over someone; listening to each other; raising a hand before speaking, etc. There are, however, no formal time limits, and hardly ever any lists of speakers. There is generally no clear-cut agenda, apart from the necessity to move forward in the operationalisation of proposals from one meeting to another. The first two meetings aim at the emergence of a maximum number of proposals, whereas the following two are more focused on the operationalisation of the proposals. The discussion is helped by the drafting, between each meeting, of reports of discussions (called '*verbale*'), given to all the participants at the beginning of the session. In the reports, proposals are generally divided into actual proposals that can be financed, which enter within the competence of the Municipio, 'signalisations', i.e., statements of local problems which do not fall within the realm of its competence, and proposals that are so minor (and therefore not costly) that they should be included in the normal administration of the Municipio. Working group discussions are therefore highly structured and proposal-oriented.

Discussion is not, however, an end in itself, as it is aimed at selecting one priority by thematic area in each neighbourhood. Decisions are not taken directly through discussion however. Discussions only allow the deciding of which proposals will be presented to the vote. Formally, any proposal can be presented by a single participant and written down on the discussion report. Most of the time, proposals are individually-based. They can be improved or refined through discussion, but they cannot be merely rejected or ranked at this stage.

Even if a majority of the working group participants disagree with a proposal, it can nevertheless be written down on the report, and be presented, at the end, to the voters. This, however, largely depends of the actual interactions taking place in the assemblies, and therefore of the power relationships between the participants. The production of the '*verbale*' implies, in some sense, taking micro-decisions, on what to write down or not. The sum of these micro-decisions defines which proposals are presented to the vote at the end of the process. The question is, therefore, about the role of collective discussion in these micro-decisions. Sometimes, especially when the notes on the discussions are taken by one of the facilitators, before writing down a proposal, he/she asks: 'Do we agree on that?'. If no disagreement is voiced, the proposal is written down; if there is some disagreement, it is further discussed. Then, either a compromise is found or the discussion is merely postponed. Very few proposals are actually rejected, unless the participant who voiced it explicitly recognises that he/she was wrong, which seldom happens.

In the end, decisions are not taken through consensus but by vote in Municipio XI. Delegates are elected by secret ballot in the first assembly of the cycle, and priorities are voted in June, after the working group discussions phase. Does the aggregative nature of the decision-making process call the deliberative nature of the procedure into question? Consensus is probably one the most demanding criteria, and as such the more contested, in the deliberative democracy literature. Apart from Jürgen Habermas himself, most theorists agree on the fact that reaching a consensus is not fundamental in a deliberative process, the most important being that the views and judgements of individuals be submitted to discussion before the actual decision is taken (Manin 1987: 75; Knight and Johnson 1994: 284; Cohen 1997: 75), which is the case in Rome PB.

A constrained empowerment?

The PB represents about twenty per cent of the overall investment budget of the Municipio. The portion of the municipal budget directly decided by the citizens varies, however, from one year to another, as no financial limit has been clearly fixed. This sometimes constitutes a problem for the participants, who do not precisely know the level of the financial resources available for their projects. This lack of transparency is largely due to the administrative nature of the Italian Municipi. As they lack financial autonomy, their budget depends of what the central commune decides to grant them every year. Municipio XI administration therefore never knows whether it will receive enough funds to finance the projects decided by the citizens.

Despite these constraints, PB assemblies are directly empowered, a genuine co-decision process taking place in Rome. One of the features of this participatory budget design is that it restrains citizen input to the micro-local level. They can take important decisions for their neighbourhoods, but cannot affect the Municipio's overall political and financial orientations. Whereas in Morsang-sur-Orge, but even more in other European (in Cordoba, Albacete and Seville especially) and Latin American experiments, citizens can have an impact on the global municipal budget, this is not the case in Rome.

Restricted to the neighbourhood level, Rome PB is highly autonomous from the municipality. First, members of the municipality do not participate in the process, at odds with the practices in Morsang-sur-Orge. In this regard, the municipality has no influence on the framing of the debates. Another sign of this autonomy can be found in the regular conflicts that emerged between some neighbourhood assemblies and the Municipio. In 2004, for instance, some delegates from San Paolo neighbourhood decided to short-circuit the process as they felt the influence of the Municipio was overwhelming. They called the participants they knew to dissuade them from attending the assembly, and organised an alternative one a week later. After some negotiations with the PB Office, the conflict was solved, but this testifies of the autonomy attained by Rome's participatory process.

The Municipio XI PB institutions are thus characterised by a deliberative decision-making process and a high degree of empowerment. To evaluate their self-transformation potential it is finally necessary to focus on the intensity of the interactions taking place in these settings. From a procedural perspective, the Municipio XI participatory design does not create highly intensive interactions. Few assemblies are indeed organised every year. In the first phase, only one assembly is organised to elect the delegates. In the second one, between four and eight assemblies are organised in each neighbourhood. In the third phase, one assembly is organised to vote for the priorities. A highly committed individual, being delegate, would, at most, attend ten assemblies per year.

The potential intensity of the Municipio XI participatory design is therefore lower than Morsang-sur-Orge's one, all the more as there are few informal gatherings or other similar occasions to interact for participants of the PB meetings. Having less frequent interactions, participants should have less influence on one another than in Morsang-sur-Orge.

Seville: The largest participatory budget in Europe

City of 700,000 inhabitants, Seville embodies the largest experiment of municipal participatory budgeting in Europe so far. It has been ruled by a centre-left municipal majority since May 2003, through an alliance between the PSOE (the Socialist Party) and *Izquierda Unida* (the former Communist Party). The PB was part of the alliance platform to be developed after the elections; and was carried out from the end of 2003 onwards. From an administrative perspective, Seville is half way between Morsang-sur-Orge and Rome Municipio XI. Using new juridical opportunities, the municipality of Seville decided, in 1989, on further decentralisation by creating a new administrative level, namely, 'districts'. This allowed the emergence of two new local bodies, District Councils – 'bringing Administration closer to neighbours and increasing the efficiency of public services'[21] – and Citizen Participation Councils (CPC), mostly opened to associations (Rodriguez Alvarez 2005). A citizen participation charter was also adopted at the end of 1990, introducing among other innovations a local petition right. Revised in 1999, the charter introduced local referendums and created new participation bodies, namely Thematic Councils (*'Consejos Sectoriales'*), to foster associative participation on specialised issues, from old people, women, social services, education and culture, to the environment, urban policies or public transportation (Font 2001).

The PB as a step further towards a participatory polity

At the turn of century, Seville was thus characterised by a broad range of public participation institutions at both district and city levels. These participative bodies remained, however, essentially informative and consultative until 2003. With the victory of the new municipal coalition in May 2003,[22] a new dynamic was given to participatory mechanisms in Seville. It was stated in the alliance agreement – mainly as an *Izquierda Unida* claim – that a participatory budget would be launched during the term. PB was understood as a compromise between representative and direct democracy, through the granting of binding decision-making power to the citizens. Paula Garvin, Citizen Participation Councillor in the municipal majority, and *Izquierda Unida* leader in Andalusia, feels in this regard directly indebted towards Porto Alegre experiment:

> When I heard about Porto Alegre, it was as if I had seen light. I said, it's a way to give power back to the people, telling them: 'take over the State'. [...] What I ask people is to cooperate with me to promote the common good, against

private interests. According to me participatory democracy is a mix between direct and representative democracy.[23]

(Paula Garvin, March 2005)

Three main goals of Seville PB can be analytically distinguished: (1) the inclusion of groups and individuals who are generally under-represented or excluded from political decision-making processes; (2) the promotion of social justice by favouring the 'redistribution of resources between zones, social groups and genders. Focusing in priority on redistribution towards the most disadvantaged'; and (3) the civic education of citizens through 'popular education in processes of co-responsibility where citizens, technicians and political representatives can learn'.[24] As in other Spanish PB experiments like Cordoba, the emphasis on social justice and redistribution towards marginalised groups seems central. This appears as a direct import of the Latin American model, and especially of the Porto Alegre paradigm, where the redistribution of power and resources towards the poor – the 'inversion of priorities' – was one of the core aims and achievements of the participatory budget. It is also interesting to note that the 'school of democracy' frame is also very much present in the intentions of the instigators of the participatory budget.

A sophisticated participatory procedure

The city was first divided into fifteen territorial zones, following the organisation of the Civic Centres, in which PB meetings generally take place. Zones are understood as a sub-division of the existing districts. Thus, Seville PB relies on three administrative tiers: the zone, the district and the city as a whole. To these three levels correspond three participatory assemblies: (1) Zone Assemblies; (2) District PB Councils; and (3) the City PB Council. The PB then follows a yearly cycle.

The participatory process starts in February, with the organisation of preparation meetings in all the zones of the city, where 'motor groups' are constituted and delegates for the 'Autoreglamento' commission elected. Motor groups, open to all volunteers, ensure a central role in the organisation and diffusion of the PB process. They are in charge of information campaigns launched to mobilise the local population. They also take care of the animation of the zone assemblies, by channelling the formulation of the proposals and facilitating the discussions. Then, the Autoreglamento commission is composed of two delegates per zone assembly. Meeting regularly between February and May, this commission is in charge of the drafting of the 'Autoreglamento' – the constitution – of the process for the year. This document is re-discussed and amended in each of the zone assemblies at the end of April, before being adopted city-wide. This makes of Seville PB a truly constituent process, as the rules of the game are constantly discussed and refined with the participants.

Once the 'Autoreglamento' is adopted, the discussion of the proposals can start. This central part of the PB cycle takes place in the zone assemblies, the fundamental decision-making body of the PB process. They are open to all residents of the zone over 16 years old. Zone assemblies are therefore formally inclusive, open to both minors and foreign residents. To foster participation, the Sevillan participatory process is highly publicised, by both the municipality and the participants. The process is coordinated by a special office, exclusively in charge of PB organisation, employing five people. This office plays an important role in the publicity of the process, by writing to the press and launching advertising campaigns (on the radio, local TV, or posters in the streets). Publicity is also ensured through a regularly updated website.[25]

Proposals to the zone assemblies have to be made in advance (fifteen days before the date of the assembly) and written down by the citizens. This allows the emergence of a high number of reflexive and constructive proposals – people have time to think about it – but it also diminishes the discursive and collective process of construction and formulation of proposals. Proposals emerging in the zones are then presented orally (but not discussed) by the proponents and then voted for or against in the assembly. Decisions in Seville participatory bodies are therefore taken through vote. Discussion is even seen negatively in these assemblies, as shows a scene that took place in one of them:

> At the beginning of the session, after the presentation of a first proposal, a woman stood up and started to discuss the proposal. She was, however, immediately cut short by Virginia, the director of the participatory budget municipal administration, who was moderating the meeting: 'We cannot start a debate. There are a lot of proposals. If you like the proposal vote for it, and otherwise just don't.'

> (Observation notes, Zone Assembly,
> Los Remedios-Tabladas, Seville, 30th May 2005)

Discussion is therefore not seen as a way to take decisions in Seville's participatory process, but on the contrary, as a loss of time and as an improper way to influence participants' opinions and votes. Decisions to vote X or Y has to be an individual one. Seville's decision-making process appears from this perspective largely aggregative. The decision-making process is also at odds with that of Morsang-sur-Orge, as elected representatives just do not have any influence on the process, not being allowed to vote, convince or persuade the voters. Seville's PB appears therefore largely autonomous.

Finally, zone assemblies also elect delegates, who represent the assembly at the district and city PB councils. One of the main tasks of the district and city PB councils, is to evaluate and rank all the voted proposals of the zone assemblies that affect the districts and city as a whole. Their main function is therefore to apply the 'social justice criteria' established by the '*Autoreglamento*'. The selection of the proposals follows a very sophisticated process, coined 'weighted vote'. First, proposals are voted in the zone assemblies. A first ranking of the proposals is therefore established given the number of votes they receive. Then, the district and city PB councils evaluate and rank them following the 'social justice criteria'. Discussion therefore also plays a role in the decision-making process as PB delegates have to agree (either through consensus or vote, both happened) on the number of points to attribute to each proposal. This offers rather interesting discussions about social justice among lay citizens that is worth evoking in some details.

PB as a way to foster social justice

There are two types of social justice criteria, objective and subjective ones. The objective ones allocate points to the proposals following some statistical data about the socio-economic situation of the population targeted by the proposal.[26] The aim is 'to give more to those who have less', following a form of territorial and social affirmative action. The subjective criteria then, discussed in the district and city PB councils, evaluate the ability of the proposals to foster multiculturalism, tolerance, social justice, gender equality, and communication among divided communities.[27] Delegates have to argue and convince each other, to reach an agreement on the allocation of points for each proposal. These micro-decisions are generally taken by consensus, even if sometimes, disagreement being too sharp and time being scarce, participants decide to vote. The social justice criteria give substance to what is meant by social justice. In this context, social justice means giving more – more attention and resources – to those who have less. In Seville, social justice is therefore implemented at both individual and territorial levels.

Despite the evident political content encapsulated in these social justice criteria, a more classical political struggle has also taken place to create such a redistributive process. The social justice criteria are part of the *Autoreglamento*. Even if discussed every year with the citizens, the *Autoreglamento* has mostly been shaped during the first year of the process, at the end of 2003. The idea to create social justice criteria, taken from some Brazilian PB experiences, was pushed forward insidiously by *Izquierda Unida*. At that time, the party was indeed divided between orthodox and reformers. The former were sceptical about the participatory budget and afraid to lose the political benefits of their participation in the municipal government by letting lay citizens decide, instead of the party. As the PB focused on areas of competence controlled by IU municipal councillors – sport, urbanism, gender and youth policies – letting people decide on these issues was therefore renouncing the application of the political programme IU representatives had been elected for. The dilemma was simple: how to implement one's electoral programme while letting people decide within the framework of a participatory process? The social justice criteria appeared as a way to filter proposals, to influence and frame them indirectly, not in their formulation like in Morsang-sur-Orge, but in their ranking. Social justice criteria thus appeared to IU members as an indirect way to apply their political programme.

Once the proposals have been ranked at district and city levels, a final list of proposals of investments, programmes and activities is established. This list is then transmitted to the Municipal Council, for integration into the vote of the global city budget. Once the budget has been approved, a last institutional body is set up, namely the 'Monitoring Commission' – '*la comision de seguimiento*'. Composed of all the district and city council delegates of the previous year, its main function is to follow, control and monitor the enactment of the PB proposals voted by the Municipal Council. Seville PB complex institutional cycle is synthetically presented in Figure 2.2.

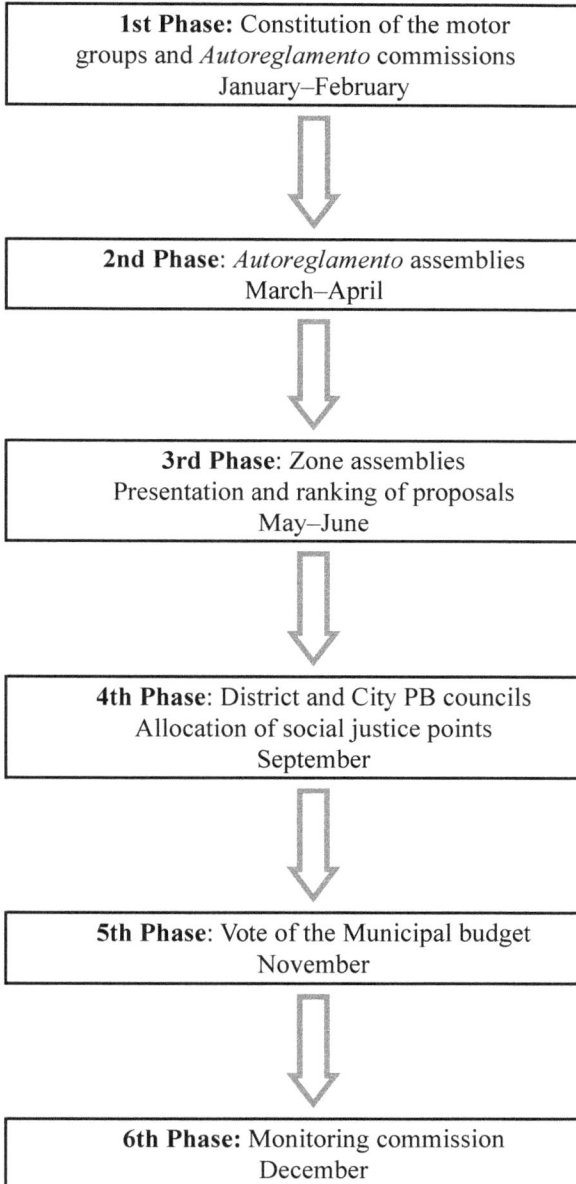

```
┌─────────────────────────────────────┐
│ 1st Phase: Constitution of the motor │
│ groups and Autoreglamento commissions│
│ January–February                     │
└─────────────────────────────────────┘
                  ⇓
┌─────────────────────────────────────┐
│ 2nd Phase: Autoreglamento assemblies │
│ March–April                          │
└─────────────────────────────────────┘
                  ⇓
┌─────────────────────────────────────┐
│ 3rd Phase: Zone assemblies           │
│ Presentation and ranking of proposals│
│ May–June                             │
└─────────────────────────────────────┘
                  ⇓
┌─────────────────────────────────────┐
│ 4th Phase: District and City PB councils│
│ Allocation of social justice points  │
│ September                            │
└─────────────────────────────────────┘
                  ⇓
┌─────────────────────────────────────┐
│ 5th Phase: Vote of the Municipal budget│
│ November                             │
└─────────────────────────────────────┘
                  ⇓
┌─────────────────────────────────────┐
│ 6th Phase: Monitoring commission     │
│ December                             │
└─────────────────────────────────────┘
```

Figure 2.2: Seville PB cycle

Seville PB process appears also extremely intensive, as it is composed of a multiplicity of institutions at different territorial levels. Intensity however, largely depends of the degree of involvement of citizens. Delegates can, for instance, easily attend one public PB assembly a week during the year. Ordinary participants, on the contrary, can only attend a few meetings a year. The decision-making power appears to be shared in Seville's participatory governance institutions between lay citizens – who present and vote for the proposals – 'active citizens', i.e., politicised actors, often members of political parties or associations who constitute most of the delegates – who discuss and apply the social justice criteria – and the elected representatives who both shaped the process at the beginning – by creating social justice criteria – and enact the decisions by integrating them in the municipal budget. From this perspective, a real co-decision process seems to take place in Seville. It is however circumscribed to the few areas included in the participatory budget – mainly sport, youth policies, gender policies and local urban projects – which represent only a little portion of the municipal budget (about 10 million Euros have been allocated for 2004, for instance – i.e., 12.5 Euros per capita). It can be said that in Seville, citizens decide a lot but on really few issues and with little money. It therefore translates into little changes in public policies, 'social justice criteria' themselves resulting in just a little more funds – 70,000 Euros – for the most deprived neighbourhoods and communities of the city (Sintomer, Herzberg and Röcke 2008b: 271).

NOTES

1. 'Only those projects accepting a method of co-elaboration with the residents will be selected'. In J.O. of 10.3.1977, p. 1356. See Blanc 1999: 177-178.
2. See especially Art. 10 of the law 'relative à l'administration territoriale de la République', J.O. 8.2.1992, p. 2064.
3. Law No. 252 of 1979.
4. Law 57/2003 of the 16th of December, 2003 – 'Ley de Modernisacion del Gobierno Local' (LM-MGL).
5. In cities over 20,000 inhabitants, 10 per cent of the electorate has to sign the petition for a proposal to be submitted to referendum.
6. James Fishkin's deliberative polls are for instance left out of this review, as they are quasi-experimental designs, aimed at testing scientific hypothesis, not at taking binding policy decisions.
7. In Denmark, the first consensus conferences were conducted on the irradiation of foods (1989), human genes (1989), the treatment of infertility (1993), chemicals in food and the environment (1995), and sustainable consumption (1996).
8. 'Each year, the majority of the 20 to 25 kilometers of new pavement has gone to the city's poorer peripheries. Today, 98 percent of all residences in the city have running water, up from 75 percent in 1988; [...] in the year between 1992-1995, the housing department (DEMHAB) offered housing assistance to 28,862 families, against 1,714 for the comparable period of 1986-1988; and the number of functioning municipal schools today is 86, against 29 in 1988.' (Baiocchi 2001: 48). For similar data, see Sintomer and Gret 2005.
9. Interview with F. Diener, Participatory Democracy Deputy Mayor, Morsang-sur-Orge, 14th January 2005.
10. See chapter four for detailed demographic data on the PB participants.
11. The 'Hello Neighbour!' initiative started in 2004, as a strategy of the municipality to answer the security problems faced by the city. This issue, understood as authoritarian and reactionary by the Left, has been answered at national level by the Communist Party through a 'conviviality and tranquillity' frame. As such, Communist municipalities have tried to develop 'conviviality' initiatives, such as 'Hello Neighbour!' in Morsang-sur-Orge and other cities on the periphery of Paris, for example, Saint-Denis or Bobigny. It mostly consists in collective lunch among neighbours.
12. The initiative 'Courtyards and Gardens' also started in 2004 as a way of offering cultural activities to individuals with low resources. The municipality contacts professional cultural companies (mainly theatre, dance and music bands) and offers them the opportunity to perform in public gardens, schools or the courtyards of collective condominiums. Individuals can also offer their gardens or courtyards as potential places for such activities, and can invite their friends and neighbours to attend the show. As in the case of 'Hello Neighbour!', the idea is to 'rebuild social links' by bringing people together around common activities.
13. Interview with Francis Diener, 14th January 2005, Morsang-sur-Orge.
14. Observation notes, Morsang-sur-Orge, Neighbourhood Council Langevin, 21th January 2005.
15. Ibid.
16. Garbatella is one of the Muncipio XI neighbourhoods.
17. Interview with Luciano Ummarino, Rome, 9th January 2005.
18. Ibid.
19. The evolution of Rome Municipio XI PB did not stop in 2005 however. The PB process was actually largely revised in 2007 after the local elections that the left coalition won easily in the Municipio XI. The town councillor in charged of the PB changed, amended the procedural design, that increasingly integrated e-participation (claims and proposals could be made on the internet, and participants could discuss on different thematic forums).
20. www.muncipiopartecipato.it

21. Regolamento de los Organos de los Distritos, Art. 3/2.
22. Seville municipality has always been controlled by the left since the first post-dictatorial munici-
    pal elections of 1979, except between 1991 and 1996. The Andaluz political system is composed
    of four main parties: the PSOE and IU on the left, the Popular Party on the right, and the Andaluz
    Party (PA), often playing a decisive role in government coalitions as it can ally either on the left
    or the right. As a consequence, it has been most of the time part of the municipal coalitions, except
    since 2003. In 2003, the Socialist Party decided to ally with Izquierda Unida rather than with the
    Andaluz Party as in the previous legislature. It has to be noted that, historically, the Left, and
    especially the Socialist and Communist parties have achieved better electoral results in Andalusia
    than in most other Spanish regions. See Porras and Soria 1993; Fdez.-Llebrez Gonzàlez 1999.
23. Interview with Paula Garvin, conducted by Carsten Herzberg, Seville, March 2005.
24. Constitution of Seville participatory budget, First Title, Statement of Principles, p. 2.
25. See www.participacionciudadana.Seville.org/PRESUPUESTOS/index.htm
26. All the proposals are submitted to two objective criteria: (1) given the percentage of the population
    affected by the proposals, they are granted from 0 to 15 points; and (2) given the socio-economic
    situation of the population affected by the proposals, they are granted again from 0 to 15 points.
27. Proposals are divided between investments and activities. Investment proposals receive points
    according to two criteria: (1) given the nature of proposals – i.e., to what extent the proposal
    focuses on uncovered basic needs and non-existent basic infrastructures or on already covered
    needs and on the improvement of existing infrastructures – it will be granted between 0 and 40
    points; and (2) if the proposal focuses on the improvement of the image and identity of deprived
    zones, it will be granted between 0 and 30 points. Activities proposals are given points according
    to five criteria: (1) given the characteristics of the population affected by the proposal, gender-
    oriented proposals will be granted up to 5 points, age-oriented proposals (focusing on youth
    or old populations) will receive up to 5 points as well, just like the proposals oriented towards
    disadvantaged groups (especially those focusing on unemployed and ethnic minorities); (2) if
    the activity proposal favours communication between different zones or different social groups
    of the city, it will be granted up to 14 points; (3) proposals favouring integration, tolerance and
    multiculturalism will receive up to 14 points; (4) proposals encouraging new cultural identities
    will be awarded up to 14 points; and (5) proposals encouraging the creation of committed and
    participatory citizenship will receive up to 13 points.

chapter three | the meanings of public engagement: how the participatory grammar reframes the role of good citizen

In Europe the absence of local public spirit is a frequent subject of regret to those who are in power; everyone agrees that there is no surer guarantee of order and tranquillity, and yet nothing is more difficult to create. If the municipal bodies were made powerful and independent, it is feared that they would become too strong and expose the state to anarchy. Yet without power and independence a town may contain good subjects, but it can have no active citizens.[1]

A. de Tocqueville, *Democracy in America.*

Is there really so little local public spirit in Europe? Are people that opposed to municipal autonomy on the old continent, as Tocqueville argues? The participatory budget cases presented here seem, however, to indicate the contrary. Some European cities have decided in the last decade – despite the limited powers and competences they are granted from a constitutional perspective – to try nurturing active citizens by creating new bodies of participation. Is this an illusion? Are these participatory experiences doomed to fail given the unfavourable context for the blossoming of a local public spirit? Tocqueville's argument is worth considering, as it subtly links civic culture, political institutions and citizens' character. The French thinker indicates the need to analyse institutions and civic behaviour in the cultural contexts in which they emerge. Avoiding the traps of a culturalist or essentialist perspective – reifying civic culture into a people's mentality or nature – it seems however, necessary to grasp the political context, at both national and local levels, in which participatory experiences develop.

The three PBs have indeed been presented from a formal point of view. To understand how people can be affected by participation in such settings, a more substantial account of the type of interaction taking place in these institutions needs to be provided. Procedural rules cannot explain by themselves, how people interact and change. These procedural rules are embedded in certain cultural, symbolic and political frameworks defining the norms of good behaviour. This chapter shows how a participatory grammar developed in the last decades, and was 'translated' differently in each country and at the local level.

First of all, grammars define common goods, rules of good behaviour, modes of coordination among actors, and are in general, embodied by specific characters and sedimented in objects and institutions. One of these grammars, which developed recently, is the participatory grammar, partly derived from the civic republican one. It defines public participation as an intrinsic good and is embodied in the good citizen character. The participatory grammar takes, nevertheless, a different shape given the country in which it develops. The emergence of a new grammar is necessarily marked by its interactions – inspiration, defiance, hybridising, etc. – with the other prevailing grammars, which are themselves partly specific to the country's history and political culture. Here, the participatory grammar takes the form of 'proximity democracy' in France, a managerial justification of participation in Italy, and a radical, but minoritarian understanding in Spain. Then, these specific participatory grammars are enacted in objects, laws, procedures and institutions. They are, for instance, enacted in local participatory budgeting institutions. These institutions, as they are sustained by the existence of groups of regular participants, interpret and filter the broader participatory grammar. This interpretation depends on the past civic practices and political experiences of the actors. The translation of the participatory grammar through the filter of the specific subculture in which the institution is embedded, thus gives rise to a specific 'group style' (Eliasoph and Lichterman 2003), defined by its discursive norms, symbolic boundaries and internal norms of solidarity. Once this style analysed, it will be possible to show how citizens are affected by their participation, as they learn to follow specific and conventional norms of good behaviour in the institutions in which they interact, and thus sometimes change.

The emergence of a participatory grammar

As mentioned earlier (see chapter one), the public sphere is ruled by implicit social norms – grammars – defining meaningful behaviour in a certain setting, enabling actors to evaluate judgements and claims (Boltanski and Thévenot 1991). As conventions, grammars have an historical trajectory and can therefore be localised in space and time. They thus have to be analysed as processes, from the moment of their emergence to their grounding in institutions, objects and laws, until their eventual decline or transformation. As such, competing grammars of public life can be distinguished. One of the most ambitious conceptual attempts from this perspective is Boltanski and Thévenot's (1991) model of 'cités' and 'common worlds'. They thus distinguish six 'cités'[2] and worlds that have been more or less salient across history. The cités have an historical trajectory, some decline – like the civic republican one – other emerge, like the 'managerial cité' (Boltanski and Chiapello 1999), or the 'ecological cité' (Lafaye and Thévenot 1993). I argue that in the last decade a participatory grammar or cité has emerged in western societies. This grammar is not a tabula rasa, and is partly influenced by previously existing orders of worth, and especially the civic republican, the managerial and the expressive individualist grammars.

The participatory grammar can be summed up in a motto: 'the common good should be the concern of everyone'. The definition of the common good should not be delegated to representatives, but elaborated collectively through deliberation in participatory institutions. The inclusion of citizens in democratic decision-making processes is necessary to enhance the legitimacy of public choices, to increase their rationality, to foster social justice, create social capital and civic bonds. The core tension at the heart of the participatory grammar lies therefore between the personal and the political, the private and the public. The question it aims to answer is how to create a common good from atomised individuals having specific interests. Given the fragmentation of society and of collective identities, the central political problem has become the creation of a public, of a community, overcoming divisions and cleavages. The participatory grammar considers civic participation as the best way to create a public. In some regards, the participatory grammar starts at home, as John Dewey (1927: 213) – one of its central theoretical inspirations – argues: 'Democracy must begin at home, and its home is the neigh-bourly community.' This grammar is therefore embedded in the promotion of the local, the personal, the proximity, seen as a pure and authentic.

The typical character of this grammar is the citizen, expressing him/herself di-rectly, i.e., without mediation, to allow a collective deliberation. As in the manage-rial grammar, horizontality, seen as the embodiment of democracy, is considered good; mediations, as introducing verticality and therefore authority, being on the contrary rejected. The central means of coordination in the participatory grammar is language – even if conceptualised in an enlarged manner, including argumenta-tion but also the expression of emotions. From this perspective, the specificity of this grammar is to enlarge the range of legitimate public discourses, to avoid the exclusionary features of impersonal argumentation attached to civic republican-ism. While the civic republican grammar relies mostly on general arguments ex-pressed at the first person of the plural ('we want'; 'we should'; etc.) or at the third person of the plural ('British people want'; 'the working class deserves', etc.), i.e., on representative discourses, a delegate speaking in the name of a group, the participatory grammar starts with an idiosyncratic subject, expressing him/herself at the first person of the singular ('I want' ; 'I think' ; etc.). The subject of the par-ticipatory grammar is an 'I', and the tension lies in the creation of a 'we' from dia-logue between separated beings. Typical discourses of the participatory grammar are therefore testimonies, personal stories and anecdotes, allowing the expression of individual needs, desires and problems. The participatory grammar takes up from the expressive individualist and the managerial grammar their emphasis on the individual agent speaking in the first person of the singular to express his/her desires and problems. The personal emphasis of the participatory grammar aims at avoiding grand discourses and ideological postures often portrayed as 'blah blah' or 'mere discourses'. The development of the participatory grammar can therefore be related to the coming of post-modernity and the decline of 'Grand Narratives' (Lyotard 1979).

The good citizen has to be practical, speaking to solve a concrete problem not to question the order of things. The participatory grammar is, from this perspec-tive, more oriented towards action than reflection. Collective discussion has to be effective, useful and therefore oriented toward potential action and decision. A typical grammatical mistake is therefore an overly general and impersonal speech unconnected to a personally experienced problem. This type of discourse is gener-ally cut short with a 'what's your point?' question.

While personal experience has to be narrated, public discussions never stop at this idiosyncratic point. Modalised discourses have to be shared with the audience. The good citizen has to show how his/her personal trouble concerns everybody and is therefore a public problem – given its collective roots and detrimental consequences for all – to be treated collectively. Generalisation should not mean depersonalisation however. The participatory grammar requires a 'distant commitment', i.e., both personalised engagement and an attempt to distance oneself from these idiosyncratic claims expressed in the first place (Cardon, Heurtin and Lemieux 1995). Grammatical correctness is always at risk between overly generalised – and therefore impersonal and inauthentic – discourses, and overly modalised ones, remaining at the personal level.

The bad citizen, being grammatically incompetent, is someone who 'doesn't care' about the common good or, even worst, someone parochial and self-interested. A typical grammatical mistake is indeed an over-modalisation, i.e., the incapacity to share one's experience or local knowledge, the narrated experience remaining personal and idiosyncratic. Conflicts emerge when positions are overly modalised or parochial, contradicting the collective strive for the common good. In this case, the individualistic or liberal grammar would be colonising the participatory imperative. Conflict can also emerge when citizens are refused an opportunity to participate or speak, especially when actors are qualified as incompetent or profane. An implicit rule of the participatory grammar is indeed formal inclusiveness: all should be able to give their say and bring an added-value to the collective decision. Motives based on competence are inappropriate in this framework, as they indicate an inherent inequality between participants.

While the participatory imperative is in part new, it shares, as well, certain features with other grammars of public life (Boltanski and Thévenot 1991), being both sources of inspiration and dissociation. The most obvious connection is with the civic republican grammar, which is also based on an equal right for all to participate, and makes of the common good the central goal of action. However, in this case the main means of coordination is not language and voice, but more directly the ballot and the representative system. The participatory imperative rejects – in part – representation, to allow the direct expression of citizens without mediations. The rejection of representation and verticality in favour of horizontal connections directly comes from the managerial grammar (Boltanski and Chiapello 1999). Delegation is seen as a form of alienation of the self's autonomy. As in the managerial grammar, the good citizen of the participatory grammar has to have a high social capital, to have good relationships with his/her neighbours, in order to convince them to participate. The good character of the participatory grammar is therefore embedded in a dense network of relationships. He/she is connected. As in the managerial grammar, the vocabulary of the project is central in the participatory realm, citizens being able to overcome traditional cleavages and divisions in a collective enterprise for a (common good) project. The focus put on the individual draws, as well, from expressive individualism (Bellah *et al.* 1985; Lichterman 1996), which puts the individual at the centre of society, in contrast to alienating collective identities. Participation would therefore be a way to realise human nature or to express oneself fully, in harmony with one's environment.

The historical and sociological roots of the participatory grammar have already been analysed in depth (see chapter two); but can nevertheless be rapidly recalled. As Blondiaux and Sintomer underlined, deliberation appears as 'the new spirit of public action'. New public bodies emerged across Europe to foster citizen participation (see chapter two) and, in the meantime, new theoretical conceptualisations were offered, proposing a deliberative definition of democracy (see chapter one). The articulation between theories and practices cannot be understood without including the concept of grammar. It can consequently be argued that a participatory grammar emerged in the last twenty years, praising the involvement of citizens at all stages of public decision-making processes, to answer some of the questions and challenges the other grammatical configurations were unable to solve. The development of the participatory grammar can be related to the decline of the civic republican grammar, embodied in the 'crisis of representation'. People no longer trust representatives blindly; they want to participate and decide directly for themselves. While the traditional distance between citizens and representatives was supposed to ensure impartiality, it is now considered alienating, politicians being deaf to the people's claims, hence the emergence of the concept of proximity and the focus on the local. The aim is still the promotion of the common good, but representation is no longer considered the best means to achieve that end. A new conceptualisation of the construction of the common good therefore emerged, articulating a craving for generality and a personal and local embeddedness ensuring authenticity. This new conceptualisation, as we saw, mostly comes from the hybridising of different grammars, and especially from the recent emergence of the opinion, managerial and expressive individualist grammars, that have been mixed up with some civic republican imperatives, like participation and the collective definition of the common good.

Deliberative and participatory theories of democracy have systematised what was starting to appear in practice, and have then been translated into second-hand literature to offer guidelines driving policy-makers in their choices. Templates of good practices have also been circulated to allow the replication of the best models (OECD 2001; Gastil and Levine 2005).[3] Advising firms have also emerged, specialised in participatory consulting. These professionals of participation are often former political or association activists who converted their knowledge and expertise to foster the spread of participatory democracy (Nonjon 2005).

Given the malleability of the participatory grammar it can give rise to very different interpretations and practical translations, from new public management and proximity democracy or community development and empowerment. These interpretations, that filter the participatory grammar, are not completely free however; they depend, in part, on the political culture within which this grammar is developed, i.e., past civic practices, historical traditions. In our cases, three declinations of the participatory grammar have been observed (Figure 3.1).

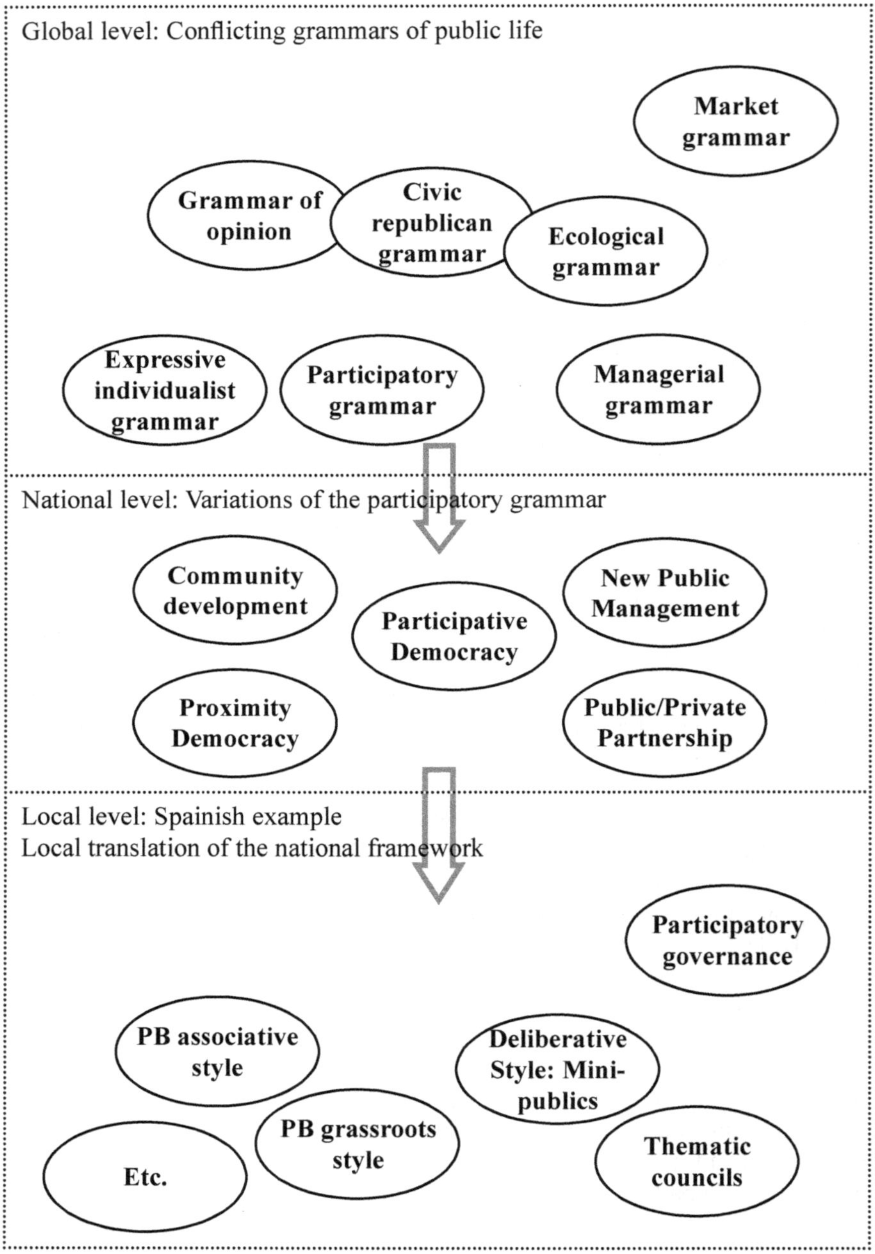

Global level: Conflicting grammars of public life

Market grammar

Grammar of opinion

Civic republican grammar

Ecological grammar

Expressive individualist grammar

Participatory grammar

Managerial grammar

National level: Variations of the participatory grammar

Community development

Participative Democracy

New Public Management

Proximity Democracy

Public/Private Partnership

Local level: Spainish example
Local translation of the national framework

Participatory governance

PB associative style

Deliberative Style: Mini-publics

Etc.

PB grassroots style

Thematic councils

Figure 3.1: Declinations of the participatory grammar

The Declinations of the participatory grammar

As noticed earlier, grammars have historical roots that can be traced back and are therefore an emanation and hybridisation of a certain political culture. As a consequence, the participatory grammar takes different forms given the national context in which it is embedded. The meaning attributed to citizen participation is therefore relatively different in France, Spain and Italy, even if they also share some common features as southern European countries. In France, the participatory grammar mainly took the form of a transformation and re-conceptualisation of French republicanism – based on the idea that the common good means generality, is located in the centre and embodied in national elected representatives. The concept of 'proximity democracy' mostly used to frame citizen participation in France makes sense in this context. On the contrary, in Spain and Italy, the participatory grammar remained more circumscribed to a certain set of actors or regions. The rise of the participatory grammar was nevertheless more widespread in Italy than in Spain, and took the form of a managerial discourse on administration modernisation and efficiency through citizen participation. Conflicting interpretations of the participatory grammar can nevertheless be observed, as more radical discourses are also voiced, putting the emphasis on the role of citizen participation in the deepening of democracy itself. Finally, the Spanish case, given the recent history of its democratic system, is marked by a weak participatory grammar; the dominant civic culture conducting citizens to apathy, moderation and depoliticisation. The few participatory voices that can be heard are therefore marginal and relatively radical, justifying citizen participation as a means to foster social justice.

The transformation of French republicanism: the emergence of proximity democracy

The appeal to citizen participation has mostly taken the form of 'proximity democracy' in the French context. The recent emergence of this concept cannot be understood unless replaced in the specific French civic tradition and its evolution in the last thirty years, with the progressive transformation of the conception of legitimacy and the common good.

The recent evolution of French civic culture has to be understood in the context of a large crisis of representative government, present in every European country but maybe deeper in France (Sintomer 2007). From 1977 to 2002, every national election (presidential or legislative) has resulted in the defeat of the incumbents. Abstention rates have also largely increased in the last twenty years, reaching 40 per cent in the 2007 legislative elections (Braconnier and Dormagen 2007), and almost 60 per cent in 2009 European elections.[4] In 2002, Le Pen – leader of the populist right – was present for the first time at the second turn of a presidential election. In 2005, the referendum on the European constitutional treaty offered a new sign of the growing distance between representatives and their constituency: while 92 per cent of the members of parliament pronounced in favour of the ratification, 55 per cent of the electorate voted against it. Polls regularly showed that a majority of citizens do not trust politicians and do not expect much from them. This distance has sociological roots too: the elected representatives do not embody a fair representation of the diversity of the national population. Women, the youth, immigrants are clearly under-represented at the Parliament and in most representative bodies, in higher proportions than in other Western democracies.[5] Intermediary bodies are also particularly weak. Political parties are far from being mass parties, despite the recent rise of membership after 2002 (Lefebvre and Roger 2009). Membership rates in trade unions are also among the lowest among European countries (together with Italy and Spain). The distance between elites and citizens has also been nourished by thirty years of gloomy economic and social climate, the rise of inequalities (Castel 1995), which put the French social model in question. Politics is no longer seen as a lever to change things, due to the negative impact of politico-financial scandals, the little room for manoeuvre in a context of increased European integration and globalisation.

This crisis is partly rooted in the exhaustion of the country's main normative frame of public action. 'French republicanism' – claimed to be inherited from 1789 and Jacobinism – has been consensual among governing political elites for a long time. Elected representatives were seen as the embodiment of the general interest expressed in elections, citizens' claims being understood as necessarily particularistic and self-centred. As Rosanvallon (2004) made clear, French political culture is defined by the conceptualisation of the common good in terms of generality. Influenced by the traditional defiance towards intermediary bodies (since Law Le Chapelier in 1791), any attempt to include citizens in decision-making processes is considered suspiciously as opening the door to lobbies and parochial interests. Local interest is framed, in the French political culture, as factions, opposed to the common good. Any claim coming from society, not expressed through the ballot box, is thus considered illegitimate (Rosanvallon 2006: 113–117). Political worth meant distance between the centre and the periphery, between representatives and the people, which allows efficiency, impartiality and legitimacy. For decades, universal suffrage has been the sole and unique means to achieve democratic legitimacy in France. But, as we saw, the decline of participation rates, the growing dissatisfaction with ruling elites and the lack of trust in the political system pushed towards reform.

The critique of French republicanism is probably as old as the model itself, but took a more decisive turn in the 1970s. The emergence of the 'second left', arguing for a more self-organised society – with the concept of 'autogestion' or self-management – was a clear sign of this change (Rosanvallon 1976; Rosanvallon and Viveret 1977). Urban social movements put into question the technocratic and authoritarian aspects of the post-war development model. From the 1960s onwards, associations have been increasingly integrated in the production of public policies and the delivery of public services. Associations have thus often developed as auxiliaries to the state. In rupture with the traditional defiance with intermediary bodies, associations have thus been recognised as having a central role in the construction of general interest. This corresponded to a will to restructure the state and transfer some of its competences to actors closer to local realities. The decentralisation wave of 1982 has to be understood as part of the same structural evolution.

The idea that proximity – especially in the allocation of services – associated with a more efficient and fair state, emerged at that time, was due to common criticisms of bureaucracy from both leftist movements and neo-liberal actors. Facing a blocked and immobile state, civil society was supposed to bring more dynamism and energy (Crozier 1995). Such discourses were constant in official reports and documents – especially from the Plan – in the mid-1970s. The organisation of the state was therefore, substantially transformed from the 1970s onwards, as illustrated in the different laws praising and pushing forward the growing involvement of citizens in decisions affecting their daily life (see chapter two). This does not mean, however, that French political culture evolved radically.

Parliamentary discussions on the 'proximity democracy' bill, finally adopted in February 2002, offer a good overview on the different conceptions of citizen participation in the French context. Some MPs, embodying traditional republicanism – and present on both sides of the political spectrum – were opposed to the possibility to include lay citizens in the discussion of public policies. They accepted the principle of the generalisation of neighbourhood councils, but feared its dire consequences for democracy: it would both weaken elected officials legitimacy and foster the expression of parochial interests. The words of a socialist MP are extremely telling from this perspective: 'Government is better at distance, while administration requires proximity. In a good democratic management, distance allows avoiding the confusion between private interests.'[6] These positions, even if they had a certain impact on the tone of the debate, were however minoritarian, a majority of MPs being ready to institutionalise citizen participation through law. A large consensus existed among MPs on the growing distance between citizens and politicians, and on the fact that participation could help solve this legitimacy crisis by fostering mutual trust, listening and dialogue between elites and the masses. They refused the reference to the term 'participatory democracy' in the law however, preferring that of proximity, despite the interventions of some Communist party members pushing for a more radical interpretation. Most MPs insisted on the fact that while only universal suffrage grants the legitimacy to interpret the common good, elected officials have nevertheless to listen and take into account the expression of citizens' private interests. Representatives keep the monopoly of the definition of the general interest, but citizens have to express their needs and interests in neighbourhood councils, playing a role of intermediation between politicians and the population.

Proximity democracy is therefore inhabited by a strong internal tension: on the one hand, it makes clear that elected officials keep the monopoly of the definition of the common good, on the other it insists on the need for dialogue with the citizens. This dialogue is permitted by the direct contact between political elites and the people, and mostly takes the form of an interpellation of the former by the latter. Conceptualised in this way, participatory democracy could not challenge the very foundations of representative government; the latter being only complemented by participatory inputs. This explains why neighbourhood councils were not granted any decision-making power in the law, being seen as mere consultative bodies in the eyes of French MPs. This understanding of citizen participation was summed up in the popular concept of 'proximity', meaning spatial, physical, sociological reduction of distance between elites and constituency to allow communication, dialogue and understanding between them (Le Bart and Lefebvre 2005).

Italy: the development of a managerial style public administration?

Even if it has been recently developing, the participatory grammar is less pervasive in Italy. Its recent emergence has mostly taken the form of a managerial discourse on the renovation of the public administration fostered by citizen participation. A more efficient public administration requires opening voice access to citizens, framed as 'users' or 'clients'. This new narrative is embedded in a broader political culture marked by depoliticisation and depolarisation, which followed the political scandals of the 1990s – coined *Tangentopoli* – and the repudiation of a divided past. In the long term indeed, Italy has been a highly politicised and fragmented society, along lines of class, religion, ideology and above all geography.

Italian civic tradition owes a lot to the French one, as it followed the revolutionary move and forbids all intermediary bodies, guilds and religious associations soon after the Le Chapelier Law was passed on the other side of the Alps. Like in France, however, the number of associations and informal groupings started to rise from the beginning of the nineteenth century onwards, in this 'great surge of popular sociability' described by Maurice Agulhon (1982). Comparison with France stops here however, as Italy did not exist as a nation until 1870 and therefore did not know the political centralisation of its French counterparts. On the contrary, the making of the Italian nation was marked by a wide defiance towards the state, Italians continuously giving their first loyalties to local communities (Koff and Koff 2000: 25–7). The late unification and centralisation of the country is however insufficient to explain the defiance towards the state. The weak allegiance to the nation also comes from strong attachment to the commune, stemming from a long history of communal government autonomy (Tossutti 2002). While the state is associated with corruption and authoritarianism, the commune appears as the embodiment of liberty. Strong local sub-cultures, therefore, developed to resist the centralising and standardising tendencies associated with the nation-state (Rokkan and Eisenstadt 1973; Caciagli 1988).

Centuries of territorial and political fragmentation have left traces. The fragmentation of Italian society took a new shape after the Second World War, with the opposition between the white and the red Italy (Kertzer 1980). Putnam has built up a strong argument on the differences between North and South Italy, the North and especially the centre around Emilia-Romagna and Tuscany, having by large much better institutional performance than the backward South, marked by corruption, inefficient public administration and a lack of economic development (Putnam 1993). Putnam explains these crude differences mostly by the higher social capital and interpersonal trust held by Northern regions' citizens – that have higher association membership rates, higher in election turn-outs or newspaper readership – in comparison with its weakness in the South. The North would be marked by horizontal bonds of mutual solidarity, while the South characterised by vertical bonds of dependence and domination. Putnam then offers an historical or path-dependency explanation of this phenomenon, tracing the roots of central Italy's civicness in a history of self-government and autonomy, while the South has been marked by vertical domination of lords over exploited peasants in the framework of a feudal archaic system (Putnam 1993: ch. 6). In some regards, the opposition constructed by Putnam does not go without recalling the traditional imagery of Southern European vertical, masculine, authoritarian political culture, opposed to the horizontal, feminine, democratic political culture of the North (Briquet 2003).

On average, indeed, Italians are marked by a high level of distrust towards political parties and politics in general, even if they consider democracy as the best form of government. Italians are known for very high levels of political disaffection, not only since the 1990s *Tengentopoli* crisis, but in the last forty years. The relationship of Italians to politics appears nevertheless extremely ambivalent (Segatti 2006), as the country has also been known to have among the highest participation rates in local and national elections in Western Europe. Strong ideological identities have generated cynicism towards other parties, but also in relation to politicians in general. The universalistic demands based on ideologies could hardly be met by the representative system, which created frustration and dissatisfaction. Then, major political events, crisis, corruption, and low levels of government effectiveness at the beginning of the 1990s, explain the high dissatisfaction with the political system. The political and financial scandals of the beginning of the 1990s completely delegitimised politics, considered corrupted, dishonest and inefficient (Koff and Koff 2000). The failures of the political system were partly attributed to the high polarisation of the history of the country.

The refoundation of the Republic in 1993 was thus supposed to embody the rupture with a divided and corrupted past. It resulted in a growing depolarisation and depoliticisation of the country. In contrast with the deep ideological divide between Communists and Catholics, the point was now to avoid conflict and rupture, to achieve practical public policies in a spirit of compromise. One of the key words of Italian political culture is nowadays 'avoiding rupture' ('*evitare la spaccatura*'). 'Spaccatura' means above all a democratic victory achieved by the exclusion of the margins or the minorities, i.e., a majoritarian imposition of a non-consensual decision (Ferrara 2001: 100–102). The point is therefore to achieve, as far as possible, consensual policies to avoid excluding part of the population. This is even reflected in the euphemistic self-designation of the leading national political coalitions, defining themselves as 'centre left' or 'centre right', despite their sometimes rather extreme political positioning.

The transformation of Italian political culture after the crumbling of the First Republic translated, as well, in a large renewal of political personnel. At the local level, new figures emerged, elected at the 1993 local elections. Without much political experience, nor formal adhesion to a political party, they based their support on civil society networks (Bettin Bates and Magnier 1995). Depolitisation had probably reached its climax (Dante 1997: 184). The following elections in 1996 were marked by a backward move of the pendulum towards a greater specialisation and professionalisation of the local political personnel. As many newly elected mayors of 1993 exit the game rapidly after their first mandate, classical political party leaders (as the party system had time to restructure and reorganise in the meantime) went back on the front-stage (Segatori 2001). This increasing professionalisation of the political elite appears as well as a form of depoliticisation, a good politician being understood as a good manager of public resources, especially at the local level.

These different trends – defiance towards national politics, and new local governments' styles – associated with europeanization and globalisation that made the state weaker, explain the emergence, in the 1990s, of a new localism. It refers to the revival of ethnic and regional movements, the shift towards decentralised structures of economic production and demands for devolution of competences to lower level government (Strassoldo 1992). It translated, in the Italian case, into a growing regionalisation and devolution of competences, as well as the development of new opportunities for public engagement.

In this context, the emergence of a participatory discourse took the form of a managerial style; increased participation being associated with efficiency and responsiveness. Participants are not framed as 'citizens' but rather as 'clients' or 'users' of public services. Linked to the lack of legitimacy of politics and the image of inefficiency attributed with public services, participation is a means to achieve more efficiency and pragmatism in public spending. This managerial discourse is committed to the realisation of 'projects' understood as concrete, consensual and pragmatic public policies, at odds with the ideological verbalism that once marked the Italian political culture.

A good illustration is the public administration modernisation law passed by the centre-left government at the beginning of 2007, also called 'anti-nothingdo-ers'.[7] Product of a large agreement across the political spectrum (apart from the far-left), and among trade unions as well, it was firstly aimed at increasing public administration efficiency by fostering careers mobility, 'meritocracy', out-sourcing, reducing costs by making redundancy easier for inefficient public servants. One of the justifications of the law was to deliver better service, by making public administration 'closer to the citizens'. One of the means to achieve such ends is also the participation in the evaluation of public services; the procedural devices remaining however vague. This law, and the vocabulary attached to it, reveals the evolution of the Italian civic grammar towards more public participation; but the latter remaining primarily associated with the modernisation and efficiency of public services.

A more radical participatory discourse has nevertheless emerged, relatively different from the consensual and dominant managerial one. Based on the inclusion of citizens' in public decision-making, especially at the local level, it is carried by political actors, mostly on the left, from *Rifondazione Comunista*, to the Greens and environmental associations, some members of the Socialist Party, and organisations linked to the anti-global movement, that federated through the New Commune Network ('*la Rete del Nuovo Municipio*'). Influenced by foreign experiences (especially Porto Alegre), and formulated through a civic republican language, participation is not understood as a way to increase efficiency, but to foster social justice, sustainable development and the nurturing of an active citizenship. It is probably at the crossroads between the main discursive justification of participation and this local radical democratic style that the norms of Municipio XI PB can be best understood.

Spain: a participatory oasis in a desert of civic passivity and cynicism

Spanish democracy is young, and differs from this perspective from both Italy and France. The recent authoritarian past paradoxically gives more legitimacy and stability to representative government and therefore presents a less powerful participatory civic grammar than the two previous cases. A participatory discourse nevertheless recently emerged as well in Spain, conveyed by the left and close in some regards to the civic vocabulary used in the Italian case. Like in Italy, the repudiation of a divided and violent past conducted to the emergence of a depolarised, moderate and consensual civic culture. Despite this general depoliticisation of society, Spain remains attached to egalitarianism, a form of anti-individualism and the centrality of the state, articulated to a republican grammar close to its French traditional formulation, considering generality and universality as the core of the political system.

While the scholarship remains divided on this question, it seems that a new political culture progressively arose in Spain with the transition to democracy. Despite the historical legacies and the burgeoning cultural changes starting back in the 1960s and largely explaining the fall of the Franco dictatorship, a new political culture arose in the 1980s (Gunther, Montero and Botella 2004: 135–7). The emergence of this new cultural matrix cannot be understood without referring to the discourse of the transition however. The transition to democracy was framed, by both political elites and the masses, as a 'period of consensus'. It has been characterised by an agreement on the need for Spain to overcome the divisiveness and brutality of the Civil War and to make a new start. Like in Italy, Spain had been divided between Communists (or better 'Republicans' in the Spanish case) and Catholics (Linz 1972), and such divisions are seen as responsible for both the Civil War and the dictatorship that followed. They had to be in some regards forgotten and overcome to start democracy anew. The first consensus of the transition was therefore the inevitability of the process of transition to democracy itself, which had performative effects. As Laura Edles argues (1995: 371):

> From a cultural perspective, the Spanish normalisation of democracy was a crucial mobilising *myth*. It was not normative epiphenomena, i.e. a by-product of the structural condition of democratisation. In other words, the Spanish transition was a 'success' because a democratic, reconciliatory symbolic framework came to emerge and, even more importantly, sustain itself throughout the Spanish transition.

A new national identity was in this framework ritualised. Every consensual moment – the first democratic elections of 1977, the drafting of the Monclova Pact and the drafting of the Constitution – gave occasion to celebrate the shared (or thought as such) symbolic framework in which the evil and confrontational Civil War and Franco era were opposed to the sacred democratic system and national reconciliation.

This consensual framework was successful in stabilising democracy but resulted in the passivity of the public. Spanish citizens got used to seeing democracy as a 'finished commodity', coming from above and promoted by leaders, in which active participation makes little difference. Hence, the low levels of political efficacy noted in most survey research (Morales 2003; Gunther, Montero and Botella 2004). Spaniards support democracy passively (Magone 2004). The Spanish political culture has therefore been labelled 'democratic cynicism', combining a strong support for democracy and a lack of interest in politics (Maravall 1982). The Spanish conception of democracy after the transition was highly formal and institutional, politics being firstly seen as the matter of parties, and above all of their leaders, citizens and civil society participation being seen as residual. Spanish civil society has, therefore, been constantly analysed as weak, rampant or passive, in comparison to the other Western democracies. Spain is, for instance, the country with the lowest number of associations per capita in Europe. In 1998, 28 per cent of the Spanish population were involved in at least one association, against 34 per cent of the Italians, 40 per cent of the French, 85 per cent of the Swedes or 53 per cent of the British (Morales 2003). Spaniards are no more disengaged today than they used to be at the dusk of the Franco regime, in which most associations were simply prohibited!

Being a good citizen in contemporary Spain firstly means remaining passive and moderate. Participation is not seen as a political virtue, as Benedicto underlines (2003: 499): 'This situation is reinforced by the absence of a cultural matrix of discourses, rites and symbols valuing political participation as the civic virtue of the "good citizen".' This public grammar cannot only be understood by the recent move to democracy, however, as other factors, linked to economic and social structures (as well as certain historical legacies) appear crucial from this perspective. First, most of the Spanish regions did not go through a fully developed industrial phase; they almost moved from an agriculture-based economy to a service centred one. As a consequence, Spain has never had mass parties like most Western democracies from the end of nineteenth to the end of twentieth century. They directly moved to catch-all type parties, lacking the support of millions of rank-and-file militants and detached from citizens' everyday life (Gunther, Montero and Botella 2004: 147–50). Hence the automatic distance between citizens and parties. Another important factor is the dictatorship legacy. There were indeed high depoliticisation pressures under the Franco regime, in which citizens were expected to be passive and obedient rather than active and participatory. Associations, unions and political parties were merely forbidden. Finally, the already evoked symbolic aspects of the transition to democracy gave the final touch to the consecration of the depoliticisation and moderation of society. The consequences of such a cultural code were therefore the moderation of opinions and practices – justified by a reference to the evil past of radicalism and polarisation.

How can participatory democratic experiences have emerged in such an unfavourable context? Participatory democracy developed in Spain as a minoritarian practice, and was hardly backed up by a nationally shared participatory grammar. It developed in certain regions and cities, with either strong national identities (Catalonia and Basque Country, Valencia) or strong politicisation traditions, like the red Andalusia. The latter is indeed known for its long history of agrarian revolts and mobilisation, and has been a communist stronghold for decades, in Cordoba even more than in Seville. Spanish participatory practices were often the result of radical political initiatives, mostly from the left of the political spectrum, i.e., the PSOE and IU, each having its own definition of participatory democracy, the former rather associative-based, the latter more grassroots style.

Unfavourable grounds for the blossoming of participatory democracy?

French, Italian and Spanish cultural configurations do not seem to constitute favourable grounds for the blossoming of participatory democracy. The three countries are marked by a tradition of high centralisation and reduced local autonomy, resulting in little decision-making power for local governments to share with citizens. Even if they have recently undergone a movement towards more decentralisation – and even a constitutional arrangement close to federalism in Spain –, local governments remain weak in comparison to other European countries. Then, overall, the three countries are among the worst in the traditional rankings of civicness: they have a higher level of distrust in politics and politicians than the rest of Europe, low levels of political efficacy, weak civil society with few individuals engaged in associations, political parties or trade unions. Given their recent political history, Italy and Spain have aimed at a rupture with a divided, violent, conflictive and corrupted past. It has resulted in the emergence of a moderated, consensual, depoliticised political culture. Cleavages are rejected, and consensus and compromise praised. In any case, these countries seem to offer the worst cultural conditions for the development and stabilisation of successful experiments of participatory democracy.

Despite these cultural hurdles, the three countries appear on the top of the list when it comes to the number of experiments of citizen participation in Europe (Sintomer, Herzberg and Röcke, 2008b). How can such a paradox be explained? The civic deficiencies of these countries might explain the need to foster participatory institutions, but why particularly empowered cases of participatory budgeting developed in such contexts? Part of the answer seems to lie in the political will of the instigators of the process, and even more in their distinctive style, largely inherited from certain historical features and local political cultural specificities.

The PB styles: Local political culture and civic customs in interaction

The participatory imperative is locally enacted by the actors, who filter the grammar according to the local political culture in which the institutions and the groups are embedded. By local political culture, I mean the entrenched civic practices and customs of a commune or region. Participatory budgets did not emerge from a *tabula rasa*, but from previous experiences aimed at fostering citizen participation (see chapter two). More broadly, the type of relationship and interaction developed between elected officials, public functionaries and citizens during the previous decades influenced the style of the group. It would be misleading however to consider that citizens passively endorse this style and do not play any role in interpreting and shaping it in interaction. It is the subtle interplay between civic customs inherited from the local political culture, the interpretation of what is a PB by the instigators of the process, and the interactions among the different actors that explain the adoption of a specific style by a PB group. A group style is understood as: 'a recurrent pattern of interaction that arises from a group's shared assumptions about what constitutes good or adequate participation in the group setting'. (Eliasoph and Lichterman 2003: 737). Three dimensions appear crucial in determining the group styles in which each of the cases are embedded: (1) the symbolic boundaries of the group (Lamont and Fournier 1992), i.e., the way it relates to the wider world, thus defining a 'they' and a 'we'; (2) the speech norms, defining what proper arguments and behaviours are, thus defining the role of the 'good citizen'; (3) the bonds among the members of the group (are they more or less cooperative or contentious, hierarchical or horizontal?), i.e., the mutual obligations actors give to one another. While our analysis follows the three criteria of a group style defined by Eliasoph and Lichterman, it differs also partly as it gives wider attention to the formation of the groups and their style, a process largely overlooked by the two American sociologists.

Most of the civic customs described here are the result of two years of regular observation of these groups. The three cases share some stylistic similarities, mostly coming from the participatory grammar they all enact. Speech norms always require PB participants to show a commitment for the common good, even if this concept is framed differently as 'the general interest', 'concrete projects' and 'basic needs'. Then, the participatory grammar requires a form of practicality from the participants, which gave rise to a specific relationship to politics seen as both politicking (idealism, political schemes and plots) and an inclination towards the common good. Again, the PB styles give rise to distinct definitions of legitimate politicisation, which might affect participants differently.

The proximity style in Morsang-sur-Orge: a bonded communist bastion

There is no formal process for the construction of PB groups in Morsang-sur-Orge. The construction of these groups directly depends of the organisers, i.e., the 'citizenry and associative life' administration, in charge of the coordination of the participatory activities of the city. Seen as non-political actors – in contrast to the local representatives – they hold enough legitimacy and neutrality, granted by their status of civil servants, to reward, generally insidiously, the right behaviours and sanction deviant ones.[8] Each neighbourhood council is indeed composed of an organisation committee in charge of the preparation of the meetings. The organisation committee is formally open to anyone but is practically constructed by solicitations and co-optation of the 'citizenry and associative life' administration, as few people volunteer spontaneously. The administration therefore selects people seen as competent, i.e., following the norms of appropriate behaviour in a PB.

The speech norms ruling the discursive interactions of the public assemblies appear central from this perspective. Public discussion plays a pivotal role in Morsang-sur-Orge PB decision-making process, most of the projects being elaborated, refined and decided through collective discussion. The first aim of the neighbourhood councils and thematic workshops is to allow individuals to express their views and judgements, which are listened to, and sometimes answered by, the elected representatives present at the meetings. The public grammar defining the civic competences required of the participants appears, therefore, in the interplay between members of the municipal majority, civil servants in charge of the organisation of the process and the regular participants of the local institutions.

First of all, to be seen as competent citizens, actors have to participate regularly in the deliberative arenas. It implies a regular physical presence in public meetings. As they are offered an opportunity to give their say, citizens who do not participate in the participatory institutions appear 'individualists' or 'couldn't give a damn people'.[9] There is indeed a strong participatory requirement pushing people to engage. As one participant once said in a public meeting: 'Those who are here are the best ones'.[10] As mere presence already means a form of support to the participatory process, those who participate easily appear as 'people who care about the common good'. A competent citizen is also someone able to mobilise his/her friends, neighbours and acquaintances. He/she therefore has to have certain social capital to be granted a good reputation. As the legitimacy of the participatory process depends a great deal on the number of participants, citizens have to be well-known, sociable and recognised as such in their community. The good citizen is a connected man.

To be considered competent, citizens not only have to participate in the public meetings; they above all have to speak in front of the assembly. It is the capacity to speak in conformity with the grammatical rules of the setting that allows actors to be granted the good citizen label. In Morsang-sur-Orge, a competent citizen cannot express self-interested, parochial or personal troubles in the framework of the public meetings. Those who express parochial arguments are indeed labelled 'ball-breakers', 'pain in the neck', 'loud-mouths'[11], etc. Explicitly interested arguments are therefore illegitimate in these public arenas. Despite the value attributed to proximity, a form of rhetorical globalisation – even if starting from a personal trouble – remains necessary to be seen as competent in this grammatical configuration. Being competent in Morsang-sur-Orge public assemblies requires using arguments framed in a way that is seen by others as promoting the common good. Interestingly, the vocabulary used by actors makes explicit references to the 'general interest'.

The common good is defined in a highly political fashion in Morsang-sur-Orge, even if political arguments have to be mobilised in a proper way. To be seen as competent, citizens should not adopt an overly critical or questioning role towards the municipal majority. Clear attacks on the municipal majority during public meetings appear to be politicking and do not grant their authors a good reputation. Partisan politics is thus excluded from the range of acceptable arguments within the deliberative assemblies. This could have led to a form of apolitical definition of civic competence, the good citizen being someone rejecting political treatment of public problems to opt for pragmatic and technical solutions. This is indeed often the case in French cases of participatory democracy (Le Bart and Lefebvre 2005; Nonjon 2005; Rosanvallon 2006). The picture is however more complex in Morsang-sur-Orge. Politicisation is valued, especially when it takes the form of membership on the left of the political spectrum, but it should not be expressed explicitly within public meetings. A participant voicing overly politicised arguments will be disqualified and labelled 'sectarian' or 'political schemer'. There is indeed a discursive division of labour between the different actors participating in Morsang-sur-Orge public discussions. As local elected representatives participate in the assemblies, the task of politicising the discussion falls to them almost naturally. They are the only ones to feel legitimate enough to talk about politics during public discussions. They regularly refer to 'the politics of the government', 'globalisation', 'the interior minister', etc., to impute responsibilities to the daily problems lived by the citizens. An excerpt from a neighbourhood council meeting where the mayor of the city intervened is pretty clear from this point of view:

François: 'I live in this city since three months and I have never had so many troubles in my life. My car was robbed twice [...] so I'd like to know what your plans in terms of security are?'

The mayor: 'It is the State that is in charge of citizens' security. We are fighting to get more resources locally, to get more policemen in the district, but it's not easy. We were even received by the interior minister, M. Sarkozy, to ask for more resources, but nothing happened since then despite his promises. He keep on saying the number of policemen increases, but it's not true everywhere. We have to fight with them to get more policemen.'

François: obviously not convinced: 'You're saying it's a struggle between you [the municipality] and them [the government]?'

The mayor: 'No! Not "you", between "us" and them!'

François: 'Ok, but what I see in the end, is that nothing is done!'

The mayor: 'It is by standing together that we'll be able to change things. [...]'

François: getting more and more aggressive: 'Ok, but you are the one to represent us, and I'm not gonna see Sarkozy myself.'

The mayor: 'No, we have to be all together. When we went to see Sarkozy, some inhabitants came with me, with a petition with thousands of signatures. And I can tell you it created another relationship than if I had been there on my own!'

(Observation notes, Robespierre neighbourhood council,
Morsang-sur-Orge, 1st of October 2005)

This excerpt illustrates the role played by town councillors – in this case the mayor – in the generalisation and politicisation of the discussion. While the discussion starts with the presentation of a personal trouble – a stolen car – a collective discussion follows about the origins of the security problems and the means to solve them. The discussion thus moves from a personal interpellation – 'I got robbed, what can you do about it?' – to a more critical mode – 'It is the government's responsibility'. Local politicians thus try to raise citizens' political awareness and eventually to mobilise them on local political issues opposing the municipality to other administrative tiers (ruled by opponent political parties especially).[12] In so doing, they map out the symbolic boundaries of the group – in a highly political manner – opposing the good local community to the conservative enemies, be they the right wing government, the European Central Bank or the WTO. The local community is thus understood as a 'besieged citadel', an island in a sea of liberalism. The image of the besieged citadel or bastion is not uncommon, and often used to characterise cities with a long Communist tradition. The bastion offers the image of a bounded local community, happy to live together, in a closed and perfect totality resisting the mainstream to keep its identity (Hastings 2003: 322–3).

The boundaries of the group not only exclude conservative institutions, but also parochial inhabitants. Local representatives often present themselves as the sole holders of the common good, facing individuals only moved by their private interests. Participation of the members of the municipal majority in these public meetings has, in this regard, no other function than the framing of the discussions to be sure that the common good – the 'general interest' in the French civic culture – is defended against local corporatism. The participatory democracy secretary is very clear from this perspective:

> The investment choices made by the citizens were pretty much those we [town representatives] would have done. And it was really reassuring for us. I was among those who were a bit scared at first, and who would have framed and controlled the process a little more, so that they won't be any trouble. So it's true, at the beginning these public meetings, were moderated, organised and controlled by the town representatives.

> (Francis Diener, Participatory Democracy Deputy Mayor,
> 14th January 2005)

The situation has not evolved radically since then. In French civic culture, the local level has been traditionally associated with special interests, corporatism, clientelism and eventually corruption (Rosanvallon 2004). In some regards, local representatives reproduce towards the citizens the criticisms of corporatism addressed by the central state to them. As they are granted democratic legitimacy, elected representatives can always use a Nimby argument to disqualify incompetent residents.

In identifying a 'they', these actors also define a 'we', creating a community with specific bonds. In the previous excerpt, the mayor explicitly transformed the participant's claim from a you/they, to an us/them conflict, thus including the resident in the definition of the legitimate local community, opposed to the right-wing national government. Even if elected officials would like to include all the population inside the community, the PB participants are clearly seen as insiders, as good citizens caring for the general interest. The bonds created among this group of good citizens, participating regularly, are relatively loose and superficial however, as the groups do not meet so regularly, and meetings have to be efficient, centred on specific issues to solve rapidly. The type of interaction among the group members are, therefore, relatively formal, as the core of group life is constituted by the PB meetings that do not imply an important personal or emotional commitment for the actors. The inceptors of the PB – mostly the municipality and the PB functionaries – try nevertheless, to strengthen the group bonds, by organising what is framed as 'convivial activities'. These activities aimed at creating 'social links', 'a good atmosphere' or merely 'to help people talking to each other', are oriented towards both the PB participants and the population at large.

Thus, to go beyond the formal collective discussion that preceded, a small buffet is often organised at the end of PB meetings. But the city has also broader 'convivial' initiatives, directed at the population at large – like 'Hello neighbours!' where big picnics are organised in the streets among neighbours – in which PB participants often play an active role. The organisation of convivial activities allows PB members to work together and thus to create stronger bonds among each other. The bonds of the group are therefore strengthened by collective action for the community. Interestingly, these two aspects – a disinterested and general promotion of the common good, and the promotion of fraternity, friendship and conviviality – are at the core of French civic culture since 1789, fraternity being understood as a necessary counter-weight to the impersonal power of the law (Rosanvallon 2004: 41–7). The type of civic customs developed by Morsang-sur-Orge PB is therefore an actualisation of a century long tradition.

If elected representatives often consider themselves as the sole holders of the common good, they nevertheless try to encourage, value and reward citizens who adopt the good posture. Criticising the parochialism of some participants, they try to encourage (what they see as) disinterested behaviours. By defining what is acceptable or not to say in these public meetings, elected representatives thus define what it means to be a competent participant. A competent citizen has to work for the common good, frame his arguments and propositions in ways that are seen as compatible with the interest of the community. If the 'good citizen' cannot be too politicised, he/she has to adopt a 'globalised rhetoric' (Gordon and Jasper 1996) that can be seen as 'politics in the noble sense of the word'. As a participant says in a documentary realised by the municipality about the participatory process: 'But politics, it's not that [he just evoked partisan politics]. And it's true that someone that would say: "I don't make politics, but I participate in the [participatory] process" [...] he is wrong, he makes politics [...] but the true one [...] not the fake one!' This sentence sums up the good way to commit in the participatory process. Being among the ten citizens selected to give their opinion on the meaning of the participatory process in the movie, this participant has been granted the status of good citizen. He is seen as competent enough to express himself in front of a camera to define what the meaning of his (and others) participation is. This sentence being selected in the movie, among the many rushes, is considered appropriate by the organisers of the process. Civic competence in Morsang-sur-Orge, therefore, means participating in the local institutions, attracting acquaintances in the process and speaking appropriately in the assemblies, framing one's argument as fitting with what is collectively defined as the common good. It appears that civic competence in Rome's local assemblies is not that different.

Democracy as concrete achievements: no-global in power in Rome Municipio XI

As inclusive institutions open to all the inhabitants of a given territory, there should not be any group *per se* in participatory budgeting arenas. Some, however, participate more regularly than others, are more integrated in the process and end up forming a group. In Rome, this process is proceduralised, as delegates are elected, and meet up every month to set up local projects. Groups in the Roman PB are therefore composed of PB delegates and facilitators, i.e., hardly ever more than twenty people in each neighbourhood. The style of PB groups in Rome is relatively different from that of Morsang-sur-Orge, in that it assigns a different meaning to the common good, less attached to generality as a political principle. Embedded in different local and national political cultures less centralised and unified than the French model, the Roman PB gives rise to a more politicised as well as a more specific approach to the common good. While in Rome, as in Morsang-sur-Orge and Seville, self-interest is rejected, the meaning attributed to selfishness and the common good is relatively different from one case to the other.

As the PB process in Rome is a mix of discursive and aggregative phases, all centred on the emergence, refinement and vote of local projects, the best way to scrutinise the style developed by the PB groups is probably to start with actors definition of a 'good proposal'. A 'good proposal' is generally defined as: (1) entering within the competences of the Municipio (thus not being unrealisable); (2) not being too expensive; (3) affecting the neighbourhood as a whole (rather than only a part of it); and (4) creating an added-value for the neighbourhood (out of the ordinary spending of the Municipio). Thus, once, at a Montagnola assembly, Antonio, one of the leaders of the group, appeared surprised when he read on the *verbale* that most of his proposals had been rejected by the technical services. He therefore asked the facilitators: 'How come all my proposals are either missing or considered as signalisations?' The facilitator answered, laughing: '*Maybe because they were all wrong*'.[13] There are, therefore, good and bad proposals in a PB assembly. Although the discussions are probably less framed than in the Morsang-sur-Orge assemblies, there is no *carte blanche* to say or propose anything. In the Municipio XI too, what is thinkable or not, i.e., what can be voiced or not by the public is defined in interaction between the facilitators and the participants. Even if the former are not part of the Municipality, they do nevertheless embody a certain definition of what a good citizen is and should be, by defining what a PB participant can or cannot say.

The discursive division of labour also includes the regular participants to the group, who recall the rules of the game when they are infringed. One of the most central discursive norms of Roman PB groups is the interdiction of self-interested arguments. This does not mean that selfish arguments are never voiced, but that they are sanctioned by the group. An excerpt, where a newcomer appeared extremely self-centred to the group and created a tensed interaction, is pretty telling from this perspective:

Mazia was coming for the first time to a PB meeting, and was apparently motivated by a personal trouble: the trees in her street had not been cut down for a long time and their branches created a danger for cars and pedestrians. She wanted to make a proposal to the PB on this issue, but was apparently frustrated when she learnt that it was impossible as this was the last PB session of the year, impeding any new proposal to be made. The other participants – regular ones – invited her to participate anyway, as she would be allowed to vote for the proposals concerning the neighbourhood. She answered: 'I cannot vote on the proposal related to street X, as I don't know it. And this street does not concern me'. She therefore decided to leave the meeting: 'At this point, as there are no problems related to my street, I'm going; because personally I don't know anything about those [other] problems.' A man nevertheless greeted her and encouraged her to come back the following year: '*At least you did* [...] *not your duty, because it's not a duty, but something good.*' Mazia, obviously upset as she was speaking faster and faster in a rather aggressive tone, made clear she would not come back as her problem was not taken into account. She was therefore sanctioned for her parochialism by the other participants: 'Enlarge your horizons. You focus too much on your own street here we're not working for our own streets egoistically, but for everybody.' Mazia, feeling attacked answered: 'I will enlarge my horizons when I'll see my problems solved.' Roberta explained to her afterwards that the delegates of the PB were not like delegates of their street or their zone, but of the whole neighbourhood. Mazia never came back to the assembly.

(Observation notes, Tormarancia working group meeting n.4, Rome, 28th March 2006)

As often, tensed interactions reveal the rules of the game implicitly followed by the actors. Usually, participants know they should not voice self-interested proposals; so they do not. In this case however, this newcomer, participating for the first time, did not know the grammatical rules of the institution. As they had been infringed, the rules had to be recalled and defined explicitly: 'here we're not working for our own streets egoistically, but for everybody'. Refusing selfishness and praising disinterested positions, the Roman speech norms appear close to Morsang-sur-Orge's. To appear as a good citizen, people have to take the position of the community, of the neighbourhood, the district or the city as a whole, but should never appear to be motivated by self-interested reasons.

The language of the common good can take different forms however. In the

Municipio XI, civic competence is not only defined by orientation towards the public interest; a good citizen has also to propose projects that are achievable and can be financed by the Municipio. Working group discussions are highly structured and proposal-oriented. Participants' speeches have to fit into one of the thematic areas and have to be seen as 'constructive', and not just as critical. While the general interest was at the core of the Morsang-sur-Orge PB, it seems that the 'project' vocabulary is central in Rome Municipio XI. A legitimate proposal has to be included in a 'project', which implies a projection in the future, planning the costs and benefits, a certain level of organisation, etc. The 'project' language is part of a broader contemporary narrative coming from the world of management (Boltanski and Chiappello 1999). The emergence of the project discourse stems from the same critique that led to the transformation of the French republican model, i.e., that of the inefficiency and authoritarian nature of the state in the 1960s and 1970s. The aspirations to autonomy, and the rejection of hierarchy, affected the public sphere as well with the deepening of decentralisation (which mostly took the form of regionalisation in Italy, see Putnam *et al.* 1993) and the promotion of a project-based public management.

Being constructive, the Roman citizen should also be aware that 'everything is not possible', that PB has strict financial limits, so that proposals should not be excessively ambitious. Facilitators constantly recall that the financial capacities of the Municipio are limited and that participants should be 'realist' and 'modest'. The rules of the games are not only recalled by the moderators, but also by the regular participants, insiders who know the grammar of the institution, as this excerpt attests:

After a few specific proposals concerning the pavements of some streets, a man in his late 50s, Giorgio, who was coming for the first time asked: 'Shall we make a general problem that tackles the whole neighbourhood or shall we focus on a specific discourse pointing out this or that specific pavement? According to me, our role is to make a general discourse about our exigencies for the neighbourhood. We should say that we consider that all the pavements of the neighbourhood should be in a proper condition. Then, all the ordinary management of the specific problems is their job [of the Municipio].' The answers of some experienced participants to Giorgio's opinion were however negative. Pietra-Emmanuella for instance: 'You're doing philosophy here. We have to point out some specific streets.' The other participants seemed to agree on that, and each one started to give the streets he/she considered particularly problematic. A woman added in the end: 'The argument of Giorgio is good, but the resources of the Municipio are limited. So we have to make specific proposals.'

(Observation notes, Montagnola working group n.1,
Rome, 18th January 2006)

Interestingly, in that case, the newcomer appeared moved by the common good, trying to avoid as much as possible promoting specific interests. Experienced participants brought him back to reality however, inciting him to be more specific and parochial, by focusing on specific problems. The grammar of the institution, even if pushing to speak the language of the common good, induces avoiding overly ambitious claims. A good citizen should therefore be competent enough to know what a 'reasonable proposal' is: not too expensive but not too narrow neither, to avoid sounding parochial.

Being reasonable, the good citizen can be politicised as well however. But, as in Morsang-sur-Orge, this politicisation should not take a partisan form. A participant voicing arguments that clearly seem 'politicking', or moved by partisan interests, is disqualified and given a sectarian reputation. The 2006 participatory budget cycle has, for instance, been advanced for a few months, to avoid mixing up with the Italian legislative and local elections of April 2006. The aim, according to the participatory budget councillor, was to 'avoid that the participatory budget be polluted by local or national political debates'.[14] Party politics appears, therefore, as 'pollution' in PB discussions. This rule is generally respected, as party politics is never openly addressed in the public meetings. When asked in interviews whether the PB was a political institution, most of the respondents answered that it should not be political (i.e., invested by political parties), but rather oriented towards the common good (conceptualised in a non-political manner). Even politicised participants, like Milena, a long-time Left Democrat (DS) party member in her 40s, and regular participant of the PB, cast politics out of the PB: 'It's good that we don't see too many party members here; the PB shouldn't be a political thing. […] When I run for delegate I never introduce myself as an activist, but as a citizen of the neighbourhood.'[15]

The refusal of political discourses is often recalled by the participants themselves in interaction. Once, in Montagnola assembly, a delegate of the previous year, made a long intervention (5 minutes), sharing his delegate experience and stressing the importance of participatory democracy; he was however rapidly sanctioned. Antonio cut him short saying: 'You already spoke too long, and eighty per cent of what you said were '*politichese*', and twenty per cent were proposals already accepted.' By '*politichese*' Antonio meant the unclear and useless political discourses and rhetoric used by professional politicians, i.e., mere politicking. Impractical discourses, not oriented towards concrete proposals or projects, are therefore clearly sanctioned in the assembly. It is impossible to express political, normative or general arguments if they are not used to justify a concrete proposal. Roman PB speech norms tend towards action, not reflection. When participants escape too far from the grammatical dominant mode, they are sanctioned by a classical: 'so, what's your proposal?' This was confirmed in the interviews made with the participants, where most of them defined the PB as a non-political process. Silvino, for instance, made it clear: 'It's not a political process and it shouldn't be. Otherwise, it is the end. If even in these things we put politics in the middle […] we lose the meaning of things.'[16]

This offers an accurate picture of the symbolic boundaries set up by Roman PB groups. Party politics is seen as impure – as being corrupted and ruled by self-interest – in comparison to participatory democracy, as working for the common good and social justice. This does not mean that the boundaries with the wider world set up by the groups were completely contentious however. The Roman groups did not have the imaginary of the 'besieged citadel' like in Morsang-sur-Orge and above all, Seville. On the contrary, PB was framed as being part of a broader group, the no-global movement, fighting against neo-liberalism and promoting social justice and democracy against the lack of transparency of international organisations' decision-making processes. The participatory budget was often seen in Rome as the direct enactment of some of the claims of the no-global movement. Far from being alone and isolated, the Roman PB was supposed to be avant-garde, supported by the movement. These boundaries were not shared equally by all the participants, however; the inceptors of the process, the moderators of the discussions, and the most politicised actors were at the forefront from this perspective.

The group bonds were relatively loose in Rome's PB. As the process is not intensive – people met a maximum of six times during the year – group members do not share much more than formal interactions during the assemblies. Usually, people go to the assembly, discuss for two hours and then go back home. There are a few socialising events afterwards like in Morsang or Seville. Participation in the PB process is indeed understood as a functional activity for most of the Roman participants. As said earlier, the Roman PB is very project oriented, so that it does not leave room for the creation of strong bonds among individuals. The 'we' created through the Roman PB is therefore relatively elusive (Lichterman 2005).

To be a competent citizen in this Roman setting, actors have, therefore, to participate actively, to mobilise their networks, but also, as in Morsang-sur-Orge, to speak appropriately. Appropriate interventions in these public discussions mean both voicing public-spirited and 'reasonable' projects, financeable by the Municipio, and therefore not overly ambitious. It implies being constructive, proposal-oriented, and not critical towards political actors. This is facilitated by the non-participation of local councillors in the assemblies. From this perspective, civic competence in Rome is different from Morsang-sur-Orge. In Morsang, actors are pushed to make ambitious proposals and eventually to mobilise against higher administrative tiers (the region or even the state) to allow these ambitious proposals to be achieved. This discursive work is done by association members and political activists in Rome, for whom the politicisation of the discussion has a different function, more ideological than merely political. Civic competence in the Roman case therefore requires being able to generalise one's arguments, to show that the local proposals are in line with the common good, not only of the neighbourhood or the city, but also at a more global level.

A radical democratic style: social justice in practice in Seville

In Seville PB groups are not composed of many ordinary citizens, but more often of experienced activists and actors with a long political history. Given the procedural organisation of the PB in Seville, it seems coherent to speak of a group only in the case of the delegates and members of the motor group – that are sometimes the same – who meet regularly all year long. The group of good citizens is there-

fore largely self-selected, composed of voluntary members of the motor groups
– open to anyone – and delegates, who have run as candidates. Hence the clear
over-representation of politicised actors in Seville PB groups, self-selection favouring the exclusion of the less resourceful actors (Gaxie 1978).

Despite regular meetings, the group bonds are relatively thin within the PB
groups. People meet for the meetings, sometimes go for a beer together afterwards, but it does not go further. Members of the group are not complete strangers
however. They are often well-know local activists, who have been active in the
local civil society for years, being members of neighbours associations, political
parties or cultural associations. In many ways, the PB meetings offer a platform
allowing different community leaders to gather and act together.

Political affiliations, even when they are mutually known, are not commonly
exposed in public. They are not seen as relevant information worth revealing to
the group and especially to newcomers. It would otherwise give an overly political identity to the group. Once, during a meeting where the members had to walk
through the city to visualise the different proposals that had been made, I had a
long conversation with one of them, Ana. Interestingly, her tone, but also the content of what she said, were totally different from what she expressed front-stage
with the others. Talking to me, she allowed herself some pretty strong and straightforward political statements:

> I'm fed up with this dictatorship of the youth! There is an article in the
> constitution that says we are all equal, independently of our race, religion,
> ethnic group, gender, etc. So how come in this country young people have
> more rights than anybody else and can disturb a whole neighbourhood doing
> noise, music [...] with the *botelon*?'[17]

She systematically stopped speaking, however, when other participants were
next to us. She nevertheless made the same type of speech a little later, while in a
bar, when only a few participants she knew (members of the PSOE, as herself) and
myself were left. Politics was therefore always present, but more in the whispers
than in the actual collective conversations taking place publicly (Eliasoph 1998).
Among friends, backstage, people allowed themselves to talk politics and voice
their convictions, which they did not do in public, especially in the presence of
public functionaries, understood as political allies of the municipal majority.

The versatility of actors (Moody and Thévenot 2001), depending on the situation, tells a lot about the norms ruling public speech in Seville PB groups. A good
illustration is offered by the discursive behaviour of one of the most politicised
participants of the process. Surprisingly, Javier, when acting as a PB delegate,
did not speak as a long Communist Party militant anymore, but as an apolitical
resident, evaluating the technical feasibility of the proposals. Taking the role of the
good citizen in Seville sometimes requires putting one's political affiliations on
the side and adopting an apolitical and technical discourse. I was indeed extremely
surprised when I saw that Javier – husband of the municipal councillor in charge
of the PB, Paula Garvin, and the central actor who conceptualised the city's PB –
had decided to run for delegate in his own neighbourhood for this year. He had no

problem in getting elected. When asked why he had decided to run, he answered: 'It's the best way to evaluate how it works in practice and I wanted to have a visual experience of what it is to be a delegate. [...] And I wanna know whether all the problems pointed out by the municipality's technicians (proposals are too expensive, hard to finance, blah, blah, blah) are true or not'. Following his group – formed of delegates of the neighbourhood and some municipal functionaries – for a visit of the zone's proposals, his very active role in evaluating the viability of the proposals, even the most trivial ones, was striking. Thus, concerning a proposal to set up a speed bumper in a street he asked one of the urban planners: 'can we really put a speed bumper here? Is it not dangerous? And what about the buses, will they still be able to pass?' Far from a role of political hardcore, he did not try to politicise the discussion about the necessity of the bumpers, its importance in relation to the more fundamental needs, etc. Knowing precisely what the aim of such visits was (he had the idea to create them) he therefore took the appropriate role, that of the good citizen evaluating whether a proposal is viable and worth investing public money. When talking backstage however, to some people he knew (some of the other participants or the civil servants) he took back his political hat, talking about the latest evolutions of the political power relationships among parties at the municipal level.

Interestingly, at the next meeting of the group, when members were supposed to evaluate the proposals and attribute the social justice criteria, Javier changed his role however. He put back his political hat. This meeting was indeed organised to rank the proposals, according to their ability to foster social justice and answer the basic needs of the population. Participants had therefore to evaluate the proposals, from the perspective of all the population, and especially of the most marginal inhabitants. Many times, in this setting, Javier insisted on the fact that speed bumpers and pavements were not basic needs of the population, even if many proposals of this type had been made. While the other participants sometimes disagreed with him, he constantly argued – in a rather political way – that people in the suburbs had much higher needs than the middle class of down town. He also voiced ironic jokes to make his point: 'Just ask people of the South District [the poorest of the city] whether they consider pavements as basic needs!'

Javier's example is significant, in the sense that if he – who has made of politics a vocation – could put his political identity on the side to play the appropriate role, anyone can, and especially the experienced activists who are the pillars of Seville PB. The normative expectations and the type of behaviour required of group members are therefore highly volatile in Seville. Publicity induces neither to depoliticisation nor to politicisation in itself (Eliasoph 1998; Hamidi 2010). Situations are ruled by different normative expectations shaping the actors' behaviour. Different forms of competences are expected from the actors, individuals being expected to move fluidly from one role to the other.

There was, however, some regularity in what appeared as good discursive behaviour, like the exclusion of self-interested speeches. A good example comes from a scene that took place in a Casco Antiguo assembly, as disagreement on a proposal led to a collective discussion on the meaning of PB and the grammatical rules of the game. The first two speakers of the evening, Raul and Andres, were both members of a cultural association, and came to defend a proposal of percussion and dancing workshops for the neighbourhood. Their proposal created a debate however, as they appeared as both proponents and beneficiaries of this proposal. As members of the association offering the workshops, they would get money from it, i.e., they had a personal financial interest in the proposal. The reactions of the audience – composed of regular PB participants – were tough; Raul and Andres had infringed the grammatical rules of the PB:

> *Paco*: It's a problem to be both the proponent and the company delivering the service [...] For instance, I proposed a yoga workshop, but it's another company that will take care of it.

> *Maria*: It's not legal, that's all!

> *Paloma*: You have to see the aim of the PB, it's not for private purposes, otherwise we wouldn't be here. We participate for our city, our neighbours. We don't participate for ourselves. If afterwards there is a personal gain, ok, but it shouldn't be direct.

> *Enrico*: We participate for our neighbours. If we want this street to be fixed, it's for the neighbours; it's not the company that is going to ask for it. It's for the needs of the neighbours. I made a proposal of concerts in the neighbourhood, but I'm not an orchestra director.

> *Antonio*: We have to work in the interest of citizen participation.

> *Enrico*: It's not moral, that's all!

> (Observation notes, Casco Antiguo zone assembly,
> Seville, 6th April 2006)

After this tough debate, the two young men argued rapidly, saying they did not know and that they would change the proposal. They looked pretty embarrassed and left the assembly right after. As some participants phrased explicitly: 'We participate for our city, our neighbours. We don't participate for ourselves.' Interested participation would even be immoral. On the contrary, the aim of the PB is to satisfy the 'needs of the neighbours'. As in Morsang-sur-Orge and Rome, the aim and justification of participation is the common good; but, it is framed in terms of 'needs' in Seville. This definition of the common good is institutionalised with the existence of social justice criteria, pushing participants to take a disinterested position, or better, the position of the least favoured in the city. A good proposal targets basic needs more than superfluous wills. The common good in Seville is not framed in terms of 'general interest' or 'concrete projects', but in terms of 'needs'. This definition – embedded in the self-definition of the institution in the *Autoreglamento* – is highly political, implying some kind of redistribution, derived from the communist local culture in Seville. Putting the emphasis on needs requires ranking them, making choices, and therefore rejecting a unitary definition of the common good, to prefer a more agonistic one. It is political in the sense that it requires creating cleavages, choosing between foes and friends (Schmitt 1939).

Being a good citizen therefore requires making proposals targeting the largest number of people and then, in priority, the weakest ones. Proposals have not only to be general but they should also be concrete and doable from a technical and financial point of view. Javier's behaviour – evoked above – is again highly telling from this perspective. All along the meeting, he sanctioned and even asked that some proposals be excluded from the list of the possible investments, as they were too general, i.e., infeasible from a technical perspective, as he said once: 'This is not aimed at any direct investment. The proponent does not say whether there is a precise problem or not, he just says we should do this or that, not in relationship to any specific problem.'[19] Like in Rome, to be valid and legitimate a proposal has to be concrete and specific, not too general. If proposals are not concrete enough they cannot be financed. This was confirmed by a joke Javier made later. He ridiculed a proposal asking for 'improvements in the Santa Cruz neighbourhood', saying: 'next year I'll propose the improvement of all Seville!' People laughed with him, even if they appeared a bit embarrassed about bashing people's proposals so much. Jokes tell a lot about the implicit rules guiding behaviour within a group.

The speech norms of Seville PB also give indications on the symbolic boundaries of the groups. One cannot but be struck by the impression of permanent battle between the different political parties in Seville. The PB has mostly been set up by *Izquierda Unida* – the PB delegate in the municipal majority being from IU, and the main areas of investment for PB proposals being those open by IU municipal councillors. The inceptors of the process and most of the regular participants – who are in fact politically close to IU positions – feel therefore constantly embedded in a local war for political domination, with the PSOE and the right. The enemies on the right are not surprising and their criticisms are well relayed by the press – local and national (especially the daily ABC) – that frequently writes anti-PB articles in its columns. The competition with the PSOE, with whom IU has a municipal alliance, is more surprising. It becomes understandable when one knows that Andalusia has historically been a 'red region', where power has always been shared (at the regional and provincial levels, but also for the municipality of Seville) between the PSOE (clearly the dominating party), IU and the Andalusian Party (Fernandez-Llebrez Gonzàlez 1999; Escalera 2002). These parties are therefore constantly fighting to tip the scales of the power relationship in their favour, i.e., to gain votes and support.

This local political culture is clearly reflected in the PB group style, especially when it comes to drawing their symbolic boundaries. The PB is seen by the participants as a ground of contention between IU and the PSOE to catch political support and popular votes. In the South District, for instance, participants constantly complained about the PSOE attitude towards the PB. Far from supporting it, the Socialist Party set up an alternative participation program – *The Integral Plan* – aimed at involving the population in the urban rehabilitation of this district, known as the most deprived of the city. In the group discussions as well, references to the manipulation and malignancies of the PSOE were frequent. Going back to the example of Javier, evoked earlier, he once asked for a proposal in a public meeting to be rejected, as he saw it as 'a political coup'. Being too general and not concrete enough, that proposal was clearly aimed (in his mind) at delegitimising the PB (that would be seen as unable to solve people's problems). It had to be manipulation by the PSOE. The boundaries of the Seville PB groups seem therefore clear: all those who do not support the PB actively are against it. These strong boundaries based on political cleavages, creates an atmosphere of a 'besieged citadel'. As a radical political experience, the participatory budget is attacked as being subversive and dangerous for the ruling elite. Island of democratic purity in a hostile conservative sea, the PB, and the political party supporting it, are at the forefront of resistance against neo-liberalism and the struggle for social justice.

NOTES

1. Tocqueville 1835 [1998]: 68–69.
2. The term in French is 'cité', but the concept has then been subsequently defined as 'grammar' by Thévenot himself and translated as such in English (Lamont and Thévenot 2001).
3. The parallel with the emergence of the managerial grammar is striking, as its principles were also synthesised in handbooks and promoted by consulting firms and management experts.
4. Sources: Post-electoral polls, Cevipof.
5. In the parliament elected after the 2007 legislative elections there were only 18.5 per cent of women, one of the lowest rates in Europe.
6. Jean Espilondo, socialist MP, 2nd session, 14/06/01.
7. '*Legge anti-fannulloni*'.
8. The position of the citizenry administration is ambiguous however, as four of its five members are also members of the Communist party, and live their professional activity as a political one. The neutrality of local civil servants appears in this regard rather problematic.
9. The French expression would be 'je-m'en-foutistes'.
10. Wallon neighbourhood council, Morsang-sur-Orge, 23rd February 2006.
11. The French expressions would be 'casse-pieds', 'emmerdeurs', 'grandes gueules'.
12. The mayor evoked for instance the mobilisation of the citizens on the issue of security, some of them even coming with her to meet the interior minister, Nicolas Sarkozy. This type of mobilisation happened on other issues like the creation of an old people's home and the opposition to the creation of a new air lane in Morsang's sky.
13. Observation notes, Montagnola working group discussion no. 4, Rome, 3rd May 2005.
14. Interview with Luciano Ummarino, Rome, 10th October 2005.
15. Interview with Milena, Rome, 14th June 2005.
16. Interview with Silvino, Rome, 17th May 2005.
17. Observation notes, Seville, 16th September 2005. The *botelon* is a typical Spanish custom – that appeared in the 1980s with the cultural liberalisation of the country, the *movida* – consisting of young people gathering together in the streets and piazzas of city centres to drink and hang out at night. It is a cheap way to socialise and have fun, and it usually gathers hundreds of teenagers and students during the weekend. It had become a public problem at the end of the 1990s, when the conservative government of José Maria Asnar decided to regulate it partially, and as a matter of fact to ban it, even if this still depends on a decision of the city mayor. The *botelon* has indeed created a lot of conflicts between the young people and the residents suffering from the noise and the dirt and mess created by such festive gathering. It was a recurrent issue tackled during the PB meetings in Seville as well in 2005–2006.
18. Javier, Casco Antiguo PB district council meeting, Seville, 26th September 2006.

chapter four | participatory democracy and its public

De Tocqueville pointed out in effect that popular government is educative as other modes of political regulation are not. It forces a recognition that there are common interests, even though the recognition of what they are is confused; and the need it enforces of discussion and publicity brings about some clarification of what they are. The man who wears the shoe knows best that it pinches and where it pinches, even if the expert shoemaker is the best judge of how the trouble is to be remedied.[1]

J. Dewey, *The Public and Its Problems.*

Participatory democracy aims at opening up the institutional machinery to citizens. Through the organisation of public meetings, assemblies and working groups, citizens are offered the opportunity to give their say and eventually to have an impact on public decision-making processes. Despite the high expectations and incantatory discourses of both political theorists and participatory democracy advocates, participation rates in public arenas remain, in average, fairly low. Those who commit themselves and get involved in participatory politics appear, in this regard, as either one of the 'happy few' or a new local elite. A closer look at the public of participatory institutions appears therefore necessary. What types of actors are ready to dedicate their time and energy for the community's welfare? Why do they participate if, in the end, so little is at stake in PB institutions? What type of competences coming from their professional activity, their militancy or their everyday life can they mobilise in the framework of PB institutions? While repeated participation is hypothesised to be a prerequisite for self-change, it might be interesting to see who are those who stay and do not exit PB institutions. It appears indeed crucial to assess who the participants of European innovative democratic institutions are, to then evaluate to what extent they can be affected by their participatory experience.

This chapter therefore aims at presenting the diversity of the participants in the three case-studies of municipal participatory budgeting. First, the question of participation in innovative democratic institutions is tackled from both a conceptual and procedural point of view. Municipal participatory budget institutions rely indeed on both a formal inclusiveness principle that nevertheless leaves room to self-selection effects, as will be seen in the second section. This necessarily raises questions of legitimacy: as these participatory bodies take binding public decisions, the representativeness of the participants appears as a central issue. In the third section, we move to a more micro perspective to assess what are the social, cultural and political backgrounds of the participants. In so doing we try to construct a typology of actors using both in-depth interviews and ethnographic material. Finally, the type of competences participants possessed before entering the participatory arenas is presented. Three main competences can thus be distinguished: local knowledge, professional competence and political experience.

The limited participation to innovative democratic institutions

Participatory democracy aims at including the maximum number of citizens in public decision-making processes. Influenced, at least in its mythology, by the dream of direct democracy, the Greek *polis* or New England town meetings, participatory democrats set up institutions aimed at being as inclusive as possible. Participatory budgeting especially – as generally brought forward by leftist political parties and social movements – have appeared due to a critique of the exclusionary aspects of representative government. Not only would representative government be in crisis, but it would also be profoundly unequal.

Two main criticisms are addressed to representative government (see chapter one). It faces first of all a problem of legitimacy, as public decisions are said to be taken by an elected cast, a powerful minority. This issue is all the more relevant today with the decline of election turn-outs, which decreases the quantitative legitimacy of elected officials. Then, representative government appears to participatory democrats as a hurdle to social justice. Far from representing the entire population, most representatives are white males, relatively old, who went to the same universities and come from the upper economic groups of society (Gaxie 1978; Bourdieu 1984; Verba *et. al.* 1995). Implying an adequacy between individuals' interests and political preferences, participatory democrats therefore fear the orientation of public policies in the interests of the dominant elite. They therefore push forward the idea of a 'politics of presence' (Phillips 1995; Goodin 2004) or 'mirror representation', participatory democracy promoting the inclusion of social, ethnic or gender groups generally excluded from public decision-making (Young 2000).

The formal inclusiveness of participatory bodies is not sufficient however to allow for a profound opening of the local political machinery to the lay citizens generally excluded from public decision-making processes. In the three studied cases, the participation rates are fairly low and offer an over-representation of middle-classes and politically left-wingers. This raises problems of legitimacy to the decisions taken in these local institutions.

Inclusiveness as a principle

As most cases in Europe and Latin America, the three PBs studied in this book are based on a formal inclusiveness principle, embodied by neighbour assemblies open to all the residents.[2] As mentioned in chapter two, there are nevertheless slight differences across cases. Rome Municipio XI is probably the most inclusive, as neighbourhood assemblies are not only open to all residents, but also to the students of the district as well as the people working on the Municipio territory; based on the idea that despite their non-residency, they are also affected by local public policies. Inclusiveness is also symbolised by the possibility offered to immigrants to participate in the process, despite they cannot vote in local or national elections. The age threshold appears as well highly inclusive, as anyone over 14 years old can participate and vote. Seville, even if participation is restricted to residents, also allows the participation of foreigners and grants participation rights to individuals over 16 years old. In both cases, the constitution of the participatory process clearly states the will to offer a more inclusive model than the one offered by representative government that restricts voting rights in national and local elections to national citizens over 18 years old. Inclusiveness thus appears as a clear political stance of both municipalities. They frame their battle for political inclusion as part of the historical trend towards more democratic participation. After the masculine universal suffrage, the granting of voting rights to women, the decrease of the age threshold, representative government needs to go a step further by including foreign and younger citizens, not only in elections but also in the production of public policies. Even if inspired by the same inclusive principles, PB is less formalised in Morsang-sur-Orge, as there is neither an official constitution of the process nor clear formal rules defining participation rights. Participation is merely said to be 'open to all the residents of the city'.

The three cities created, therefore, bodies open to the self-selection of the participants. They are more inclusive than institutions based on formal selection criteria (inclusion of stake-holders only, or of representatives of organisations, for instance), but offer more bias in terms of the socio-demographic composition of the public than randomly selected institutions. As many political science studies have demonstrated, political participation, even in an unconventional fashion like the participatory budget, generally concerns individuals with certain educational, cultural and political resources (Gaxie 1978; Verba *et al.* 1995). The inequalities PB aims at subverting would therefore re-emerge from its very selection mechanism based on self-selection.

Interestingly, despite the will to be as inclusive as possible, none of these PBs implemented random selection procedures of the participants. While random selection can offer a fairly representative sample of a population, this issue was never tackled when PBs were set up in these cities. This is probably due to the political culture and imaginaries of the inceptors of such processes. The three cases belong indeed to communist led cities, and the organisers generally acknowledged they had never thought about institutionalising random selection. While mini-public experiences mushroom nowadays in Europe, these communist militants were unfamiliar with them and more directly influenced by the Porto Alegre model. More broadly, their democratic ideals refer much more to the Paris Commune, the soviets or even to the Zapatist movement, than to random selection experiments. For them, direct democracy means a general assembly, not a randomly selected sample; despite the self-selection effects this might imply.

Participatory democracy and the problem of legitimacy: the limits of participation

Participatory democracy is on all the lips but, somewhat surprisingly, few people are actually interested in getting involved in local democratic institutions. Participation rates in the three cases are low, as usually about 1 to 5 per cent of the population is involved more or less intensively in the PB process; which is within the average of the other European PB experiences. This clearly raises problems of legitimacy, as such a small fraction of the population can take binding decisions that will affect all. Two questions need to be addressed from a quantitative point of view: (1) what is the overall participation rate in the three cases; (2) what is the socio-demographic composition and political orientations of the public of the participatory budget institutions. Both aspects – the quantity and the quality of the public – appear crucial for the democratic legitimacy of participatory processes.

Only a small minority of participants

From a quantitative perspective, the three cases offer rather low attendance rates. In Rome Municipio XI, only 978 people participated in the process in 2003. Involvement increased in 2004, as 1,498 participated at the different phases of the process. This means that, in 2003, the participants represented 0.70 per cent of the entire population of the Municipio and 0.82 per cent of the electorate, and 1.08 per cent of the whole population and 1.26 per cent of the electorate in 2004. Participation appears therefore extremely low, but is even lower in Seville, as 2985 persons participated in 2004 and 3352 in 2005, which represent about 0.42 per cent of the total population and 0.58 per cent of the electorate in 2004.[3] It should also be noted that the turnover rate is extremely high in Seville, as most of the participants in 2005 had not participated in 2004. Thus, in September 2005, the administration had a database of 6146 individuals who had participated at some point in the PB process in the last two years. This means that no more than 1 per cent of the electorate has participated at some point in the PB. There is no official data concerning the participation rates of Morsang-sur-Orge participatory assemblies, as the municipality never took care to produce a wide quantitative study. The database of the 'House of Citizenry' in charge of the coordination of the participatory process counts about 550 people who participated since 1999. There is nevertheless a high turnover rate, and it is evident that less people participate every year. It is also evident that some irregular participants are not registered in the official database. It can nevertheless be stated that at least 3 per cent of the total population has participated in the participatory process since its creation, which represents about 5 per cent of the electorate.[4] The participation rates are therefore clearly higher in Morsang-sur-Orge than in the two other cases, which is mainly due to the size of the respective cities.

Overall, however, the participation rates in these participatory bodies remain extremely low, especially in comparison with the participation rates of the local and national elections in these cities.[5]

Table 4.1: Participation rates in the three PBs

	Total PB participation in 2004	PB participation rate compared to the total population in 2004 (in %)	PB participation rate compared to the constituency in 2004 (in %)
Rome	1498	1.08	1.26
Seville	2985	0.42	0.51
Morsang	550*	2,85	4,35

* Estimations

The over-representation of white politicised middle-classes

This limited participation is supposed to be compensated however by the heterogeneity of the economic, social, cultural and ethnic backgrounds of the participants. Innovative democratic institutions are indeed supposed to open administrative bodies to more underprivileged actors than the traditional ruling political elites. The data on the socio-demographic backgrounds and political orientations of PB participants does not perfectly confirm this incantatory discourse however.

The heterogeneity of PB participants has first of all to be compared to the socio-demographic characteristics of the cities as a whole. The Municipio XI is part of a global multi-cultural metropolis of almost 3 million inhabitants and Seville, with 700,000 inhabitants, appears as well as a very diverse city. From a socio-cultural point of view, Municipio XI and Seville seem more heterogeneous than Morsang-sur-Orge. The unemployment rates are higher (16 per cent in Rome, 18 per cent in Seville vs. 10 per cent in Morsang-sur-Orge), and the social structure seems more mixed than in Morsang-sur-Orge.[6] It goes from lower working classes (with the presence of industries in Rome and Seville) to students (one of the biggest universities of the city, the University of Rome III, is based in the Municipio XI, and Seville counts a high number of students) to top-rank managers, and therefore cannot be considered a purely middle-class city like Morsang-sur-Orge where the rate of people working in the public sector is at about 17 per cent of the active population (against 7 per cent at the national level).[7] In Seville, 23.5 per cent of the occupied active population work in the secondary sector, much more than in Morsang-sur-Orge and Rome Municipio XI. From a cultural point of view, the proportion of foreigners in the total population is higher in Morsang-sur-Orge, representing 8.7 per cent of the total population,[8] while in Rome the same figure was of only 5.7 per cent in 2001. Officially it was even lower in Seville with only 2.4 per cent of foreigners. The number of illegal residents is nevertheless considered rather high, so that the city is probably much more culturally mixed than these data reflect. The origin of the immigrants is more diverse in the Italian and Spanish cases, with minorities coming from Pakistan, Bangladesh (36.8 per cent of the Municipio XI foreigners come from Asia) and African countries in the Municipio XI, and a lot from Latin America (45 per cent of the total) and Africa in Seville. The Andalusian city is also characterised by the importance of the gypsy community – of Spanish nationality however – present in the region for centuries. With a strong cultural identity – they embody the Flamenco culture in the city – deep social problems and difficulties of integration, the gypsy community is the strongest marker of Seville's cultural diversity. Municipio XI also hosts one of the biggest camps of Rom gypsies in the city. Morsang-sur-Orge does not count such organised communities, and 66.5 per cent of the foreign residents come from EU countries. It seems therefore that Rome and Seville are more heterogeneous cities than Morsang-sur-Orge, especially concerning the amount of foreigners and the highest diversity of the job patterns in the population.

Table 4.2: Socio-demographic composition of the three cities

	Unemploy-ment rate	Rate of foreigners in the total population	Rate of under 25-year-olds in the total population	Rate of over 60-year-olds in the total population
Rome	16	5.7	–	19.5
Seville	18	2.4	29.6	19.8
Morsang-sur-Orge	10	8.7	31.8	17.2

Are these general trends reflected in the socio-demographic characteristics of PB assembly participants? The most comprehensive data available comes from the Municipio XI, where quantitative studies focusing on the composition of the public have been conducted in cooperation with a Roman research group. In the two other cases, only a qualitative analysis from observations and interviews can be provided. From a gender point of view, participation is rather equal in Municipio XI assemblies, with a slight over-representation of females. Thus, in 2004, 53 per cent of the participants were females. The traditional male domination is however reflected in the gender of elected delegates, 60.9 per cent of them were males in 2003 and 58.1 per cent in 2004.[9] The same phenomenon can be noticed in Seville, where women were over-represented in voting assemblies (54 per cent of the attendance[10]), but largely under-represented when it comes to representative positions. The traditional sexual division of labour seems therefore to be reproduced in PB assemblies. The open access to discussion assemblies seems to allow women to participate equally, but when elective mechanisms are introduced domination reappears. This is confirmed by the situation of Morsang-sur-Orge, where no delegates are elected, so that in most assemblies women were just slightly under-represented (46 per cent of the attendance[11]). Other studies seem to confirm that participatory budgets – and participatory democracy more generally – do not reproduce the gender bias of other political arenas (Bacqué, Rey and Sintomer 2005; Sintomer, Herzberg and Röcke 2008b). This could be explained by the less directly political nature (for some participants) of local democratic institutions dealing with proximity issues. When politics reappears, especially with representative mechanisms, women step back. It will be seen however that under certain conditions women can be politicised with repeated PB participation.

While PBs appear to suffer less from gender biases than other political arenas, they are affected by all the other classical exclusionary mechanisms, and first of all by the under-representation of youngsters. From a generational perspective, there is indeed in the three cases a clear over-representation of participants over 50 years old. In 2004, 36 per cent of the participants were over 51 years old, in the Roman case. There were no participants under 19 for the two first years, while in 2005 and 2006 dozens of high-school students, between 16 and 18 years old, and other students, participated at some stage in the Roman process.

Despite the over-representation of elder participants it has to be stressed that there is a greater diversity in the generational composition of the Municipio XI PB assemblies, than in Morsang-sur-Orge and Seville. In particular, young people between 20 and 30 years old, among them many students, are much more present. The clear over-representation of elderly people in PB assemblies should be investigated further, but can be linked to both their 'biographical availability' (McAdam 1989) – the free time retired people have – and from their attachment to a territory in which they often lived for decades. This is also confirmed by the over-representation of own-owners in PB assemblies. 60.5 per cent of the participants in the Roman territorial assemblies in 2004 were owners of their house or flat.[12] Being a property owner appears to be a strong determinant of participation in the PB process. The same conclusions can be drawn from the interviews conducted in Morsang-sur-Orge and Seville, where most of the interviewees were owners of their apartment/house. Attachment to the territory is also a financial and juridical embeddedness.

The higher diversity of the Roman PB public in comparison to the two other cases is confirmed by the occupational structure of the participants. In 2004, 13 per cent of the participants were students, 25 per cent were employees, but only 5 per cent were unemployed. Furthermore, few students and freelancers can be found in Morsang-sur-Orge, while employees are clearly over-represented. Unemployed and precarious people are also completely absent from the assemblies. On the contrary, in Seville, the participants have a much more working-class background. Many women participating in the voting assemblies are housewives, some of them being even illiterate. Depending on the neighbourhood, it seems as well that some unemployed and precarious individuals participate in the process. There is however a gap between voting assembly participants and delegates, who have generally a higher social status, with higher educational and political capital.

There is no official data in any of the cases on the cultural origins of the participants. Ethnic minorities appear however, largely under-represented in all of the cases. Some Municipio XI neighbourhoods – like in 2005, at the Ostiense territo-rial assembly where a Lebanese delegate was elected through the mobilisation of about forty foreigners living in a squat in the neighbourhood – have nevertheless seen migrants participating sporadically. Similarly, in some of the Sevillan neigh-bourhoods members of the gypsy community participate in the voting assemblies, even making proposals for the promotion of their cultural identity. Nothing similar in Morsang-sur-Orge, where few foreigners participate. In some of the more de-prived neighbourhoods however, second or third generations of Maghreb migrants show up. They remain extremely marginal in the process however, hardly speak-ing up during the assemblies. Finally, from an educational perspective, little data is available apart from the Roman case. In the Municipio XI, 24 per cent of the participants were university graduates and 41 per cent had finished high school. In this sense, the participants in the PB institutions have a higher cultural capital than the overall population of Municipio XI. This is probably the case for the most active participants in Morsang-sur-Orge and Seville as well.

The public, in all of the three cases, is marked by a clear over-representa-tion of associations and political party members. Having a previous political or associational experience is a strong determinant of PB participation. From this perspective, the ambition to open up the institutional machinery to apolitical citi-zens might be doomed to fail, the majority of those participating being already politicised. Overall, however, at least half of the participants have no experience of public participation in the past. 40 per cent of Municipio XI participants are members of an association. Large disparities can nevertheless be noted between neighbourhoods, from 50 per cent in Garbatella and San Paolo, to less than 15 per cent in Ottavo Colle/Tintoretto. It also appears that 20 per cent of the Roman participants are members of political parties and 30 per cent of a trade union.[13] Concerning the political orientation of the participants, the data is extremely clear: the left is overwhelming in Roman PB assemblies. 51 per cent of the respondents declared to be on the left, and 30 per cent on the centre-left, while only 10 per cent declared being on the right or centre-right.

The political origins of the PB, initiated by *Rifondazione Comunista* in the Municipio XI, seem, therefore, to have a strong influence on who participates. The same observations can be made in the two other cases. In Morsang-sur-Orge, politicised participants are mostly from the left and centre-left. Members of the centre-left PTA (Parent Teacher Association) FCPE are also extremely well repre-sented in the PB process. There are nevertheless many non-politicised participants as well. In Seville, the dichotomy between the public of the voting assemblies and delegates seems to hold again. The political diversity of the former can be con-trasted to the highly politicised orientation of the latter, mostly on the left (PSOE and IU). Most of the delegates cumulate political and associative affiliations, be-ing members of neighbours associations (*asociacion de vecinos*), extremely pow-erful in Spanish local politics, or the PTAs, through the AMPAS movement.

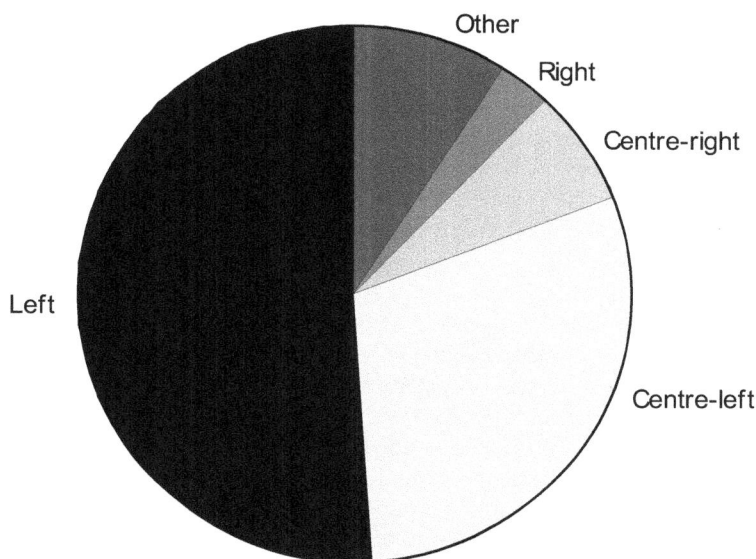

Figure 4.1: Political orientations of Municipio XI participants[14]

The circles of participation: groups of good citizens and irregular participants

Not all citizens participate at the same level of intensity within PB institutions. Beyond the quantitative picture presented above, a more detailed account of the intensity of citizens' involvement is necessary. A first step from this perspective is to consider that PB institutions are composed of circles of participation.[15] These circles are both quantitative and qualitative. From a quantitative point of view, some participate more than others, some are regular participants – the pillars of the participatory process – others come occasionally, and some exceptionally. But the circles of participation tell as well a more qualitative story, about the degree of integration of the citizens within PB institutions. To exist as such and stabilise, participatory institutions need to create groups of regular participants that I call 'groups of good citizens'.[16] Regular participants, as integrated in the process, are those who respect, recall and enforce the grammatical rules of the participatory bodies. The stabilisation of such groups is therefore necessary for the institutionalisation of PBs. The group of good citizens is, in general, composed of between five and ten citizens. The bonds of trust and solidarity between the members are the glue of the group of good citizens. Regular participants can be said to form a group as they share, respect and enforce the grammar of the assembly. Having in common the same mutual expectations, they form a relatively stable group, with its own style (see chapter three). The formation of these groups – extremely important in the process of self-change itself – is different from one case to the other, being institutionalised through delegate elections in Rome, voluntary participation in Seville within the motor groups, and a mix between voluntary participation and co-optation in Morsang-sur-Orge. In the three cases, it can nevertheless be argued that politicised actors play a great role in them. Being acquainted with political participation, they have the skills and competences, and above all the habit to speak in public that they can easily reinvest in PB assemblies.

Then, the second circle is composed of irregular participants, who assist a few meetings every year. Most of the time, they come to the assembly in relation to a specific problem they have faced recently. In Rome and Seville, they only participate in the election of the delegates or in voting for the proposals, remaining most of the time silent and reproducing delegation mechanisms that participatory democracy aims to overcome. In Morsang-sur-Orge, they are irregular attendants of neighbourhood councils and thematic workshops. They cannot be considered as a mere audience, as often they speak and voice their grievances in the assemblies.

The interactions between irregular participants and good citizens are of great interest, as they allow the drawing of the boundaries of the PB grammar. By definition, irregular participants master the grammatical rules of the PB assemblies much less than the members of the group of good citizens. If they manage to learn these rules, irregular participants might be 'dubbed' by the PB group, and thus integrated. Irregular participants form therefore a pool in which the group of good citizens – in constant search of new members to gain legitimacy – might extract new recruits. If, on the contrary, they do not respect the discursive rules of the game, they might be sanctioned, criticised or ridiculed, in such a way that they never come back (see chapter six). Irregular participants do not attend all the meetings as they do not feel at ease in them; not mastering the grammar of the institution, they are often unconsidered, ashamed and marginalised. As a consequence, they do not feel as if they were allowed to participate more regularly and to take a more central role in the PB. Therefore, they step back. On the contrary, those feeling esteemed, appreciated and valued will tend to participate more. Participation is indeed linked to a politics of recognition (Rui 2004). As the social-psychologist Serge Moscovici underlined (1992: 81): 'The benefit we expect [from participation] is social recognition of our effort to participate in a significant way to the different common activities.'

Finally, the third circle of participants is composed of the population of the city as a whole. Even if not mobilised in the PB it composes the pool from which all the participants are drawn, and it plays an important implicit role: the PB has been created by the representatives it has chosen. A majority of the population should therefore be in favour of the PB, so that exceptionally, it can participate in relation to a specific problem. The mobilisation of this wider circle happens in some exceptional occasions, often ritualised, like the inauguration of the PB processes (with, for instance, the draft of the *autoreglamento* in Seville), and to a lesser extent, the general neighbourhood assemblies at the beginning of each year in Rome and Seville. In Morsang-sur-Orge, the population can mobilise for a local referendum for the creation of a municipal police, proposed by a PB thematic workshop, or a 'Citizen Summit' organised to draw a balance of the participatory process of the city. The population as a whole is concerned by the PB, as well, in the sense that it receives information about PB choices in the municipal journal or, with special PB mailings addressed to the whole population. Even if the readership rates are unknown, information can still be considered as a low intensity form of participation.

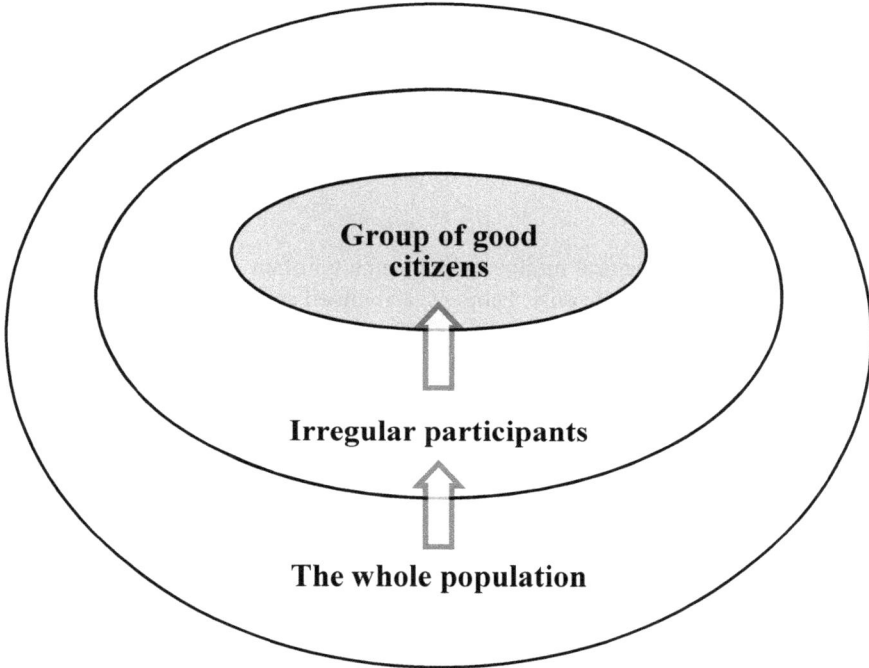

Figure 4.2: The circles of participation

The Characters of the participatory budgets: why and how people get involved

Who are the people ready to spend their time and energy for the common good, despite the frustrations it often creates? What do they find in participatory budgeting motivating them to come and stay? Four main motivations, at the roots of PB participation, coming up in interviews, can be distinguished: (1) self-interest; (2) civic duty; (3) social integration; and (4) personal enrichment. They seem to fit with at least three of the four types of retributions of activism severed by Daniel Gaxie (1977: 128–39) for political parties, namely material retribution (professional positions in the party or the public administration), personal enrichment (acquisition of a political culture) and social integration (creation of social capital, comradeship, pleasure of acting in common).[17] The symbolic gratifications (prestige, honour and distinction) do not seem central for PB participation, which is not so symbolically rewarding outside of the institution itself, little prestige being associated with PB participation, apart from the feeling of being a good citizen.

Four motives to get involved

Self-interest: One of the main reasons people started participating was material self-interest. In some regards, PBs reward participation: the more you get involved the higher chances you have to get your problem solved. As the issues dealt with in the PB assemblies are those brought by the participants, PB mobilisation can easily be rewarding. Interested motives were, most of the time, hidden, are they clash with the participatory grammar, and were, therefore, often sanctioned by the group of good citizens when voiced (see chapter three). It nevertheless emerged regularly, especially from certain categories of actors. The fact that a majority of participants were property owners indicates, as well, the importance of material self-interest.

Civic duty: Another central motive, which came up often in both interviews and public discussions, is civic duty. People get involved and participate because it is important; important for the good of the community, or in itself, as citizens have to be active. The civic duty motive could also be coupled with political or ideological considerations, people considering participation as a good in itself.

Social integration: Another motivation, probably less central and that can be considered an externality of participation, is social integration, which was often framed in an idiom of pleasure and emotions. Some people actually love it. They can meet people, talk and socialise. Civic engagement appears, therefore, as a means to create social capital, to make friends, spend time or get useful. This type of discourse is often derived from the will of both the municipality and the citizens to re-create conviviality and social links that are declining in contemporary societies.

Personal enrichment: Finally, while people might not get involved for this reason in the first place, learning and personal enrichment might be good reasons to stay. It was indeed hard to meet a regular participant not acknowledging the enriching value of participation, people feeling that they were learning about their city, local politics, technical issues, or about their neighbours. Personal fulfilment and civic engagement are therefore far from being contradictory (Lichterman 1995). These outputs of civic participation – and the process leading to them – will be tackled at length in chapter six.

Characters on the public scene

These different motives are not mutually exclusive, and highly involved participants can actually share them all. Some categories of actors refer however – both in public discussions and in interviews – to certain types of motives more than to others. I therefore constructed what I call characters, actors that I came across regularly during my observation, sharing some common features, in the way they present themselves and speak in public, in the type of motives they use.

Characters are neither ideal-types nor roles; they are more fluid than ideal-types, but less flexible than roles. On the one hand, ideal-types – as idealisation of reality[18] – do not take into account the role of context and situation in shaping people's behaviour and discourses. The aim here is, on the contrary, to show how certain individuals embody certain characters in a situation, but can change if the situation evolves. The concept of role could have therefore been more adequate. A role is usually defined as a normative expectation of meaningful behaviour belonging to a specific situation (Joas 1993). Roles do not cause or determine individual and collective behaviour, as deviation is always possible – even if sanctioned. They shape them in interaction. However, being essentially situationally specific, the concept of role does not carry the personal resources and structural components that shape actors' behaviour. Characters are, therefore, more rigid than roles. They guide individuals towards a certain set of roles. Situations generally do not make available only one type of role and adequate behaviour as different parts can be played by individuals, and the role they take in the end depends on the character they are, stemming from their social and cultural position.

To evaluate the impact of participatory experiences on people's trajectories, it appears indeed necessary to know how they got on the boat, i.e., who they were when they started to participate. It is the confrontation between people's histories, memories and trajectories – as recorded in life-history interviews and systematised into characters – and the grammatical norms regulating public interactions in participatory institutions, that can explain people speeches and behaviour, as well as their potential trajectory reorientation.[19] When they start participating people come with their own competences, stemming from their previous experiences, with their own degree of politicisation, their abilities to speak in public, certain motives that pushed them to participate in the first place and representations of what a good citizen is and should be. Some distinctive characters have thus been observed all along the fieldwork; types of people participating in a certain way, presenting themselves in a similar manner in public and in interviews. The similarities between the words and the deeds of some participants in places as different as Rome, Morsang-sur-Orge and Seville was sometimes striking. These characters were therefore constructed from the observation of regularity in discursive behaviour in public assemblies and face-to-face interviews, even if some discrepancies often occurred between these two different types of discourses (Eliasoph 1998). Each character was not present in all the cases however and, sometimes, different characters overlapped in the way individuals presented themselves. Overall, six characters have been constructed: (1) the good neighbour (2) the parochial old lady; (3) the young leftist; (4) the experienced militant; (5) the concerned parent; (6) the community leader.

The good neighbour

This character is one of the most common in the three studied cases. It is as if the participatory budget had been created for him/her, embodying the concept of 'lay citizen'.[20] The good neighbour is generally over 30 and less than 60, younger and older participants having other specific features. He/she works (is therefore not retired) generally as an employee, even if he/she can also be a professional. The good neighbour is thus generally from the middle-class or the upper middle-class. He/she has a relatively high cultural capital, having often completed a few years of university. Having less free time than students or retired people, the good neighbour has to be highly motivated to participate in the PB, as it takes either some of his/her work time (some even taking days off to be able to attend the meetings) or leisure time. The clearest feature of this character is their embeddedness in the city and community. They care about the city and are ready to mobilise for it. Their motives are generally full of references to the local level, be it the street, block, neighbourhood or city. Not uninterested in national or global issues, capable of rhetoric globalisation, this character is nonetheless primarily focused on where he/she lives. This localism is therefore connected to a strong apolitical orientation.

The good neighbour generally votes at all the elections however, and most of the time at the centre of the political spectrum, being relatively moderate. The good neighbour does not have strong political convictions however, and often moves from one party to another, like Antonio in Rome: 'through time I voted a bit of everything, from Fini [president of *Alleanza Nazionale*, a right wing party] to Bertinotti [secretary of *Rifondazione Comunista*], passing through the Radicals [centre-left party] and blank'.[21]

The good neighbour is a volatile voter, who does not vote by ideological conviction but as a civic duty. To the question 'do you usually vote in elections?', these interviewees generally answer, like Nicole in Morsang-sur-Orge: 'Always. I always expressed myself. Because you have to take your responsibilities and say what you think. It is even a duty.'[22] She also stated she often voted blank, which is frequent among this type of participant. If the good neighbour votes, he/she does not belong to any political party, or to any politically oriented association. At best, he/she is part of a cultural or sporting association, eventually a PTA when he/she has kids. This character is apolitical in the sense that he/she has no strong political conviction and frames his/her participation as civic and not political. As says Nadine, a 38-year-old participant in Morsang-sur-Orge and member of the FCPE (generally politically close to the Socialist Party): 'I don't feel I'm doing politics [when participating in the PB], I feel I'm a citizen. Whatever my opinions [...] whatever my personal political ideas, I have the opportunity to participate.'[23] Politics is associated by this type of participant with pure ideology or even corruption. What the good neighbour looks for is concrete solutions to practical problems, in the words of Alessandro, from Rome: 'whoever you are, from the left, the right, the centre, the important thing is that you make public services work for the citizens. Then everyone has his political idea [...] but this is not the most important'.[24] The good neighbour has therefore a non-political definition of the common good. Even if he/she frames his/her commitment as a way to foster the general interest, this is understood as non-political, or even anti-political, as stated by Nicole:

> I prefer to put politics on the side and to say: 'we are people living in the same city [...] there is a common good, and we fight for it, that's all'. You can be

Communist, from the right, the left, whatever side, as long as you consider there is a common interest you just go. Politics should not impede all this investment from the people.[25]

The good neighbour is someone who cares about the local community, and tries to act to solve its problems and improve daily life. In many ways, PB offers a new channel of participation for individuals who used to mobilise individually by writing letters or having personal appointments with the mayor, or calling the municipality to underline a problem. Antonio is a good example of this kind of behaviour, as he presented himself in the first assembly of his neighbourhood:

I'm someone who gets angry all the time. I'm fighting all the time. And I'm tired to hear, each time I complain or try to do something, 'but who are you?' I answer that I am an Italian citizen who pays his taxes. I get angry all the time about the wastes and misuses of public funds. […] About cars that are stolen or crushed, about recycling, about cleanness of the streets, etc. […] I am not belonging to any political party, but I believe in the revolution of how to spend taxes.

(Montagnola votation assembly,
Rome, 4th of February 2005)

The good neighbour was not inactive before the PB, he/she was just an isolated revolted individual. They indeed often present themselves as someone 'revolted' or 'who fights'.[26] Another common motive used by the good neighbour is that of the rationalisation of the use of public funds. The good neighbour appears indeed as a rational taxpayer. Most of the good neighbours are indeed owners of their house or flat and therefore care about the value of their property. They feel that the rationality of public policies is directly connected with the value of their property; the public and self-interest being linked from this perspective.

Finally, the good neighbour has a strong sense of community and sociality. He/she often complains about the anonymity of modern urban life and the development of individualism. He/she is therefore the kind of person who says 'hi!' to his/her neighbours, gives his/her seat to the old lady in the bus, holds the door open in the metro, respects the highway code and does not drive too fast, he/she is a person who generally recycles his/her domestic waste, collects the dejections of his/her dog in the street. Kind of Amélie Poulain of the neighbourhood, the good neighbour is convinced that this kind of small and individual good action can make changes at the macro level, and are crucial to 'make the world a better place'. Their participation in the PB therefore appears to them as a natural continuation of their daily behaviour.

The good neighbour is a central character of both Rome and Morsang-sur-Orge PBs, but seems less present in Seville. I was actually surprised by the similarities between some participants in the French and Italian cities. Some used almost the same words in interviews and in the public meetings, expressing the same defiance towards politics and the same commitment for the common good. In the Spanish city, in contrast, most of the active participants (not only those who vote for proposals, but those having a deeper commitment as delegates or members of the motor group) are politicised, being members of political parties (PSOE or IU) or associations with clear political orientation (especially the neighbours associations).

The parochial old lady

This character could appear restrictive, as including age, gender and political features. It seems, nevertheless, perfectly relevant for the three case-studies. We know there is a clear over-representation of the over 60-year-olds and retired participants in PBs, and that there are roughly as many women as men in the process. For clear demographic reasons (women having a higher life expectancy), there are therefore more retired women than men participating in the PB. Most of them have specific motivation and public behaviour marked by what is generally defined by the other actors as 'parochialism'. This does not mean that only retired women are labelled parochial, or that all females over 60 are parochial. There were nevertheless a fair number of them in the cases studied. The parochial old lady generally comes from the middle-class or the upper fractions of the working class. Retired, she has time to commit herself, her participation appearing also as a way to fight the isolation she suffers. The case of Rita, in Rome, appears paradigmatic from this perspective.

I met Rita, a 69-year-old retired teacher, at the first assembly of Garbatella, one of the Municipio XI neighbourhoods. She appeared pretty different from the other participants of her working-group. While the others were politicised and tried to promote a form of environmentalism, she appeared to care essentially about the rehabilitation of her street. After an hour of collective discussion on the need to develop cycling paths in the Municipio, justified by environmental reasons, during which Rita remained mostly silent, she had the opportunity to voice her proposal:

> My priority is the rehabilitation of via Cialdi, where I live. This street has really become dangerous lately [...] First of all, the pavements are full of holes and need to be rebuilt; otherwise there are clear risks of falling in the street, for old people like me and my husband. [...] Moreover, there are always cars and scooters on the walkways, which make it complicated to walk ...[27]

She concluded by proposing to transform a 'deserted little park' into a parking area as she had 'problems to park in her street'. The other participants smiled, but did not pay much attention to her proposals, and moved rapidly to other issues. Her proposals were nevertheless written on the meeting report as valid ones.

A few meetings later, while Rita was not present, Valentina, an integrated and highly politicised participant, realised that Rita's proposals were still on the list of the potential investment projects for the neighbourhood. She reacted to what she saw as a form of parochialism with an ironic tone: 'We have a lobby of via Cialdi here!' She specified: 'I'll boycott these proposals with all my energies ... these proposals kill me.' Rita had left after the first meeting, as her proposal had not really been welcomed, as she told me: 'the others were completely uninterested in what I said'.[28] Her participation was clearly linked to these requests; being ignored – not to say rejected – she stopped participating.

Rita's PB experience is in many ways symptomatic of the trajectory of the parochial old lady in the participatory assemblies. For the parochial old lady the personal troubles at the roots of her mobilisation can be dog's dejections on the pavement, the installation of a bus stop in front of her house, the lack of parking lots in her street, the noise made by scooters at night, a feeling of insecurity in the neighbourhood, a damaged pavement becoming dangerous for old pedestrians, i.e., all the little nuisances that can make life a nightmare for her. Similarly, Monique, participant in Morsang-sur-Orge PB, intervened once in her neighbourhood council about the noise made by buses in the morning, and asked whether the municipality could give her money to pay for double-windows to isolate her house from the noise of the street. She was bashed publicly, symbolically punished to have used a self-interested argument publicly.[29] Mobilised by a personal trouble, the parochial old lady has generally a hard time convincing the audience that her problem is a priority for the neighbourhood as a whole. She is therefore often sanctioned for voicing self-interested proposals. Losing face publicly and failing to influence public decisions, she stops participating rapidly. The parochial old lady is therefore an irregular participant.

This PB character is not only parochial however, it is also nostalgic of an dreamed golden age, when neighbours talked to each other, knew each other, and where not yet 'devoured' by modern individualism. In this regard, the parochial old lady shares a sense of community with the good neighbour. The parochial old lady is also apolitical, even if adhering to a form of conservatism, derived from the nostalgia of a more controlled society. The parochial old lady is characterised by a form of moral conservatism – that does not constitute a systemic political orientation however.

The parochial old lady is a central character in Morsang-sur-Orge and Rome assemblies, where she participates actively, speaks and makes proposals. Given the more formalised aspect of Seville PB, the parochial old lady generally makes written proposals, attends voting assemblies but does not take a wider role in the participatory process.

The young leftist

Organisers of the participatory process always complain about the under representation of youngsters (rightfully, see above) and, as a matter of fact, only relatively politicised ones participate. They remain nevertheless rather minoritarian, except in some Roman neighbourhoods. The question is however, how can leftist individuals, committed to radical political ideals, get interested in these often down to earth discussions where the most common issues are the rehabilitation of pavements, street cleaning or public transportation?

The young leftist is generally a student, between 18 and 30, coming from middle-class or upper middle-class families and his/her parents are generally politicised on the left, from the '68 generation. The main reason the young leftist gives to his/her participation is linked to the value attributed to political participation in itself. Related to a criticism of representative government as a system based on delegation, the young leftist is generally committed to direct democracy. His/her participation relies on strong ideological grounds: making people participate is a good thing. Even if they both share this commitment to participation, two types of young leftists can nevertheless be distinguished. On the one hand, there are the members of radical social movements or political associations. They live their participation in the PB as a natural continuation of their other forms of political commitment. They generally know the experience of Porto Alegre, make references to the Zapatist movement and are generally convinced of the necessity of direct democracy. On the other hand, younger students who do not belong to any political organisation yet, despite their clear political orientation on the left, live their experience in the PB as a first formal act of participation. Not ready to commit themselves in an organisation with a clear ideological orientation, they commit in a more flexible structure like the PB assemblies. This second type of young leftist is in general younger than the first one, often still a high school student.

The young leftist is not present similarly in all the cases however. Given the high number of students living in the Municipio (due to the location of *Roma 3* University) and the presence of radical social movements in the territory, young leftists are plentiful in Rome's PB. They come from social centres (there are two in the district), housing rights organisations, international solidarity associations, or simply from the local high school collectives. For the first type, they often started to militate in the student organisation of their high schools or universities, called '*collectivo*' in Italy. They are generally part of the anti-globalisation movement, from the 'Genoa generation'. Some of them, like Valentina, an active participant in Garbatella PB assembly, have indeed started their political trajectory with Genoa anti-G8 mobilisation in 2001. Like the participatory budget secretary – Luciano Ummarino – who comes from one of the local social centres, *La Strada,* the Municipio XI PB experience is seen by young leftists as the embodiment of a radical democratic ideal. The ideological and political affinities between the initiators and facilitators of the PB, and the character of the young leftist, allows the latter to get involved easily.

One of the main reasons these young Roman leftists participate in the PB assemblies is that they are supposed, more or less implicitly, to represent their organisation or association. Some political organisations, as important actors in local civil society and ideologically close to the political project of the participatory budget, feel they have to participate and be represented in the assemblies.

All the activists close to the anti-globalisation movement of the Municipio do not participate to the PB assemblies however. What are personal or political features of those engaged in Municipio XI PB that can explain their participation? Members of civil society organisations, they have to be trusted enough by their organisation to represent it in the assembly, and as such, have to be members of the organisation for some time already. They might also have some personal interests or competences in the issues tackled in the PB. The young leftist has, therefore, to be interested in urban planning, local management, or the environment to participate regularly. The case of Valentina is pretty telling from this perspective. She is a 26-year-old member of one of the most important Roman housing rights associations, *Action,* engaged in a radical political action based on the occupation and squatting of empty buildings, to offer shelter to immigrants. But she is also interested in environmental issues. A bio-chemical engineer, graduated from Rome University, and committed to environmental issues such as recycling, renewable sources of energy, the development of non-polluting means of transportation, Valentina sees the PB as a realm where the motto 'think globally, act locally' can be enacted concretely. She therefore appears as the proponent of clean means of transportation (bike, but also public transportation vs. cars, etc.) in the PB assembly. It seems clear that her previous professional skills, which made her interested in environmental issues and urban planning, led her to the PB assemblies, where local actions were achievable and her skills mobilised.

Valentina's case shows that certain young leftists, given their trajectories, have higher chances in getting interested in the PB than others. The young leftist appears as a central character in some of Rome's Municipio XI neighbourhood assemblies, playing an important role in the framing of the discussion (see chapter five). The situation appears more in contrast in Seville, as the radical political scene is much more critical of the PB experience. Linked to anarchist political parties and unions, Seville's young leftists see the PB as a 'reformist experience' – a compromise with institutions – far from their radical ideological postures. Some nevertheless occasionally commit themselves in the PB assemblies; they are not in general members of any political organisation or social movement yet.

With few students living in the city, the character of the young leftist is simply absent in Morsang-sur-Orge. Local civil society is rather embryonic and there is no organisation that could be associated with the anti-globalisation movement apart from ATTAC, which does not count many young members in Morsang. As most of the associations are connected to the Communist Party, the young politicised individuals hardly participate in the PB assemblies at all, and generally opt either for associative commitment or for joining the PCF.

The experienced activist

Even if PB assemblies are not composed of a majority of already politicised actors, the latter are nevertheless active in participatory governance institutions. The experienced activist is, in general, a male, between 40 and 65, from the middle-class or the upper fringe of the working class. He is often an employee, especially working in the public sector. I did not meet any right-wing activists during my fieldwork in any of the three case-studies. Right-wing militants do not participate actively in PBs, or do not express it publicly, putting on their 'citizen' hat rather than the 'militant' one. On the contrary, left-wingers were clearly over-represented among the experienced activists. In the three cases, the most common type of experienced activist was a member of the Communist Party. As these PBs were set up by Communist Parties, communist militants felt at ease participating in these settings. Members from Socialist and Left Democratic Parties are also well represented in PB assemblies in all of the three cases. Some of the experienced militants also have a unionist past.

The cynics argue that militants participate to recruit new members and to get a grip on a new political activity developing in the territory. Apart from the interests of the political parties they belong to, it might be interesting, at a more micro-level, to focus on the trajectories of the militants who became involved in the PB process. The experienced activist, who participates actively in the PB, is often one who did not achieve the political career he was expecting to have.[30] He is a disappointed activist. The case of Joaquin, in Seville, is pretty explicit from this perspective. Joaquin is a 58-year-old employee at the Spanish Telecom company. Member of *Izquierda Unida* since 1994, he has been involved in political activity 'all over his life', starting in the 1950s with participation in the Christian workers movement. He was then active in the 1970s among the neighbour associations that played a crucial role in the destabilisation of the Franco regime. He finally decided at the beginning of the 1990s to join IU, and got year after year of increasing responsibility in the party. He was, as well, elected president, at the end of the 1990s, of a local neighbourhood association, which led him to engage in collective struggle against local urban projects. Despite all his commitments, everything has not been fine in his activist life. Joaquin was expelled from the district direction of IU in 2003, in what he calls a 'coup d'état'. His eviction was due to internal power relationships and disagreements on the local strategy. Since this episode, he does not have any representative role in the party. The ousting has been a personal shock for him; a difficult time to go through, about which he still appears to be pretty sensitive to talk about. As an 'unemployed activist', with time and energy to invest, the PB appeared as a good alternative path to political mobilisation at the local level. His commitment in the PB process appears therefore as a recycling of his activism, a bifurcation in his militant career, due to his eviction from the IU directing board, and the emergence of a new window of opportunity for political participation. Since the creation of the PB, he is one of the most active participants, and started at the beginning of 2006 a campaign to promote and defend the PB in case of change in the municipal majority at the next election. He thus created an 'apolitical association' – even if most of the members are close to the Communist party – to defend the PB, and rapidly became its president. Disappointed by political activism, he was ready to invest himself fully in the PB experience.

If the participatory budget attracts experienced leftist activists, only some of them invest in this arena fully, due to their specific personal and political trajectories. In search of a new channel of commitment, some experienced leftist activists find in the PB a way to reorient their political career. For others, the PB can appear as a stepping-stone for a coming political career. The PB can indeed work as a space for notability for political activists, willing to deepen their political commitment and reach some elective functions. The case of Arthur, young leader of the Socialist Party and of the Parent-Teacher Association, FCPE in Morsang-sur-Orge, illustrates how political activists can use the PB as a stepping-stone for a political career. Despite his young age – 35 – his participation to the PB appears almost natural to him and others, given his central position in Morsang-sur-Orge's political scene.[31] As one of the leaders of his neighbourhood council, speaking well in public and knowing the tricks of the trade, he increasingly appeared as a skilled future local politician to the other participants. PB participation thus allowed him to enlarge his network and develop his local reputation. The PB represents, therefore, a specific moment in experienced activists' trajectories. As a new opportunity for participation, they can use it as either a means of reconverting their activist skills and experiences in another arena or as an accelerator in the process of notability.

The experienced activist is a central figure in Seville, where the majority of active participants (the delegates) are members of either a political party (PSOE or IU) or a neighbour association (that often have political orientations). The PB is thus controlled and framed by political activists in the Spanish case. It is much less the case in the Municipio XI, where some members of RC or DS participate, without being overwhelming, however, the young leftists being in general more numerous. Members of political parties were largely present in the first year of the process, but soon realised that little political gain could be extracted from the PB. Most of them therefore, stopped participating after one year. In Morsang-sur-Orge, apart from a few exceptions, few political militants participate in the PB assemblies. This might be due to the presence of the members of the municipal majority (mostly from the PS and the PCF) who appear implicitly to the militants as their delegates even in the PB assemblies. The voice of the party being already represented they do not need to participate further.

The concerned parent: the 'gang of mums' case

This character is close to the figure of the good neighbour, but his/her mobilisation is framed in a specific manner, centred on issues of kids, education and schools. The concerned parent is, in general – but not always – a mother, following the traditional sexual division of labour in families. From a socio-economic point of view, she can have a rather diversified profile, going from working-class to the upper-middle classes. Given the role they take in the assemblies, the concerned parent is, in general, relatively young, as she has to have kids, most of the time, young ones. She is generally in her 30s. Some of them are members of Parent-Teacher Associations, who are very well represented in PB assemblies. The FCPE, in the case of Morsang-sur-Orge (much more than the other national PTA, the right-wing PEEP) and the AMPAS in Seville, are among the most powerful associations in the PB process, as their local presidents participate and try to mobilise their members as much as possible. There is hardly any neighbourhood council in Morsang-sur-Orge where a member of the FCPE is not active. The connection between the PB and schools is, in general, rather strong; the assemblies, especially in the French and Italian cases, taking place most of the time in primary schools. Members of the local PTAs, but also the teachers and the school administrators, are from this perspective pretty well informed of the organisation of PB assemblies.

The specificity of the concerned parent character is her constant reference to kids, as the embodiment of disinterestedness and the common good. Kids – their defence, protection, promotion, – are often the highest value in PB assemblies, as they are seen as innocent and good. Debates about kids are, therefore, generally highly consensual, as it seems impossible to criticise a proposal justified by kids interests. The concerned parent character appears therefore highly legitimate and respected in PB assemblies. The mobilisation of a group of young women in one of Morsang-sur-Orge Neighbourhood Councils to promote the rehabilitation of a public park is pretty telling from this perspective. Anonymous strangers at first, they got to know each other in the mist of collective action, and ended up defining themselves as 'the mums gang'. The way they describe their mobilisation and motivation is interesting in the construction of the concerned parent character:

> *Patricia*: I live in the neighbourhood since four years and I have a two-year-old son. I used to go to the park with him, I went two times, but I never came back. It is a luxury to have a park so close. But the problem is that it is dangerous: the playgrounds for kids are broken or obsolete; the environment is not adapted (with rocks, cigarettes on the ground, etc.). So in the end the park is not used by kids or their parents, but by teenagers who squat there, smoke cigarettes, etc. I sent a letter to the mayor and I got in contact with Patrick Bardon [a town councillor]. We got together with four-five mums and started to think about what could be done about it. Basically we went door-to-door to speak with people of the neighbourhood to get their opinion and possibly their support. People gave us a lot of ideas that we didn't have at first.

> *Tatiana*: It's true that this park is really dangerous for kids. I have two, and once I found my son with a syringe in the hands [...] I decided to send a letter to the mayor as well. Afterwards we met with Patricia and others and decided to make this letter about the rehabilitation of the park and went door-to-door in the neighbourhood. But I insist, it is not a petition. A lot of people are ready to go back to this park. We let the park to other people and it's a pity. We didn't force anybody to sign, we didn't threat them with a knife, but we got almost 200 signatures.

> (Observation notes, Robespierre neighbourhood council,
> Morsang-sur-Orge, 26th November 2005)

Interestingly, these women presented themselves not as citizens, nice neighbours, nor taxpayers, but as concerned mothers. They introduced themselves by specifying the number of kids they had and their age. They framed their own collective identity as a group of 'mums' caring about kids' quality of life. As innocent and pure, kids appear as a legitimate and consensual cause to defend and promote. Whatever the political orientation, everybody would agree on the need to do as much as possible for kids. As Nina Eliasoph (2002) argues, often, references to the children stopped conversations, rather than helped them to generalise. In this case, participation is framed as totally apolitical, as the letter of support for the mum's project is defined in non-political terms, Tatiana making clear: 'this is not a petition'. The concerned parent does not participate for political reasons, and shares many of the features of the good neighbour, even if she defines the common good through 'the kids', more than by evoking 'the community' or 'the public interest'. Politics does not appear as a central concern for this character, who nevertheless generally votes, and for moderate parties.

The role of concerned parent is also highly present in Rome Municipio XI, is partly constructed by the procedural design itself. One of the thematic areas of discussion is indeed 'youth policies', dealing with projects for the creation of structures or activities for kids. Most of the participants to this working group were either young students or women in their 30s taking the role of the concerned parent. Once, in Garbatella assembly, as candidates had to introduce themselves before the election of delegates, Silvia presented herself as:

> a mother, with a very young child. 'If you vote for me, I will take care of the future of the kids in this neighbourhood. [...] I have already a proposal to make: I thought that we could create an outdoor playground for the kids of the neighbourhood.'

> (Observations notes, Garbatella working group, 19th January 2006)

The motivations and frames used by the Roman concerned parents seem, from this perspective, close to those of Morsang-sur-Orge.

The concerned parent has a slightly different profile in Seville, as she appears as having rather working-class origins, often being a housewife with little education, but a lot of free time as she often does not work in order to take care of her kids. In general, the concerned parent is not highly committed in the PB process however, participating only in the proposal phase and not in the successive ones, reserved to the delegates. Their proposals aim at offering decent conditions for kids to play or 'helping the teens to getting out of the street'.

The ethnic community leader

The community leader is a marginal character in most of the PB assemblies I observed. Most of the participants were indeed national citizens, few foreigners or immigrants participating in the PB institutions despite the formal access open to them. Foreigners are under-represented in PB institutions, and become visible only when a leader participates. The community leader is most of the time a man, relatively young (less than 40 years old), well integrated in the country. He masters the national language enough to communicate in PB assemblies. From a socio-economic point of view, the community leader is, in general, no better off than the other members of his community. He lives in rather precarious conditions. Most of the time nevertheless he works; his occupation giving him a form of legitimacy as he appears to be socially integrated. Despite his low cultural and educational resources, the community leader is often politicised, situating himself on the left. Like Mohammad in the Municipio XI (see below) who said, in an interview: 'I love politics, really, I find it really interesting. Not only in Italy, but outside as well.'[32] He then tackled different political issues during the interview: the Israeli/ Palestinian conflict, taking openly the side of the Palestinians, the war in Iraq that 'costs billions, which could be so useful for the people', the political situation in Lebanon (his country) or France. The community leader is politically committed, caring about the fate of his community or of the poor people in general.

Mohammad, 32 years old, was elected PB delegate in 2005. With a really low economic and cultural capital, he seems nevertheless able to speak about everything, and especially about politics. He left Lebanon when he was 13, 'because of the war', and then worked in different European countries, before settling down in Italy 16 years ago. He seems well integrated in Italy, and speaks Italian fluently. He got involved in the PB process as a 'speaker' of the immigrants he is living with (in the squat of the *Coordination Fighting for Housing*). He is not a community leader *per se,* as he is not representing a unitary ethnic or religious community. The migrants he lives with indeed come from different countries (Peru, Ecuador, but above all from Morocco and North Africa), and pushed him to run for PB elections: 'they don't speak Italian very well, so they told me to go for it'. At the first assembly, about 40 people from the squat came to vote for him, many women with veils, some illiterate who had to ask for help from the facilitators. Mohammad is a Muslim, but feels he represents all the migrants, the people with low incomes in the neighbourhood. As a zone delegate he does not try to promote the interests of his community only, he seems concerned about the neighbourhood as a whole: 'it would be important to have a school for kids of the neighbourhood, or a public park [...] also to take care of the holes in the pavement or of the noise made by the clubs on Saturday night'.

The community leader is present in some of Rome's Municipio XI and Seville's neighbourhoods. Most of the time, they come from rather deprived neighbourhoods where migrants live, far from the city centre. In Seville, the main community mobilising in the PB are the gypsies, especially in the poorer neighbourhood of the city. While the gypsy community is very present in the voting assemblies – making many proposals to promote their cultural identity – I never met any clear community leader participating more actively as a delegate. In Morsang-sur-Orge, the figure of the community leader is almost absent. Even if foreigners represent a small portion of the population, a population from foreign origins (being from the second or third generations of migrants, who mostly live in social housing neighbourhoods) they are almost invisible. As most of the marginalised classes, they hardly participate in the participatory process, the ethnic variable being added to the lack of cultural and economic capital in the exclusion of these groups.

The case of Kamel, a 26-year-old irregular participant in Wallon neighbourhood council can, nevertheless, be evoked. Even if he cannot be considered a community leader as he participates on an individual basis, not representing any organised group or well-defined community, he is seen by the other participants as the voice of 'the youth' of his housing project neighbourhood in the NC. I met him in the fall of 2005, after the urban riots of November, which had reached Morsang-sur-Orge too. That evening he participated in the NC to push forward the idea to 'offer a premise ['*un local*'] for the youth of the neighbourhood ['*la cité*']'. How can someone like Kamel – '*un jeune de cité*' – participate in a PB assembly? What are the social conditions for the inclusion of this type of subaltern actor – so hard to reach – in participatory processes?

First of all, he is not a teenager any more, being 26 years old. Then, he has a certain educational level: he has a Baccalaureate and two years of business studies (a BTS). He has known a form of upward social-mobility, as his father, a Moroccan immigrant, – Kamel is French – was employed as a manual worker all his life. Kamel works in a Parisian airport as a 'stopover agent'. His trajectory thus gave him the educational, professional and cultural resources to 'understand politics'. He thus told me he always voted and he even mocked the teenagers of his neighbourhood – 'who don't know who is on the left and who is on the right. They think UMP is from the left [he laughs]'. He told me as well that he would like 'to give civic education classes for the kids. […] Not political ones, but objective ones […]. Telling the rights and the duties, and recalling the values of the Republic: Liberty, Equality, Fraternity.' He told me he participated in the PB assemblies because they 'put citizens in the front-stage'; even if 'they always talk about the same things, the pavements, etc., and never about the problems of the youth'. The community Kamel represents implicitly – not for the 'constituents' but for the other participants – is therefore the youth of the neighbourhood, who create problems and are generally from the second and third generations of post-colonial immigration.

It is no surprise, however, seeing that the mobilisation of a community does not follow ethnic, religious or cultural cleavages in Morsang-sur-Orge and in France, in general. Organisation along ethnic or cultural lines is rejected by the Republican and universalistic French civic culture. Ethnic associations are thus often disqualified as being 'communitarian' in France. Other categories are nevertheless constructed, more transversal, at least in their formulation, like 'the youth' or 'the youth from the cité' (Neveu 2003), who embody a problematic population – associated with delinquency, violence and nuisance. On the contrary, in Rome and Seville, the communitarian leaders are emanations of associations – a housing rights association focused on migrants, in the case of Mohammad and gypsy cultural associations in Seville. These differences stem from the different civic cultures of these countries and the type of organisation of civil society emanating from it.

Even if the heterogeneity of the PB public is limited, different type of actors interact in these assemblies to create rich communicative moments. Each case does not present the same level of diversity however. Table 4.3 illustrates schematically the representation of each type of actor for the three cases; 0 meaning the quasi-absence of the character and 4 its omni-presence. Rome Municipio XI appears as the most diverse case, all the characters being represented. On the contrary, Morsang-sur-Orge appears more homogeneous with a large majority of middle-class, non-politicised, middle-age and old actors. Seville offers a middle-way between the two cases, with nevertheless a clear over-representation of experienced activists, but also the presence of non-politicised actors, foreigners, and individuals with popular backgrounds.

Table 4.3: Types of participants in PB assemblies

	The good neigh-bour	The parochial old lady	The young leftist	The ex-perienced activist	The con-cerned parent	The com-munity leader
Morsang-sur-Orge	3	2	0	2	2	1
Rome Municipio XI	3	2	2	2	2	1
Seville	2	1	1	4	1	1

When citizens can mobilise their skills: the discursive inclusiveness of participatory democracy

Evaluating whether and how people have learned and changed in the course of their PB experiences requires firstly knowing the type of skills, competences and knowledge they previously mastered. Based on life history interviews and early observations, I discovered different types of knowledge and competences mobilised by citizens during public meetings and collective discussions. These competences were mobilised by actors along a discussion to support their arguments and convince the audience of the validity of their claims. Mobilisation of knowledge had therefore a persuasive aim. The initial competences mostly came from the actor's previous experiences, be they personal, professional or political ones. Three types of competences have therefore been sorted out: (1) local knowledge; (2) professional experience; and (3) political competence (Sintomer 2008). They will be studied successively in a comparative perspective.

Local knowledge: proximity politics and emotional expression

The most common competence PB participants had when starting to get involved was local knowledge, linked to their repeated practice of the territory. Local knowledge appears as a crucial concept in the justification of participatory experiences, as it relies on the idea that citizens are those who know best the local realities linked to their daily life, and as such are able to improve significantly public policies, rationality, justice and acceptability when involved in decision-making processes. This idea is not new however; and was already fully developed by Aristotle. He considered that each individual has 'a share of excellence and practical reason' and thus at least a partial understanding of the matter at hand. Aristotle praised the soundness of practical knowledge; users of the law being better judges than those who make it, 'just as the pilot will judge better of a rudder than the carpenter, and the guest will judge better of a feast than the cook' (1995: 1282; Bickford 1996: 406). Use and practice would thus be the conditions for a sound judgement.

This theoretical perspective is nowadays directly mobilised in most participatory institutions. The character of the citizen-user (of public services) has thus made its apparition in contemporary political vocabulary (Rouban 1991; Fischer 2000). Local knowledge is both embedded in proximity and direct practice. The regular and reiterated practice of a territory is at its roots. The question raised by the mobilisation of practical knowledge is that of its sharing with others, as it is aimed at convincing the audience and influencing public decisions. Being necessarily linked to an individual and relatively idiosyncratic practice, speakers use different rhetorical means to share their local knowledge. It can be procedurally fostered, mobilised and shared in different ways: discursively in the framework of public meetings, or more directly through field visits requiring citizens' emotions and sensations, and especially their view.

In Rome and Morsang-sur-Orge, local knowledge is mainly mobilised discursively in public meetings. It generally takes two different rhetorical forms: embeddedness and testimony. On the one hand, it requires a local embeddedness ('I live here since X years'), indicating the reiterated practice and observation of the territory, founding judgement not on epiphenomena but on recurrent problems. Reference to local embeddedness appears as a necessary condition to get enough legitimacy to speak up in the assembly, to grow oneself and thus acquire a higher worth and status than that of a mere individual. On the other hand, practical knowledge is often expressed through anecdotes and examples, drawn from a recurrent problematic experience that pushed to participate in the first place. The case of the group of women in Morsang-sur-Orge – self-qualified as 'the gang of mums' – who mobilised for the rehabilitation of a park in their neighbourhood can be evoked again. Their interventions started with 'I live in Morsang-sur-Orge since X years', 'I have a child of that age', and 'I go to the park regularly'. Different examples and anecdotes were then offered to back up arguments on the dilapidation and dangerousness of the park, as Tatiana evoking her 'two-year-old son with a syringe in the hands'.[33]

Anecdotes, like testimonies, are modalised discursive forms, which are appropriate as long as they mean: 'this can happen to anyone'. As Iris Young (1996) and Lynn Sanders (1997) underline, the use of testimonies, anecdotes and personal stories has two main functions. On the one hand, they allow the audience, who has not experienced the scene directly, to imagine and represent it better, and thus to understand it. At odds with the impersonality of argumentation, testimonies allow reaching audience empathy, and arousing emotions that will enlarge judgements. Given the weakness and fallibility of imagination and the impossibility to really put oneself in the shoes of another (Young 1997; Polletta 2005), personal stories allow visualising a situation, making it present though discourse. Then, the possibility to express modalised discourses of this sort allow equalising partially communicational resources. While all actors – given their cultural, political and therefore discursive resources – are not able to reach immediately a general argumentative discourse, the opening to personal stories and anecdotes allow enlarging the circle of legitimate speech. The democratisation of access to public discourse could nevertheless also mean its depolitisation and the decline of critique (Cardon,

Heurtin and Lemieux 1995). Participants mobilising local knowledge are therefore mostly from popular backgrounds with a limited experience in terms of political participation and public expression. They are mostly good neighbours, parochial old ladies, concerned parents and sometimes community leader characters.

Local knowledge takes the form of testimonies in public meetings, but it can also be presented in a more direct manner by mobilising the view of the other participants. A common practice in Rome PB is to use pictures to illustrate personal testimonies and budget proposals. As it relies on a personal experience, practical knowledge is more convincing when it can lean on other means than the mere discursive interactions. The direct visualisation of the problems at stake, allowed by the bus tours organised in the framework of Seville PB, appear highly efficient from this perspective. These tours are aimed at helping PB delegates evaluate and rank proposals (i.e., in the attribution of the social justice criteria) by seeing directly the problems on the field. Experiencing directly the cold in a primary school, or seeing the deprivation of one of the poorest neighbourhoods of the city – with deteriorated buildings, kids running alone in the streets or broken bottles of alcohol everywhere on the floor – does not leave the judgement of an individual immune. The absence of mediation – the sensation being lived directly by the actors, or seeing with their own eyes, without verbalisation – might foster a more powerful sentiment of injustice. These immediate experiences are, in general, complemented by the testimony of some concerned actors. In Morsang-sur-Orge, 'pavements meetings' are also organised regularly before the start of public works. These direct experiences allow the nourishment of subsequent discussions in neighbourhood councils.

Given its idiosyncratic feature, local knowledge requires a discursive work of sharing. This sharing effort allows the enlargement of the legitimate discursive modes in the public sphere, letting free access to testimonies, but also to forms of visualisation (pictures, maps, videos) and direct experiences (tours, street meetings). Accepting the use of practical knowledge as legitimate would, therefore, allow a double democratisation of the access to the public sphere, on both content and form. This would furthermore allow the emergence of new public problems, raised by actors until then excluded from both representative mechanisms and argumentative logic.

Professional and political knowledge: mobilising specialised competences in participatory arenas

Participants of innovative democratic institutions can mobilise competences linked to their daily life, and also to their previous professional and political experiences. While the participatory bodies warmly welcomed local knowledge, they were more reluctant towards the expression of other forms of citizen competence. Based on professionally or politically acknowledged expertise, these civic skills put into question the technical legitimacy of elected officials and municipal experts. Professional and political competences do not necessarily raise new public problems; they rather offer alternative solutions to those presented by traditional decision-makers.

Professional knowledge gives both a technical legitimacy (especially through the use of a certain type of language) to arguments, and enriches the debate cognitively by bringing new information to the table. Some professional profiles are more represented than others in the assemblies. Given the municipal competences in the three studied cases, discussions often deal with urban planning projects, public transportation, the environment, culture or leisure activities. Rare, but important, figures in PB assemblies are therefore the architect and the urban planner, who share their professional knowledge and expertise to qualify or disqualify proposals. In this regard, citizens are not equals in the assembly, according to the skills previously acquired in the professional sphere.

Thus, in the framework of a public meeting dealing with urban planning budget decisions in Morsang-sur-Orge, Annick, urban planner and regular participant to this workshop, put into question the diagnosis made by municipal technicians. Referring to public works she had coordinated in Strasbourg, she harshly criticised a municipal plan she considered dangerous for both pedestrians and cars. Speaking with authority, using a technical language (budget data, statistics, specific terms, etc.), she appeared more competent than the municipal technicians who, in a small city like Morsang-sur-Orge, appeared in contrast like amateurs. Annick's words easily convinced the audience, against the initial opinion of the experts.[34]

The traditional expertise of municipal functionaries is thus questioned and enriched by expertise coming from other professional milieus. By multiplying the sources of expertise and the pool of knowledge, decisions should be more rational, less biased by the limits of a unique source of information. The idea of the cognitive input offered by a plurality of positions is indeed at the core of the deliberative paradigm (Mendelberg 2002).

The turn to professional knowledge often fosters the emergence of technical controversies however. It appears as a form of counter-expertise, putting into question the monopoly of expertise granted to municipal services (Callon, Lascoumes and Barthe 2009). The inclusion of professional knowledge in PB discussions is indeed part of a broader phenomenon, linked to the rise of a 'knowledge society': the increasing educational levels in most developed countries question the legitimacy traditionally granted to politicians and experts, as citizens (especially from the middle and upper middle-class who participate actively in PB) have become at least as competent technically as the elected officials (Rosanvallon 2006: 60-61). While the argument of the incompetence of the masses has historically justified the exclusion of the people from places of power (see Madison 1790; Manin 1997), the increased educational levels seem to push for a growing inclusion of citizens in the production of public policies.

The mobilisation of technical competences by certain citizens, even if rare, allows the avoidance of censorship of citizens' proposals by municipal experts. Professionals do not have the monopoly of technical knowledge however; certain activists being able to mobilise specialised skills acquired through previous participation experiences as well. Militants have a large experience of participation and knowledge on the functioning of public arenas that allow them to appear immediately competent in situations. Political competence can thus be mobilised in two different manners. On the one hand, activists have certain specific knowledge acquired through their associative commitment on a particular political question (linked to housing rights or environmental innovative solutions for instance). Thanks to this specific political or technical knowledge, activists can enrich the discussion cognitively and influence the final decisions. On the other hand, militants can also mobilise their previous participation experiences, which gave them specific skills and competences in terms of meetings, organisation and moderation, public expression, mastery of the codes of the public grammar, ways of organising collective action, relationships with elected officials and local notables. These types of skills make the functioning of the public meetings at the core of PB decision-making processes easier, and gives activists a prominent role in the process. Militants can, therefore, either 'technicise' discussions by bringing their own counter-expertise on the table, or politicise it by making underlying political stakes emerge.

The case of an experienced activist, Gianni – president of the neighbourhood association *Grotta Perfetta* – in a PB assembly of Rome Municipio XI, can be evoked. The way Gianni mobilised his technical and juridical competences using his memory of previous public controversies in the neighbourhood, his knowledge of the internal power relationships among the administration and the state of certain key dossiers, in order to foster the emergence of a countervailing power against the lack of transparency of the municipality in the attribution and property of certain parcels, within the framework of the local urban plan is worth being presented:

> The issue had first been raised by Ierma, a young participant, who waxed indignant about the refusal of the municipal administration, a year ago, to create a public equipment on an unused parcel. The municipality argued that

Table 4.4: Characters' competences

	Local knowledge	Professional knowledge	Political competence
The good neighbour	*High*	*Medium*	*Low*
The parochial old lady	*Medium*	*Low*	*Low*
The young leftist	*Low*	*Low*	*High*
The experienced activist	*Low*	*Medium*	*High*
The concerned parent	*High*	*Medium*	*Medium*
The community leader	*Medium*	*Low*	*Medium*

this was a private parcel, which surprised Ierma and many participants. This is when Gianni decided, intervening in the discussion: 'We have to fight and ask for the cadastral register to the municipality. If they refuse, we have to be ready to go to court. Legally, the municipality has to provide us with this document.' Ierma, obviously satisfied to have received such a support, went on: 'Yeah! I'm ready to go to court. If the municipality has these cadastral maps it has to give them. It's a right! Otherwise it'll be pointless to say that the PB is useful or important!'

(Observation notes, Roma 70 neighbourhood assembly,
Rome, 3rd June 2006)

Gianni was thus able to tell what the legal options were, and which solutions had already been envisioned and abandoned. He therefore allowed taking a better, more informed, collective decision. Using his political experience, he was also able to mobilise people to start a micro-collective action. It therefore makes no doubt that when activists put their competence into the game, the discussions, and therefore the decisions as well, are different. Those who able to mobilise political knowledge are the most politicised participants, i.e., experienced militants (like Gianni) and young leftists.

Confining citizens in apolitical roles and impeding deliberation?

Participatory budgeting is characterised by a double inclusion of ordinary citizens, which could allow for a significant democratisation of the public sphere. On the one hand, the procedural inclusiveness should allow a broad range of actors – and especially ordinary citizens, traditionally excluded from political arenas – to make their voice heard. On the other, the discursive inclusiveness of participatory budgeting, argumentation not being the only legitimate mode of expression, the narration of personal testimonies and stories being even valued, should allow citizens with little 'epistemological authority' (Sanders 1997) to speak up.

These radical ambitions have been partly deceived on both points, however. Firstly, even if it gives them a new institutional opportunity to voice their claims, participation of the subaltern classes in the PB institutions remains limited. Politicised and educated participants are over-represented, even if the disproportion is less important than in more formal public arenas. Then, despite the legitimacy granted to testimonies, anecdotes and personal stories, the voice of those able to construct solid argumentative claims remain dominant. Besides, the symbolic opening of participatory institutions to non-argumentative discursive modes might confine citizens to apolitical roles, thus reinforcing insidiously their domination. The risk is high for citizens to be confined in roles of 'neighbours', 'residents', 'users', 'parents', unable to enrich the discussion in other ways than through the mobilisation of their personal and idiosyncratic experiences. Competent enough to express their personal claims and needs, ordinary citizens might not be granted enough legitimacy to be heard on political and technical issues, still reserved for experts. When citizens have put on the resident hat, it might indeed be difficult to put on another one within the same arena as the other participants' expectations derive from past self-presentations of the actors. Moving from the role of neighbour, voicing his/her personal problem, to that of expert is not as easy as it seems.

This might furthermore create a problem for deliberation. How can deliberation emerge if citizens are confined to apolitical roles of parents and neighbours? What kind of public discussion can arise between individuals sharing their personal experiences? Is this type of discussion a favourable ground for the nurturing of a competent citizenry? How can the collective weighting of the pros and cons of a course of action occur, if what is expected from participants is merely to voice their needs? Would deliberation therefore be impossible in PB institutions? It will be seen in the following chapter that deliberation is indeed scarce in PB arenas, but that under certain procedural, social and political conditions it can nevertheless emerge.

NOTES

1 Dewey 1923: 207.

2 The only European exceptions, to my knowledge, are that of the city of Pont-de-Claix, near Grenoble in France, and Albacete in Spain, which include some form of random selection of the participants. Random selection is also relatively common in French neighbourhood councils.

3 At the 2003 local elections, the electorate was of 581,939 persons. Sources: *Servicio de Estadistica del Ayuntamiento de Sevilla – Resultados de las elecciones locales 2003 en Sevilla y Distritos.*

4 In 2004 the number of people enrolled on the electoral lists was indeed of 12,657. Source: Ville de Morsang-sur-Orge.

5 In 2001, the participation rate at the local elections was 76.6 per cent in Rome Municipio XI. In 2003, the participation rate at the local elections was 58.55 per cent in Seville. In 2008, the participation rate to the local elections was 59.6 per cent in Morsang-sur-Orge.

6 The socio-demographic data for Seville concern in general the whole province, not only the city. Sources: Junta de Andalucia, Instituto de Estadistica (2005) *Sevilla, Datos Basicos 2005.*

7 Sources: INSEE, *enquête sur l'emploi 2005.*

8 This is only a bit superior to the 5.9 per cent at the national level in 1999 in France. Sources: Data from Table A.1.5 in SOPEMI (Systeme d'Observation Permanente des Migrations) (2001) *Trends in International Migration,* Rome: OECD.

9 The only available data are for 2003 and 2004. See Ummarino 2005 : 162–96 ; La Riva Sinistra 2004 : 151-157.

10 Data from the author, gathered in 20 Seville PB assemblies.

11 Data from the author, gathered in 27 Morsang-sur-Orge PB assemblies (only neighbourhood councils and thematic workshops are counted here).

12 Data from d'Albergo 2005. Data was collected during the AT assemblies.

13 Sources: d'Albergo 2005 and AT assemblies

14 Sources: d'Albergo 2005 and AT assemblies

15 The circles of participation described here are present in the basic arena of participation of each PB, the assembly, which generally takes place at the neighbourhood level: the neighbourhood councils in Morsang-sur-Orge, the territorial assemblies in Rome Municipio XI and the zone assemblies in Seville.

16 The categories of 'group of good citizens' and 'PB groups' are used interchangeably from now on.

17 It seems from this perspective that these retributions can partly be extended further than to political party membership, to all collective action engagement.

18 See Weber 1978. For Weber, the use of ideal-types aims precisely at offering an abstraction of reality, thus mapping exhaustively the social world. If identities are not reified per se in the concept of ideal-type – as some actors can share different features of a type – it nevertheless relies especially on actors motivations, being thus based on an inner conception of the self, in keeping with Weber's comprehensive sociology, which does not fit with the overall approach of this investigation

19 By trajectory, I mean the totality of the experiences lived by an individual over his/her life. Different types of trajectories can be distinguished: the political trajectory (the electoral choices, party, union or association membership, newspaper readership, etc.) the educational, the personal, the professional trajectories. Trajectories are considered to be the result of both subjective decisions and the objective constraints limiting the different options on this path, coming from both the social structure and the individual socialisation. See Passeron 1989.

20 The good neighbour should not be confused with the good citizen, the latter is not a specific character, but the integrated members of PB institutions. I call a member of the group of good citizens a 'good citizen'. Each of the six characters presented here can therefore become members

schools of democracy

of the group of good citizens of their PB assembly.

21 Interview with Antonio L., president of a tourism agency, Rome, 7th February 2005.

22 Interview with Nicole C., secretary in a small familial company, Morsang-sur-Orge, 24th February 2006.

23 Intervention in the movie on the PB process directed by the municipality, 'Participatory Democracy: Utopia or Necessity', Morsang-sur-Orge, January 2006.

24 Interview with Alessandro M., assistant manager in an insurance company, Rome, 1st of March 2005.

25 Interview with Nicole C. (see note 22)

26 Nicole, Alessandro and Antonio used these words many times during the interviews.

27 Observation notes. Garbatella, working group meeting n.1, 17th February 2005, Rome.

28 Interview with Rita, retired teacher, Garbatella, Rome, 21st February 2005.

29 Observation notes, Cachin NC, Morsang-sur-Orge, 18th January 2005.

30 The point here is not to offer a psychological interpretation of their political trajectory in the vein of Ted Gurr's (1970) relative deprivation, but rather to understand how the closing of some opportunities implied re-orientating one's commitments towards other arenas.

31 Interview with Arthur, Morsang-sur-Orge, 30th January 2006.

32 Interview with Mohammad, Rome, 4th March 2005.

33 Robespierre neighbourhood council, Morsang-sur-Orge, 26th November 2005.

34 Urban planning workshop, Morsang-sur-Orge, 12th December 2005.

chapter five | much ado about nothing? why and how public deliberation hardly change people

The ideas of either party may change in the course of the conversation. It may be, for example, that a certain agreement is arrived at by the partners in the course of the conversation. One might convince the other. Then something from one passes into the other. It is assimilated into his or her individual structure of ideas. It changes this structure, and is in its turn modified by being incorporated into a different system. [...] The special feature of this kind of process, that we might call a network-figure, is that in its course each of the partners forms ideas that were not there before, or pursues further ideas already present. But the direction and the order followed by this formation and transformation of ideas are not explained solely by the structure of one partner or the other but by the relation between the two. And precisely this fact that people change in relation to each other and through the relationship to each other, that they are continuously shaping and reshaping themselves in relation to each other, is characteristic of the phenomenon of social interweaving in general.[1]

N. Elias, *The Society of Individuals*

4:45 pm, the meeting room of the primary school is still empty. After five minutes, three members of the organising team arrive and start to put chairs in circle. At 5 pm the first citizens arrive, seat and start to chat in small informal groups. At 5:15 pm about twenty people are seated – forming a big circle – one of the organisers introduces the meeting, welcomes everybody, recalls the conclusions of the previous assembly and evokes the questions on the agenda for today. In the two following hours, participants will speak, express their views, give their opinions, laugh, shout, speak in an aside with their neighbours, and listen to other people. At about 7:30 pm, the moderators invite the speakers to conclude. A quick summary of the debates is made, and people stand up and go. Outside, in the courtyard, a few residents will stay about half-an-hour, speaking about the neighbourhood's problems, the political situation of the municipality or the different local gossips running at the time. At about 8 pm, once the room put in order, the organisers invite the last people still present to leave and go back home. They will see each other again one month later.

This stylised scene took place in February 2006, in Garbatella, one of Rome's Municipio XI neighbourhoods. But at the time, when this scene ended, another one, relatively similar, if one's adds a few tables and elected representatives from the municipal majority to the scenery, started in Morsang-sur-Orge in the Parisian suburb. Those kinds of scenes have taken place and multiplied everywhere in Europe and America in the last decade. Participatory democracy is indeed a rather fashionable political experience at this time, especially at the local level. Many social science studies assess the transformation of decision-making processes of many public bodies, citizen participation being henceforth considered a necessary step in the production of legitimate public policies (see chapter two). The basic institution of participatory democracy, and PB especially, is the public meeting or assembly, i.e., the public gathering of more than two persons to discuss. If one asks the participants of the introductory scene to describe what happened in the three preceding hours, they will answer that they 'talked', 'discussed' or 'exchanged ideas'. On the contrary, social scientists generally define what they observed as 'deliberation', 'argumentation' or 'public discussion'. The equivalence between lay citizens' public discussions and deliberation, as defined by democratic theorists, cannot be taken for granted however. It has been constructed through a collective work of conceptualisation and definition of the social reality by certain political actors and committed scholars, all trying to push forward participatory democracy as a political ideal. The promoters and practitioners of public engagement are indeed nurtured by the theoretical literature on deliberation, while deliberative democrats are inspired and try to promote concrete citizen participation experiences. Does the comparison between the new dominant democratic paradigm and the discursive practices of some participatory bodies make sense? Are the interactions taking place in participatory arenas of a deliberative nature or do they rather take other discursive forms, like rhetoric, strategic or polemic sequences?

Beyond the definitional issue, it will be argued here that social sciences dealing with communicational phenomena in the public sphere should try to understand *when* deliberation happens. Deliberation does not exist institutionally or formally, it does not spring magically from good procedural rules, it depends on a multiplicity of social and situational conditions. If procedures appear as a necessary condition for the emergence of deliberation, they are not sufficient. In this regard, I argue that there is nothing like deliberative institutions *per se*, but only deliberative interactions, moments when deliberation emerges; the institutional setting playing an important role in this social process. How can we explain that sometimes some discursive interactions are highly fruitful and constructive while at some other times they end up being extremely confrontational, agonistic and defensive? How can the emergence and vanishing of argumentative sequences in participatory arenas be assessed? In a word, what are the institutional, social and situational conditions for the emergence of deliberation in the cases we studied? The answer to this question will then allow the evaluation of the effects of these deliberative sequences on individuals. Does deliberation mean politicisation of the discussions? Does it foster individual preference change? Does it mean increased cognitive capacities and better-informed choices? The observation of more than a hundred and twenty public meetings in the three studied cases indicates that deliberation – when it emerged – does not affect significantly people's long-term opinions and civic practices. One of the explanations of this unexpected result is that deliberation is different when participants have a direct interest in the issues at stake. Two models of deliberation (interested and disinterested ones) will therefore be constructed.

I first show that deliberation is scarce, as the discursive interactions in the public arenas I studied offer a large variety, thus sketching a plurality of discursive regimes in participatory institutions. I thus present the diversity of the discursive modes observed over my fieldwork in the second section, to then investigate the favourable (procedural, social, political and situational) conditions for the emergence of deliberation. In the third section, I assess the (limited) impact of these deliberative sequences on actors. Finally, I offer an interpretation of the failure of deliberation to shape people's opinions or interests in the cases I studied, discussing the results in relation to the literature to construct a tentative generalisation.

The scarcity of deliberation in the public sphere

Deliberation is scarce. Having observed over two years more than 120 public meetings in three different settings, in which discussion was central, I rarely saw deliberation happening. This does not mean deliberation never happened, but that each meeting gave rise to different types of discursive interactions, from bargaining, rhetoric, polemic, monologues and soliloquies to sharp argumentation. As will be seen, despite good procedural conditions, deliberation among ordinary citizens only takes place in exceptional moments, when a variety of conditions is met. This firstly depends on the definition of deliberation adopted here.

A strict definition of deliberation

Deliberation is not understood as any type of collective discussion, but as *a reasoned exchange of arguments aimed at taking a collective decision*.[2] Each term is important, in what can be considered a strict definition of deliberation. First, deliberation is a collective exchange of arguments, requiring weighing the pros and cons of a certain course of action.[3] It does not necessarily exclude emotions, anecdotes or personal stories from the picture, but considers they can nurture deliberation only in so far as they open up a collective discussion nourished by contradictory interpretations of the moral or political meaning of otherwise personal and idiosyncratic stories or testimonies (Young 1996; Sanders 1997; Mansbridge 1999b; Polletta 2005). In this regard, deliberation necessarily requires a form of generalisation from the personal views and opinions that are expressed, to evaluate discursively the collective consequences of a certain course of action. A deliberation is therefore a collective discussion in which certain types of propositions are voiced, called arguments, i.e., propositions backed up by reason rather than by threat, power or money. Deliberation is therefore analytically different from bargaining – in which threats or interests are mobilised and negotiated. Even if backed up by reason, arguments are different from scientific demonstrations. They are propositions backed up by reason that do not aim at truth but at collective agreement and verisimilitude.

Then, this collective exchange of arguments is aimed at taking a decision. The collective decision might not necessarily become a public policy however; it might indeed be a consultative decision or one affecting the group internally, in its organisation for instance. Discussion is just not an end in itself – like in clubs or debating societies. It is therefore different from a conversation, in which reasoned exchanges of arguments can take place between actors, but are not aimed at action.[4] The action-oriented feature of deliberation has two decisive effects. First, as a decision is at stake, deliberation has to be conclusive. There are therefore time constraints, which is different from conversations that can always be stopped and continued in the future. Second, and more importantly, the fact that discussion is aimed at taking a decision shapes the behaviour of participants, who are, to some extent, bound by the arguments they voice. For both moral and pragmatic reasons – words might have an impact – it is considered that the participants will take the discussion more seriously than in a conversation in which their words have no effect.

It is no doubt that given such an exigent definition, deliberation is scarce. It both requires institutional settings based on discursive decision-making (decisions are taken through discussion, rather than through aggregative means or authoritatively by a leader) and a certain competence from the actors, in order to reach a certain discursive quality. The two central features of deliberation are, however, analytically distinct, as summed up in Table 5.1. A collective discussion can be ruled by an exchange of arguments, but not aimed at taking a decision; it will therefore be defined as a reasoned conversation. Non-argumentative conversations are, in contrast, coined casual conversations. On the contrary, a collective discussion aimed at taking a decision is not necessarily ruled by arguments.

Table 5.1: Types of discursive modes

	No decision	**Decision**
Argumentation	Reasoned conversation	Deliberation, monologue
No argumentation	Casual conversation	Bargaining, polemic

While conversations are left on the side here, public discussions are at the core of this investigation. What matters therefore is to evaluate in which conditions collective discussions, aimed at taking decisions, can become deliberations. The aim of this chapter is to evaluate the conditions of felicity of the emergence of deliberation in comparison to other forms of collective discussion. This approach allows for the understanding of the quality of the discursive interactions taking place in the public sphere. Different discursive modes have thus been observed, from bargaining and polemic (personal attacks) to monologues (arguments are voiced but are not answered and do not give rise to collective discussions). Before moving to the empirical part however, a discussion of the limits of literature on the empirical analysis of the emergence of deliberation is necessary. Surprisingly, the theoretical and empirical literature on deliberation has remained, until now, naively optimistic about the possibility of deliberation to emerge. I argue this stems from both an under-conceptualisation of deliberation itself and from a lack of rigour in empirical research.

A lack of analysis of the conditions of emergence of deliberation

One of the dominant approaches on deliberation argues that publicity is the crucial factor for the emergence of deliberation. Following a Kantian tradition taken up by Habermas, a large fraction of deliberative theorists see publicity as the crucial social mechanism orienting people towards the common good. In certain public settings, self-interested arguments would merely be inexpressible. The force of publicity is then attributed to the pre-suppositions of language by Habermas (1984), to the strategic will to convince actors with unstable preferences for Elster (1995), or to the submission to certain social norms for Fearon (1998).

Were it purely normative, one could buy the argument. However, a growing number of deliberative theorists try to enrich their approaches with the analysis of social science studies of past or present deliberative experiences. Leading figures have thus studied the discursive sequences of constituent assemblies (Elster 1995), citizen juries (Goodin and Niemeyer 2003) or deliberative polls (Fishkin 1997; Fishkin *et al.* 2002). Designing quantitative studies based on pre/post surveys, their research aims, above all, at evaluating preference change through deliberation (Delli Carpini *et al.* 2004). The main problem with these approaches is the lack of analysis of the discursive sequences *per se*. They focus either on the external perspective – the procedural design – or on the micro-level of preference change, but not on the (social and discursive) process linking the two together. As Ryfe underlines (2005: 54):

> Researchers have been less interested in deliberation itself than in measuring its effects. Whether they use laboratory, survey, or participant-observation methods, the authors of most empirical studies assume that deliberation ensues when certain structural conditions (such as equality and autonomy) hold. [...] In the process however, deliberation itself remains essentially unexamined.

Deliberative democrats are more interested in the effects of deliberation than knowing whether deliberation took place *tout court*. The process of deliberation is therefore entirely overlooked.[5] Deliberative democrats do not enter the black box of deliberation and end up being unable to assess whether it is collective deliberation, information from documentation materials, or pure randomness that explains preference changes.[6] The only way they investigate this crucial question is by asking – in the final questionnaire – 'what made you change your mind on this issue'. (Fishkin *et al.* 2002; Goodin and Niemeyer 2003). They therefore do not assess whether deliberation took place at all, and whether it was of a rather good or bad quality.

Surprisingly, far from the rigour and conservatism of the theoretical analysis, they generally derive from their approach a rather minimalist definition of deliberation in their empirical studies, as Robert Goodin in his study of Australian citizen juries, who defines deliberation as: 'Collective conversations among a group of equals aiming at reaching some joint view on some issues of common concern.' (Goodin and Niemeyer 2003: 633). Any collective discussion would thus become a deliberation, independently of the type of propositions that are voiced. Deliberation would thus emerge automatically from public bodies adopting discursive decision-making procedures.

I argue, on the contrary, that any 'collective conversation among a group of equals aiming at reaching some joint view on some issues of common concern' is not necessarily a deliberation. It can be bargaining, polemic or monological discursive sequences. Deliberation is a specific form of discursive interaction, requiring a collective exchange of arguments and reasons (that can however be based on and backed up by personal experiences, testimonies, i.e., emotional narratives) in the aim of taking a collective decision. All discursive sequences in public arenas are not deliberative. On the contrary, the few sociological studies dealing with discursive interactions in non-experimental public institutions appear sceptical about the quality of collective discussion in these settings. Deliberation appears to be of a rather low quality, or even non-existent (Bacqué and Sintomer 1999; Blondiaux 2000). It is especially the case when public arenas involve lay citizens, more than professional politicians, which is the focus of attention of most empirical research on deliberation.[7] When it comes to discussion among lay citizens, it seems that a large fringe of participants try to avoid argumentation and justification of their viewpoints at any cost. Considering their opinions as private matters, prime markers of their identity, people would not be ready to justify them publicly, and even less to change them as an outcome of deliberation (Conover *et al.* 2002).

Even if actors come to express themselves, to discuss collectively, and eventually to take binding decisions, the result of the interaction is not necessarily a deliberation. It requires interventions following each other, people listening and answering each other in a constructive and argumentative manner, which seldom happens. The repeated observation of public meetings in PB institutions does not confirm that only disinterested arguments, oriented towards the common good, are expressible in public arenas. Personal testimonies, feelings, and private matters are regularly presented in these public settings. Participants can bargain, engage in polemics, exchange impressions, and sometimes deliberate.

The three discursive modes of PB institutions

To answer the shortcomings of the deliberative democracy literature, I offer a different but complementary methodological approach to the study of deliberation: namely direct observation and ethnographic research. To understand the nature of discursive interactions taking place in the public sphere, one needs to observe them in detail, to follow the voice and tone of lay citizens, to hear the difficulties and breakdowns of interpersonal communication, and sometimes the emergence of deliberation. Direct observation and the transcription of public meetings of participatory institutions, allow the gathering of some incredibly rich material – hundreds of discursive sequences and interactional situations, full of citizen voices and discussions. It allows the discernment of the regularities in the practices of actors, as well as the irregularities, the moments of crisis and tension. And far from my initial hypotheses, deliberation was not the norm of the participatory institutions I studied. On the contrary, the direct observation of public meetings indicates that the norm of public interactions resembles much more a succession of monologues and proposals, than a truly interactive deliberation. This is why I consider that social sciences dealing with communicational phenomena in the public sphere should try to understand *when* deliberation happens.

My ethnographic study does not indicate that certain types of arguments are inexpressible in public settings, but rather that personal interventions are evaluated differently by the audience – sanctioned, rewarded or ignored – given the norms regulating interactions in public. These norms are often not powerful enough to impede people voicing arguments that appear inappropriate or incompatible with the discursive norms of the group. The norms regulating interactions in a certain social setting, are not integrated immediately and automatically by actors, they have to be learned progressively (Talpin 2006); hence the existence of a plurality of discursive modes. I observed three different discursive modes in PB institutions: (1) polemic; (2) bargaining and (3) argumentation.[8] The distinction between the three primarily stems from the way claims are backed up and justified by actors. Their differences do not derive from the actor's intentions, but from the words they use in public.

First, I saw – very rarely however – polemical sequences, participants using personal attacks to criticise others' positions. Far from fostering constructive deliberations, polemical sequences often lead to discursive messiness. It mostly occurred in the French case, opposing citizens to elected officials, the former criticising the latter. A citizen got his car stolen, asks the mayor in a public meeting: 'I got robbed, what can you do about it ?'[9] Or a group of teenagers asking for the creation of a 'premises in the neighbourhood', and in both cases, participants were bashed, ending in the second case with youngsters leaving the meeting obviously angry.[10] Sometimes the participants bash each other, condemning their self-interested motives. An excerpt from a NC meeting in Morsang-sur-Orge is very telling from this perspective:

> The meeting started with a discussion about the new urban planning project of the neighbourhood. However, at a certain point, Josiane – a woman in her late 60s – started to speak in a rather aggressive way on a completely different topic: 'I'd like that the bus stop in front of my house to be removed! I don't feel at home any more since it's been put there. Would it be that complicated to move it fifty meters? What should I do for that? I'm fed up! I'm really fed up! You have to do something about it!' Jacky, member of the technical services of the municipality, answered rather harshly: 'There's nothing to do about it! I'm sorry! It would require a lot of permits and official authorisations. And it doesn't depend of us any more; it is a competence of the agglomeration community.' The answer was not sufficient for Josiane however: 'OK, but this bus stop was not here when we bought the house! Otherwise ...' Given the increasing tension of the discussion, Francis, the participatory democracy official, intervened: 'You know Madam, It's not to duck the question, but ... you know, *the problem with bus stops, is that they are great as long as they are in front of other people houses.*' The audience became more or more critical. Jokes started to burst forth: 'It's always better in front of other houses, hum!'; 'you should move out!'; 'OK, we got your point, this is useless!' The discussion became a mess and finished in an atmosphere of disgrace for this woman.

> (Observation notes, Morsang-sur-Orge, 4th November 2005)

This excerpt illustrates how parochial arguments can be expressed publicly in Morsang-sur-Orge assemblies – the publicity of the interaction does not make them disappear as argued by some deliberative democrats – but are heavily sanctioned. In this case, this woman received a double sanction, as she was both publicly ridiculed by the comments of the other participants – and especially those of a local councillor, granted an important symbolic capital – and was then labelled 'ball-breaker'.

The second discursive mode is bargaining, participants trying to foster their self-interest through public participation, to negotiate with the authorities to obtain what they want. The explicit use of self-interest to justify claims was rare however, as it was both relatively non-functional (because inefficient) and socially disqualifying (see above). Most of the time however, people try to offer at least a minimal public good justification for their claim, in keeping with the norms of civic engagement. These were argumentative sequences, and some empirical evidence is provided below. However, argumentation does not always mean deliberation. An argument has to be answered (criticised or endorsed) to start a deliberation. Most of the time, however, as will be seen below, PB allowed for the development of monological argumentative sequences: arguments were voiced but not answered. The rule of PB discursive interaction was not deliberation, but a succession of monological (argumentative) sequences not answering each other.

The main division line between polemic, bargaining and argumentation, therefore, lies in the types of justifications used to back up claims: do speakers justify their claims with personal, interested or common good arguments? While ethnographic research allows the drawing of conclusions on the regularities of interaction patterns, they also require paying special attention to exceptional moments, when the routine is broken. Deliberation embodies from this perspective a breakdown with the routine of PB discursive interaction. The question then is to evaluate how public discussion in PB assemblies can sometimes mean deliberative sequences and, at some other times, mere bargaining, polemical or monological sequences. When does deliberation happen? How come the power of publicity does not always play fully to allow the emergence of deliberation?

Necessary conditions for the emergence of deliberation

If deliberation is scarce in PBs, it can, nevertheless, emerge under certain specific social, political and institutional conditions. These conditions are therefore worth investigating in depth, to understand better the phenomenon of deliberation among lay citizens. I argue that the main conditions for the emergence of deliberation in non-experimental political settings are:

- Procedures
- Disagreement
- Leaders
- Stakes

These favourable conditions are more or less salient in the different cases, but were, nevertheless, always present when deliberation happened. They also take different forms given the cases as, for instance, conflict and disagreement are not framed similarly when they emerge between politicians and lay citizens, or among citizens themselves. While these conditions for the emergence of deliberation were drawn from observation of the discursive interactions, these four features are partly generalisable to other participatory arenas.

The power of procedures: Laissez-faire vs. structured discussions

One of the crucial prerequisites for the emergence of deliberation is the organisation of the discussion. Deliberation does not emerge spontaneously from the interactions taking place in the public sphere. On the contrary, *laissez-faire* discussion is the best way to let powerful actors, those with the highest discursive skills and cultural capital, capture the floor. The focus on procedure is central in the deliberative democracy literature, in which good deliberation means a procedurally fair exchange of arguments. Fair deliberative procedures especially imply publicity and formal inclusiveness (everyone should be able to participate), and the exclusion of internal constraints (everyone should be able to give his/her say) (Cohen 1989). In practice, the organisation of the discussion around fair procedures includes different elements however: scenography and size of the groups, limits framing public interventions (mutual respect, time limits, list of speakers, etc.), selection and style of the facilitators.

Scenography and size of the discussion groups

Organised discussion has to be fostered by some basic procedural designs. The spatial organisation of the meetings appears from this perspective important: everyone should be able to see each other when talking. People need to see and hear each other properly to answer each other and be fully responsive. The organisers of the three studied PBs were well aware of the importance of scenography for deliberation. Thus, once, Paula Garvin (local leader of *Izquierda Unida* and inceptor of Seville PB) was giving her feedback and impressions on the assembly of the day, and underlined the 'distance between the stage and the audience [...] the whole thing looking pretty formal'.[11] She insisted on the symbolic importance of putting 'the speakers and the audience, at the same level', and concluded with a political interpretation of the phenomenon: 'those are the little power mechanisms of everyday life. [...] We don't pay attention to them, but that's when they are the most powerful. We're just reproducing the same thing as the others; without even thinking about it'. Assemblies therefore generally take the form of circles of chairs, facilitators avoiding divisions between the speakers and the audience.

Besides spatial organisation, the size of the discussion group is also a crucial factor for deliberation. This issue is dealt with in a contrasted manner from one case to another. In Seville, where zone assemblies gather a high number of participants (up to a few hundred) the organisers decided to limit the role of discussion for reasons of effectiveness. Decisions are therefore taken though vote. Discussion is restricted to the application of the social justice criteria, which gathers only elected delegates, i.e., never more than a dozen participants. In a small city like Morsang-sur-Orge, the idea of splitting assemblies has never been raised. Public meetings never gather more than thirty people; so that the organisers never had the impression that affluence impeded the quality of the discussion. The awareness of the importance and difficulty of public communication pushed the organisers of the Roman PB to design it in such a way as to foster the quality of discussion, with the organisation of working groups – by thematic area – gathering between four and ten people. The experience of Montagnola neighbourhood assembly is pretty telling from this perspective:

> The first two meetings of the year had been chaotic. The thirty participants had indeed refused to split into working groups, against facilitators' advice. It resulted in a discursive messiness, people not listening to each other, speaking over the other, moving from one topic to the other. At the third meeting, participants decided to divide in three working groups, gathering respectively between six to eight people. Discussion dynamics thus changed drastically. I followed one of the working groups, where discussion was calm and constructive, the facilitator sometimes asking 'not all at the same time' or 'one after the other'. A speaking turn was organised, proposals were written down, and those cutting short others systematically sanctioned. Deliberation therefore emerged, based on the collective evaluation of arguments and proposals. In a few months, due to the imitation of some basic discussion rules, citizens had learnt to deliberate. The better organisation of the debate allowed moving from agonistic and sometimes aggressive exchanges, to a much more cooperative and constructive atmosphere.

> (Observation notes. Motagnola neighbourhood,
> Rome, January–May 2006)

Size makes, therefore, a significant difference to the quality of deliberation. Not only do smaller groups make discussion more constructive, they also increase the number of speakers during the meetings. The smaller the size of the group, the higher the speaking rate (number of speakers per session): it was 79 per cent in Rome, 68 per cent in Morsang-sur-Orge, and 40 per cent in Seville.[12] It has to be stressed, however, that this data does not take into account the inequalities between participants' interventions – some speaking many times and for a few minutes, others just once and for a few seconds. Nevertheless, the speaking rate might be an important factor in the emergence of deliberation, as it increases the diversity of the viewpoints expressed, and therefore, can foster the expression of disagreement.

Another procedural means to increase the number of speakers, is to organise 'turn taking', everyone having to give his/her opinion on the issue at stake. While, in general, the floor is captured by a few speakers, the discussion takes a different shape when everyone has to give his/her opinion. While people with few oral skills lack the confidence to speak up spontaneously, they take the chance offered to them to express themselves. This again can increase the pool of expressed arguments, and therefore favour the emergence of disagreement and the breaking off of monological sequences. This discursive procedure is not institutionalised however, and therefore depends on the style of the facilitators. Furthermore, some problems remain with this discursive trick. It becomes indeed increasingly difficult for people to express dissent as a certain number of persons have already expressed their views. Rapidly, indeed, a clear majority emerges for or against a proposal, and actors have to be extremely self-confident to express counter-arguments or dissent at that point. Said differently, this is a powerful way to construct consensus (Mansbridge 1980). And it will be seen in the next section how important disagreement is for the emergence of deliberation

Organisation of the discussion and facilitation

Spatial organisation, small groups and 'turn taking' are not sufficient for deliberation to emerge. Other factors, like the procedural organisation of the discussion and the style of the facilitators, play crucial roles, as shown in the comparison between the Morsang-sur-Orge and Rome Municipio XI discussions. Morsang-sur-Orge appears as a good example of *laissez-faire* discussion. A facilitator organises the discussion and is in charge of the agenda. He/she is, in general, either an elected official or a public functionary. Despite the existence of a clear agenda – prepared by an organisation committee composed of residents – the discussion is not properly organised. A topic is introduced by the facilitator, then additional information is added by elected officials or technicians, thus substantially framing the discussion, and then lay participants can give their say or ask questions. They generally say little, and often remain silent. There is therefore little discussion on the topics on the agenda. However, often at the end of the meetings, participants come up with issues that were not initially on the agenda, generally related to personal troubles they have, that actually motivated their presence at the meeting.[13] What follows is a messy discussion, where lay citizens, upset at having remained silent for so long, express themselves aggressively, while elected representatives and civil servants try to answer the questions and evoke possible solutions. It hardly gives rise to good discursive sequences, where problems are stated, alternative solutions and course of actions weighted, and collective decisions taken. It more often gives rise to adversarial and polemical discussions, where no proper counter-arguments are stated, and no decision taken.

On the contrary, the facilitation style can be proceduralised, as in the case of Municipio XI PB, where discussion is based on a trivial but crucial tool, a report, where every problem or proposal is written down.[14] People have first to state and define the problem they identified. Then, in a second column, they have to propose a solution to the problem. Discussion generally occurs at both stages, to define the problem correctly, and then to evaluate the possible courses of action to solve it. A report is thus written at the end of each meeting for each thematic area, and then addressed to the technical services of the Municipio, who are required to provide an answer on either the problem (Is it adequately framed? Is it of the competence of the Municipio? Is there something planned to solve it already? etc.) or the solutions (Are they technically viable, of the competence of the Municipio, financially realisable, etc.?). The answers of the technical services then serve as a basis for the further discussion of the projects at the following meeting. As a consequence, Roman PB discursive interactions were, in general, highly effective and organised.

The organisation of the discussion appears, therefore, as a crucial element for the emergence of deliberation. *Laissez-faire* discussion hardly end-up in what is defined as deliberation. On the contrary, when attention is paid to the spatial layout of the meeting, when the size of the group is small enough to discuss properly, listen and exchange arguments, when there is even material support (like the Roman '*Verbale*') framing the discussion in a constructive manner, and when finally everyone is invited to give his/her say on the issue at stake, deliberation is on good grounds. Other factors, both social and situational, are nevertheless necessary as well, the first being the public expression of disagreement.

The difficulty and necessity of expressing disagreement in public discussion

As said earlier, deliberation is scarce. In public arenas, most people voice arguments, diagnosis problems and evoke possible solutions in a monological way. Personal interventions do not answer each other and hardly end up in a constructive exchange of arguments and counter-arguments in search of a common good. Deliberation relies on argumentation, but it also requires an *exchange* of arguments.

Most of the time, it was the absence of conflict, dissent or disagreement that impeded the emergence of deliberation. It can appear trivial, but when everybody agrees from the beginning or when people do not care or bother to express disagreement, deliberation cannot emerge. Most of the empirical literature on deliberation has stressed, until now, the importance of heterogeneity or diversity for deliberation. Deliberation usually does not occur among fellow men. Mutz and Martin (2001) showed, for instance, that a more heterogeneous social network prompts a more deliberative frame of mind. Huckfeld showed as well that heterogeneous discussion networks create more reflexive political choices (Huckfeld *et al.* 2004). Heterogeneity and the diversity of views are necessary, but not sufficient, conditions for the emergence of deliberation. What matters however is the discursive expression of diversity. Indeed, for many social, situational and pragmatic reasons heterogeneous groups might remain fully consensual, not expressing any disagreement.[15]

I thus observed, over my ethnographic study, some very sophisticated deliberations, but only when some disagreement was voiced. An excerpt from a discussion that took place in Garbatella neighbourhood assembly in Rome is pretty telling from this perspective:

> Participants decided to split into working groups at the beginning of the meeting, and I followed the one dealing with urban and environmental issues.

It was composed of six people, three women and three men. The discussion was immediately organised by Valentina, the youngest participant, but experienced activist in a social centre and a housing rights association. She proposed to start with a short introduction by each participant and then asked each of them to voice their priorities in terms of urbanism for the PB.

Maurizio, a man in his early 50s, member of the environmentalist organization *Legambiente* (as he introduced himself immediately), was the first one to speak: 'Personally, what I want is to fight against the influence of cars in the city. It's unbearable and dramatic for the environment. [...] I want to make two proposals: the creation of bicycle paths and the creation of a 'Zone 30' – limiting cars' speed – in the centre of the neighbourhood.'

His intervention spurred some strong reactions. Franco, a man in his 70s, immediately voiced a counter-argument: 'It's not a problem of urbanism or roads [...] it's not a technical problem, it's a problem of culture. Culture is to know what are one's rights and duties. [...] It's really nice to change the rules, but where are the policemen to make them respected?'

Maurizio answered by reformulating his argument. He found an ally in the person of Stefano, a man in his early 30s, regular participant of the PB process: 'I think speed bumps would be enough. And it doesn't cost that much. [...] If we were a civilised and educated people everything would be easy of course, all these discussions would be useless [...] but we're far from it. [...] That's why we need speed bumps.' He, therefore, answered Franco's cultural arguments, to justify a technical solution from both a political ('we cannot change people's culture') and financial perspective ('it doesn't cost that much').

(Observation notes, Garbatella working group,
Rome, 17th February 2005)

In this case, a deliberative sequence emerged: a problem was identified and framed as an environmental issue. Solutions were then offered: the limitation of the use of cars, by the creation of a cycling path and a 'zone 30'. The procedural organisation of the discussion was probably good enough to allow the emergence of a constructive discussion. The small size of the group, and the facilitator organising turn-taking, played a crucial role too. As one participant was speaking after the other, people listened to each other. The procedural and situational conditions of the discussion, therefore, made possible the expression of disagreement. The expression of disagreement – by Franco in this case – pushed Maurizio (and Stefano) to offer a more comprehensive justification of his proposal, and thus to argue.

The importance of disagreement for deliberation is even clearer in a neighbourhood council meeting of Morsang-sur-Orge. A few teenagers of the neighbourhood had decided to participate to ask for the creation of some premises in which to gather in the evening. A sharp deliberative sequence developed due to a double disagreement – hence the tensed atmosphere of the meeting – the mayor, present that evening, rejecting the request pretty harshly: 'No! Otherwise, it is always squatted in an unpleasant way'; the teenagers, and especially Kamel, arguing back 'I don't agree ...'[16] A highly argumentative sequence developed thanks to the publicly voiced disagreement. They weighted the pros and cons of the creation of such premises, and took a decision.

If disagreement is so important for the emergence of deliberation, it is scarce however. The public expression of disagreement is a difficult move. Most of the time people consider their opinions to be private matters, which do not need to be discussed, justified and eventually modified after a discussion with strangers. It seems that there is, in most public arenas, a strong cultural force pushing people to respect the opinions of others, therefore refusing to contradict or convince them. This might be linked to group dynamics – in relation to what Goffman (1959) calls the 'principle of unanimity' – especially when participation is organised at the neighbourhood level. Diana Mutz (2002) argued convincingly how difficult it is for individuals, embedded in cross-cutting social networks, to express their views or simply to talk about politics, as people are afraid of losing their social relationships. It seems, however, that this phenomenon is embedded in a deeper cultural trend, linked to a form of democratic tolerance or political liberalism that gives each citizen the right to express his/her opinions. In such a context, it appears inappropriate to contradict anonymous strangers, or to try to make them change their mind (Eliasoph 1998; Conover *et al.* 2002; Duchesne and Haegel 2006). Criticising an opinion would be like denying the status of citizen to an individual. Dissenters are therefore under a strong social pressure to remain silent.

Despite all these difficulties, sometimes disagreement is voiced, allowing for the emergence of deliberation. How can some be ready to argue, to exchange their views in a collective and public discussion, given the risks attached to it in terms of reputation and social integration? What are the social and situational conditions for the emergence of disagreement in public arenas? Two factors appeared crucial from this perspective: the role of leaders and the stakes of the discussion.

The role of leaders: Expressing dissent and politicising discussions

Some actors play a more important role than others in the expression of divergent views and the emergence of conflict within the group. Actors have indeed to be confident enough about their ideas and standpoints to voice them explicitly and to be ready to argue with others. From this perspective, activists and political party militants have a decisive influence on the quality of PB discussions. Holding strong preferences, they have the cultural and political resources necessary for the expression of dissent. Then, belonging to a group or a collective also fosters the expression of dissent, as it allows sharing the risks of expressing divergent views with others. In the case of Garbatella, evoked above, politicised actors like Valentina, Stefano and Maurizio played a crucial role throughout the discussion, both in the way discussion was organised and in the expression of counter-arguments. One of the clearest signs of the importance of leaders and politicised actors is the vacuum created by their absence. Maurizio, Valentina and Stefano were indeed absent at the following meeting of Garbatella's working group, which ended up being of a mediocre discursive quality. Proposals followed each other without justification nor counter-arguments, as no disagreement was expressed. While it is often assumed that activists are anti-deliberative agents, preferring direct action to cooperative discussion (Young 2001), it seems that in Rome and Seville deliberation could not have happened without the commitment of local militants.

In Morsang-sur-Orge, given the presence of elected representatives in public meetings, dissent and conflict generally emerged between citizens and members of the municipal majority. An excerpt of a disagreement that emerged in a neighbourhood council meeting once, illustrates rightly the nature of the discussion that can derive from it.

This meeting, taking place in the more deprived neighbourhood of the city, was in some regards unique, as it attracted a few teenagers living in social housing residence. Their presence was not random however, they had been mobilised by social workers active in the neighbourhood and this took place a few weeks after the French 'banlieue riots' of the fall of 2005 (*French Politics, Culture and Society* 2006). The meeting was all the more special that the mayor was present. After an hour of discussion about different local issues, the teenagers asked to speak. The group of four young males, between 16 and 20, looking kind of 'banlieue style', wearing caps, sneakers and joggers, contrasting with the rest of the public, mostly white and old:

Frank, one of the teenagers, asked: 'I wanted to know if you had a project for us?'

The mayor appeared confused about the request: 'What do you mean? I don't understand.'

Frank: 'Premises for teenagers.'

The answer from the mayor was this time pretty clear: 'No! Otherwise, it is always squatted in an unpleasant way. We had a lot of experiences of this kind of thing in the past, and it always ended up badly when we gave a room to the teenagers.' [...]

Kamel, the eldest member of the group, appearing as their speaker: 'They ask for a place to meet and gather together, to play games. The municipal room is not enough. For the moment, they meet in basements in awful conditions.'

Henry, an elder participant of the meeting: 'We could ask the owner, Efidis, to create a premise for the youth?'

The mayor seemed however sceptical: 'Efidis are like us, they know how it works [...] And it costs something, you know. There used to be a gym here, at the free disposal of the youth of the neighbourhood, and they completely destroyed it a few years ago. And it's gonna be the same thing now.'

Kamel: 'So we leave them in the basements?'

The mayor: 'They can meet up at some parents place. We don't have this kind of request anywhere else, I don't understand. It is the only neighbourhood where I see teenagers gathering in basements.'

Frank: 'We started to make a petition. We made it and we got the basement, but it was destroyed afterwards.'

The mayor: 'But meeting up in the basement is not human. And if we do something we're sure that in three weeks there won't be anything left.'

Kamel: 'I don't agree!'

The mayor: "We saw with the gym, teenagers from the neighbourhood destroyed it. I cannot take the responsibility to invest thousands of Euros for something that will be destroyed. You are the nice ones, but the others are not all like you.'

Kamel: 'You don't trust us?'

The mayor: 'No!'

This was probably understood by the teenagers as an insult and can be interpreted as a grammatical mistake from the mayor. While the teenagers where trying to look for support in the NC, the mayor showed a great deal of authoritarianism and refused to put the question on the agenda, thus impeding the autonomy of the assembly. Especially, some regular participants to the NC (not young ones) seemed rather favourable to the idea of offering a premise to the teenagers, especially given the recent riot movement. The mayor however impeded such a discussion. All the teenagers, except Kamel, left, saying ironically: 'Thank you!'[17]

The discussion with the teenagers stopped at that point, and the NC moved back to the daily issues of the neighbourhood. No decision was taken that evening but a good deliberative sequence occurred. The main reason was the emergence of disagreement due to two main actors: the mayor – who refused teenagers' proposal – and Kamel – who opposed the mayor, saying at some point 'I don't agree'. Such a level of disagreement remains however a rare phenomenon in Morsang-sur-Orge PB assemblies. The counter-arguments of Kamel were listened to and answered by the mayor, who moved her position along the discussion. The presence of public officials therefore allowed the emergence of disagreement, conflict and therefore of a good deliberative sequence. The types of deliberation taking place between lay citizens and elected representatives, and among citizens alone, are relatively different however. When citizens discuss with each other they try to search for the best collective solution to a public problem, the presence of politicians in the discussion transforms it into a bargaining process, citizens trying to attract resources and to obtain promises. At the end of the previous excerpt, Kamel concluded saying 'it's fair's fair'. The presence of politicians might therefore transform deliberation into a clientelist relationship (Lefebvre 2005).

The politicisation of the discussion, and the expression of disagreement, are therefore mostly assured by the elected representatives in Morsang-sur-Orge.

Given the weakness of the local civil society, the discursive work of creating conflict has to be done by the elected representatives, who appear as the clear leaders
of the discussion. There is nevertheless a gap between the participatory practices
of Rome and Morsang-sur-Orge. While Roman activists can act as a counter-veil-
ing power against the municipality (Fung and Wright 2003), the whole process is
dominated by elected officials in Morsang-sur-Orge. If leaders are crucial to the
emergence of disagreement and deliberation, the type of leader necessarily frames
the nature of the deliberative interactions.

The stakes of the discussion: Deliberation in empowered participatory institutions

Discussions are not ends in themselves in PB institutions; they aim at taking binding decisions about the allocation of part of the municipal budget (up to 10 million
Euros in Rome and Seville). Even if these participatory institutions can be considered marginally empowered – the proportion of the municipal budget 'decided' by
the residents being relatively modest – the mere fact of having to take decisions
changes the dynamic of the discussion. The crucial difference made by the stakes
of the discussion is that they lower the cost of dissent, or better, make it worth expressing (Sunstein 2003a: 23-5; Ryfe 2005). Stakes push people to express their
views – not to keep them private – if they want (as their presence in the assembly
indicates) to make a difference on the final decision. The importance of the stakes
can be illustrated by comparing cases of decision-free discussions with discussions aimed at affecting public policies.

Decision-free discussions happen when participants talk about issues out of the
realm of the local government competences. Arguments can be voiced, but disagreement is silenced, as no decision has to be taken. An excerpt of a Neighbourhood
council discussion on the issue of a new law about French kindergartens (the PSU
law, '*Prestation de Service Unique*'[18]) is pretty telling from this perspective:

> Francis, a town councillor, started to evoke the reform: 'The aim of this law is
> to liberalise the kindergarten system. Parents will be able to let their children go
> for only a few hours a day, and not for the full day as it used to be.' Participants
> reacted straight off. Isabelle, obviously surprised, was the first one: 'That's
> terrible! That's terrible for the future of our kids! OK, it's more convenient for
> the parents, but what about the kids?' Francis answered: 'I think this is the true
> question: what is the priority, parents or kids? I guess the law tries to take into
> account the complexity of modern life, with flexible schedules, part-time jobs,
> precariousness etc.' Isabelle went on with the same line of argument: 'Parents
> want kids, but then they throw them to the kindergarten and that's it. It's really
> terrible for the future of these kids, it's gonna destabilise them, disturb them
> [...] It's terrible!'

> (Observation notes, Neighbourhood council Langevin,
> Morsang-sur-Orge, 21st January 2005).

This excerpt could lead one to think that deliberation without disagreement is possible. Arguments were voiced and the discussion reached a certain level of generality. But arguments went all in the same direction, everybody agreeing on the damageable character of the law. It is not, however, that a consensus was magically created from the beginning, but rather that disagreement was not expressed publicly. A juxtaposition of similar arguments does not make a deliberation, but a collective plea. Once the discussion on the PSU was over, my neighbours started to talk in an aside, and one of them said: 'But me, personally, I don't think that this PSU idea is so stupid. I'm for performance and efficiency.' This argument would have clashed with those expressed publicly by the other participants, as they rest on different ideological grounds. This participant did not dare expressing his counter-argument publicly, however. He probably did not feel competent enough to do so, but above all, he certainly tried to avoid a useless conflict. For disagreement to be expressed, it has first to exist latently, but its expression has to be seen worthy by actors. In that case, no decision had to be taken; the debate was an end in itself. Expressing dissent was therefore not worth it for the participants who would have had to accept the discursive and social costs (in terms of reputation especially) of a dissonant argument. It is indeed socially and pragmatically risky for individuals to engage in adversary conversations and to put their opinions on the table. The stakes make the expression of disagreement worthwhile by giving a value and an interest to argumentation. This conclusion is rather dull for the prospect of a deliberative participatory democracy, as most experiences of public participation are consultative. Even in relatively empowered cases like PBs, disagreement and deliberation are exceptional, and only an addition of favourable conditions can make deliberation happen.

In the end, it is no surprise, given the four conditions identified for its emergence, that deliberation is scarce in the public sphere. A final question needs, however, to be raised: if deliberation is scarce, does this mean self-change is scarce too? Do people change only when good deliberative sequences take place? What is the individual impact of deliberation? Does deliberation result in preference change?

The difficulty of opinion change in PB institutions

Even if rare, deliberation happened under certain conditions in the PB cases I studied. According to the literature, deliberation should affect people by shaping their preferences, or at least making them more robust because they are more informed. Deliberation should draw people's attention to new arguments, shed a new light on some issues, increase the pool of available information, which should foster better-informed preferences. Are these hypotheses confirmed by our observations?

One of the clearest signs of the individual impact of deliberation should be preference change.[19] Surprisingly, however, little opinion change happened during the public discussions I observed. Participants' opinions – those expressed in public – remained mostly stable and the cognitive quality of their opinions did not increase drastically. It seems that participants did not convince each other. Each participant gave his/her say, some answered, voiced counter-arguments, but

I never witnessed a participant saying: 'You're right, and I am wrong.' Moreover, none of the interviewed participants acknowledged to have changed their mind through discussion.

Changing position publicly, or acknowledging one's mistakes, is a difficult move; this does not mean non-speakers, or people with weak preferences, were not affected by deliberation. Deliberation could contribute to opinion formation instead of opinion change. One of the aims of deliberation is indeed also to convince those who do not have an opinion yet. Speakers, those with strong preferences, try to convince the audience – those who have no opinion and do not speak – to opt for their position rather than for a rival one (Elster 1994). This process is however largely invisible to the observer. Different scenarios can nevertheless be distinguished in the process of opinion formation.

First, monological sequences – the most common case – can have an influence on silent participants (those with weak preferences on the issue at stake, therefore remaining silent), helping them to form an opinion on an issue they did not know or care about before. In that case, it is argumentation rather than deliberation that made the audience change (or make up) its mind.

Then, when disagreement emerges between speakers holding diverging (strong) preference, different arguments are offered for and against a certain course of action. The speakers of the two or more conflictive positions hardly change their mind in that case – I did not observe it – but, again, the audience, having weak preferences, can go on one or the other side. In that case, consensus being broken and dissent made explicit, decisions concluding the discussion are taken through vote, to gain time. This happened regularly in Seville for the attribution of the social justice criteria. The vote of the non-speakers (there were in general few abstentions) indicated that they had made up their mind in the course of the discussion.

Finally, even more rarely, some participants with strong preferences, having defended a certain position publicly, changed and ended up with a different position at the end of the deliberative process. An example of such a slight evolution comes again from Garbatella urban planning and environment working group in Rome Municipio XI PB. At the last session of the working group, participants had to browse all the proposals made in the previous meetings to select the three or four more significant ones. Surprisingly, Franco, one of the most regular participants to the working group, defended the speed bumpers proposal. While at the first meeting he had criticised and rejected it, he had changed his mind with time. Asking him why, he answered: 'I thought about it again at home, quietly, and I arrived at the idea that this was a lesser evil.' It seems, therefore, that public deliberation with activists at the first session induced an internal deliberation for this participant (Goodin 2003). If changing position publicly during a discussion is difficult, to avoid losing face and acknowledging one's defeat in the verbal battle, adverse arguments can, nevertheless, have an impact and convince the speakers in the end.

If Franco's position evolved on a specific technical question (how to decrease cars' speed in the neighbourhood), he has not been convinced by the environmental arguments expressed by the activists, however. Franco's opinion change therefore happened marginally, on a technical question, but his ideological frames remained intact. The political arguments based on the need to diminish the use of cars for environmental reasons were not sufficient to change Franco's ideological frames. When an opinion is relatively stabilised, acquired through years of experiences, new arguments, even if repeated over four successive meetings, are not enough.

Even if exceptional, this example indicates opinion change is possible when deliberation is of good quality and repeated over time. One of the reasons opinion change was so rare could, therefore, be that the quality of PB discursive interactions was not sufficient. Consensual and monological discussions were indeed the rule in most PB assemblies. Conflicts and disagreements were scarce while, in general, discussions were very cooperative, proposal oriented and practical. Often, people made a precise proposal, it was written down by the facilitator, and then a new speaker talked about a different topic. The routine of PB discussions was rather a succession of monologues, than a constructive deliberation. In some regard, this was what most participants expected and it allowed constructive public discussion about the best public policies to set up. This discursive style was effective, in keeping with the first goal of participatory budgeting: letting citizens shape the city's public policies.

If organised, practical and consensual discussion can be functional in terms of public policy achievement, it is not sure that it goes hand in hand with self-change and participant politicisation. A dilemma seems therefore to exist between participatory democracy's external and internal goals: changing public policies or empowering people. As these two goals imply different types of interactions, it is not sure that they can be perfectly compatible. Praising highly organised and practical public discussions – as Archon Fung (2004) does for instance – might imply accepting the depoliticisation of both issues and subjects.

Why deliberation had limited individual impact

If the quality of PB public discussions was probably most of the time insufficient, it was not always true; sometimes deliberation happened, but opinion change remained scarce. How can we explain that even when deliberation emerged so little conviction occurred? The quality of deliberation – in comparison to other participatory arenas – is surely one of the reasons, but other factors can explain the stability of individual preferences. First, orators could be insufficiently convincing, their arguments being too weak to convince the audience. Then, the audience could fail to listen to these arguments adequately, not being ready to be convinced. Finally, and this will be the main point here, preferences seem overly rooted in the previous experiences of actors, to be changed by words. It can even be argued that preferences being directly linked to interests, actors have few chances to change, unless they see their interests under a new light.

The failure of conviction and information?

One of the reasons why opinions remained stable could be that speakers were not convincing enough to make the others change their mind. As Dryzek and List (2003: 9) emphasised, deliberation should:

> draw people's attention to new arguments about the interdependence of issues, confirm or refute the internal consistency of such arguments, make explicit previously hidden premises and assumptions, and clarify whether controversies are about facts, methods and means, or values and ends.

In PBs, speakers could have failed therefore to draw the attention of the audience to the interdependence of issues or to the consequences of some choices over others. This is not what I saw, however. When deliberation emerged, it was precisely when some speakers argued about the consequences of a certain course of action. People argued, even if answers and counter-arguments were rare. The argumentative part of deliberation was present, but it rarely convinced the audience.

Another reason why preferences remained overall stable could be the absence of new information brought in the debate by the participants. One of the central claims of the cognitive hypothesis is that in a deliberative arena most people do not have the same ideas, experiences and opinions. By sharing them, they may increase the pool of information available for discussion and, as such, should increase its quality (see chapter one). One of the reasons of the scarcity of preference change in PB assemblies could, therefore, be the small amount of new information brought to it by the participants. The idea of scarcity of information does not fit with these PB cases however. New information was brought either directly by participants – be it their local knowledge, professional and political competences (see chapter four) – or acquired during participation, as in the case of Seville city tours, explicitly aimed at increasing information on the proposals to evaluate. Local knowledge was important in raising a new problem or disqualifying potential solutions (Fischer 2000). The most informed participants – especially experienced activists – also brought new information to the table, and it sometimes reoriented the discussion. When people had information on the legal status on certain land plots they increased the pool of available information, and it had an impact on the discussion, that stopped or got reoriented. In any case, all the participants interviewed stressed the informative nature of the discussions. This does not mean individual preferences were changed however. Collective discussions were re-reoriented, some solutions disqualified, others became cognitively more robust, but participants rarely changed their preferences.

From this perspective, it does not seem that the scarcity of preference change stemmed from a failure of argumentation or a scarcity of information. Both were present, but insufficient for changing individual opinions

.

A lack of mutual listening?

Another factor that could explain the scarcity of preference change could be the failure of listening in PB assemblies. A crucial condition for preference change is indeed the capacity of the participants to listen to each other. If speech is central for deliberation, listening might be even more important, as Diego Gambetta (1998: 20) argues:

> If agents show up late at meetings, pay no attention to one another's speeches, jump the queue, speak all at once, or shout when they have no argument, the conditions for deliberation are simply not there. Deliberation of course, relies on a grander factor, freedom of speech. Free speech, however, achieves functional significance only if somebody is prepared to listen.

One of the reasons why so little preference change occurred in PB assemblies could therefore be that participants failed to listen to each other. Not listening to others' arguments, people could not be convinced. However, this is not what I observed in PB assemblies. Of course, some of the PB meetings were messy, but most of the time discussions were well organised, people speaking one after the other. People could, at least, hear each other. As seen earlier, the procedural organisation of the discussion is a necessary condition for deliberation to emerge. It might however be necessary to go further in the definition of the term 'listening'. Listening to an argument might mean more than respecting the speaker by not speaking over him/her. Silence is a necessary but not sufficient condition for the emergence of deliberation and therefore for preference change. The 'I will listen' evoked by Benjamin Barber seems to imply more than mere respect:

> 'I will listen' means to the strong democrat not that I will scan my adversary's position for weaknesses and potential trade-offs, nor even (as a minimalist might think) that I will tolerantly permit him to say whatever he chooses. It means, rather, 'I will put myself in his place, I will try to understand, I will strain to hear what makes us alike, I will listen for a common rhetoric evocative of a common purpose or a common good.' Good listeners may turn out to be bad lawyers, but they make adept citizens and excellent neighbours.

(Barber 1984: 175)

This might be the difference between the type of listening observed in PB assemblies, and the 'I will listen' of Barber. PB participants might just be tolerant minimalists, politely letting their adversaries express their views without ever challenging their own. They listen to others' positions, but will always consider their own preference as superior. As said earlier, there is a logical contradiction between persuasion and tolerance, and in general, people opt for tolerance. Each citizen is allowed to express his/her opinion, and in the name of democratic tolerance it appears inappropriate to contradict people, or even to try to make them change their mind. Deliberation, on the contrary, requires a form of intolerance, or the presumption that one's own opinion is the best, at least until a different position has not been proved true.

The stability of caused preferences

The difficulty of preference change in PB assemblies, linked to an ethic of toleration, might be related to the participation of politicised actors in these institutions. They have, by definition, rather strong preferences. Having pre-defined positions on issues, resulting from sometimes a long experience of militancy, politicised actors can hardly change their position in the course of the discussion. It would mean betraying their own goals and ideals, in which they have believed for long. It is all the more difficult to change position and be convinced when these opinions have been coherently organised for years within an ideological scheme. As convincing an argument can be, it might be politically, cognitively and emotionally difficult to change, as Daniel Gaxie (2002: 167) argues: 'For someone relatively involved politically, rupture with past and highly valued opinions is costly. This cost limits or slows down opinion change.'

Opinion change is not only a matter of cost however. Otherwise, I would have witnessed preference change from apolitical citizens, for whom the cost was lower. Preference change is also, and to a large extent, a matter of socialisation, that deliberative democrats tend to overlook. Deliberative democrats have an under-socialised conception of preferences, as it appears clearly in Manin's seminal article (1987: 351), when he writes:

> Individuals 'have certain preferences and some information, but these are unsure, incomplete, often confused and opposed to one another. The process of deliberation, the confrontation of various points of view, helps to clarify information and to sharpen their own preferences. They may even modify their initial objectives, should that prove necessary'.

The incomplete, incoherent or contradictory nature of preferences has been demonstrated for long (Converse 1964). Apart from highly politicised actors who hold a well-defined and coherent set of values – even if an ideology can itself be ambiguous or incoherent – most individuals do not hold very sophisticated opinions. But who said the strength of a conviction was proportional to its coherence? Maybe the contrary is true. The logical connection established by Manin between preference confusion and the capacity to change is far from evident. In general, despite their incoherence and inconsistency, opinions are strong and stable.

Political preferences are indeed largely determined by the primary and secondary socialisation endured by individuals. Preferences are affected by a diversity of biographical elements, linked to the specific experiences that marked the trajectory of individuals. As Offe argues (1997: 88), preferences are caused:

> After all, preferences that we observe are by no means randomly distributed across historical time and social space. In fact, we can fairly reliably predict at least some of the preferences of a person if we know his or her family background, national identity, economic position, associative involvement, age group, educational background, etc. Preferences emerge from and are shaped by a formative context, or background conditions.

If preferences only depended on the free choice of individuals, they could eas- ily be changed. Being deeply rooted, political preferences cannot be changed by a two hour discussion. Interestingly, the definition of individual preferences as 'caused', is at the roots of the deliberative paradigm. Including the institutional conditions in the formation of individual preferences, deliberative democrats ar- gue that provided there are adequate procedural conditions, individual opinions can be enlightened (Sunstein 1991). This fails to note that the origin of individual preferences is to be found in the institutional context, but also in some more struc- tural features (evoked by Offe above) to be found in individual trajectories. This does not mean individual preferences cannot change, but that it has to be, at best, a long term process.

Preferences appear all the more stable when the topics of discussion direct- ly touch on individuals' interests. In PB meetings, most of the discussions deal with issues directly affecting the private interests of, at least, some participants. Interests have, at least partly, a structural component, linked to the social, eco- nomic or territorial situations of individuals and groups. This does not mean that a new light cannot be shed on individuals' interests, allowing actors to take a larger picture, taking into account their long-term interests too. It does not mean either that the interests at stake in PB meetings were always private. They were, most of the time, collective interests: that of blocks, neighbourhoods, the city as a whole or of a certain category of the population. But even when linked to collective or pub- lic interests, preferences might be more stable than deliberative democrats thought at first. This explanation of the failure of collective discussion to change individual opinions indicates two different models of deliberation.

Two Models of Deliberation

Two models of deliberation can therefore be distinguished. On the one hand, there is disinterested deliberation, in which individuals have no personal interest at stake in the discussion. The ideal-type of this model is judiciary deliberation: jurors have no direct interest (personal or collective) in clearing or sentencing the defendant. The aim of deliberation is, in this case, to find the truth. Participants might therefore be easily convinced if presented credible new information; all the more as their preferences were relatively weak in the first place. This model gives prominence to argumentation and discussion in the formation of (public) opinion. It is the dominant perspective on deliberation. The second model, fitting our cases, is an interested type of deliberation, in which participants have a direct interest in the topics under discussion. In this case, preferences appear – as being connected to interests – much more stable. The stability of individual preferences does not only stem from past experiences and socialisation, it results from the type of preferences at stake. This model can be qualified Aristotelian, as the Greek phi- losopher had a conception of rhetoric in which individual preferences could not be unfairly influenced by skilled orators, as they were rooted in individual interests (Aristotle 1993).

The second deliberative model is based on the idea that a good judgement is not necessarily an impartial and detached one, but on the contrary, a situated judgement, embedded in individuals' life worlds. One of the arguments of Aristotle against impartial deliberation was indeed the risk of manipulation. Having no direct interest at stake in the discussion, citizens might easily be charmed by charismatic speakers distorting their judgement. As Garsten argues (2006: 126):

> Having his own good at stake exerted an influence on the direction of his thoughts, perhaps acting as an anchor pulling him back to the matter at hand, as a standard against which he could easily measure the worth of various arguments and feelings, and a motivation to pay attention. Because he was an interested party, a deliberator applied his interest as a criterion in making his judgements, basing his judgements on his determination of what was good for him.

The superiority of interested deliberation, therefore, stems from the type of judgements it allows. When interests are at stake, it means that preferences are connected to individuals' experiences and daily life, i.e., to local knowledge. For Aristotle, bad judgement always stemmed from the absence of experience in the matter at hand. This does not mean that partiality should be the bottom line of deliberation. It has to be considered as a necessary starting point, even if it might render opinion change more difficult.

These two models of deliberation have also different consequences in terms of preference change. Impartial deliberation relies on short-term preference change, opinions being formed or shaped in the course of the discussion. In the long term however, impartial deliberation has little effect on individuals, as these preferences were directly related to the specific arena in which they were formed. Most of the empirical evidence on preference change in citizen juries and consensus conferences thus indicate the limited long-term effects of these types of participatory institutions (Hansen and Andersen 2007: 543–547; Talpin and Wojcik 2010). On the contrary, interested deliberation does not allow much preference change in the short-term, as opinions are connected to individual interests. In the long-term, however – as will be seen in chapter six – such participatory experiences might have important effects on individuals. These individual effects do not directly stem from deliberation however.

Table 5.2: Differentiated impact of the two types of deliberation

	Type of deliberation	
	Disinterested	**Interested**
Short-term: impact on preferences	Preference change or formation	Little preference change
Long-term: impact on civic practices	Little impact	Trajectory bifurcation

NOTES

1   Elias (1939b) [1991]: 57.

2   For a relatively similar definition see Manin 1987.

3   One of the rationales for the definition adopted here is that in the most canonical conceptualisations in the literature, deliberation is restricted to argumentation. As the aim of this chapter is to evaluate part of the deliberative democracy literature, it appears more accurate opting for a restrictive, but dominant, definition, and then confronting it to my empirical results. See Elster 1986; Cohen 1989; Gutman and Thompson 1996; Habermas 1996.

4   My definition of a conversation is different from that of Gary Remer (2000), for whom conversation is a collective discussion in which speakers and listeners constantly alternate (in contrast to the oratory mode, in which the roles of the speakers and the audience are fixed). I also disagree with Remer in considering conversations as a form of deliberation, as in that case, deliberation is disconnected from decision

5   With some notable exceptions however, see Mansbridge 1980; Fung 2004.

6   See for instance Fishkin, Luskin and Jowell 2002: 484: 'Another question is how much of the information gains and changes in policy preferences came from the briefing materials, versus talking, reading and thinking about the issues in group discussions, versus the large group sessions with policy experts, versus large group sessions with politicians, etc.'

7   For an interesting empirical analysis of the quality of deliberation in parliaments, where actors have different skills than ordinary citizens, see Steiner *et al.* 2005.

8   For a comparable typology, see Bacqué and Sintomer 1999 : 141-4.

9   Observation notes, Robespierre neighbourhood council, Morsang-sur-Orge, 1st October 2005.

10   Observation notes, Wallon neighbourhood council, Morsang-sur-Orge, 21st November 2005.

11   Given the number of attendants of this assembly (over 200) the organisers had exceptionally decided to set up a stage with microphones for the speakers.

12   In Rome, only speakers in the working groups were counted, as the other meetings – to elect delegates or vote – were not aimed at collective discussion. Thus, 340 of the 430 participants to the Roman working groups I observed spoke up at least once.

13   For a good example, see the excerpt with Josiane, in Robespierre neighbourhood meeting, above.

14   The Roman 'verbale' seems close – in its format – to the "Beat Plan Forms" evoked by Archon Fung in the case of Chicago Community Policing. In both cases, systematic forms and reports were provided to the participants to help them identify the problems and propose alternative solutions. Fung qualifies this as a "deliberative problem solving" process. See Fung 2004: 61-8.

15   I use here a minimal definition of disagreement, understood as the expression of a counter-argument during a collective discussion.

16   Observation notes, Wallon neighbourhood council, Morsang-sur-Orge, 21st November 2005. This example is developed in the following section.

17   Observation notes, Wallon neighbourhood council, Morsang-sur-Orge, 21st November 2005.

18   The PSU has been set up by law n.78/203 of January 2005.

19   I make a difference between opinion change and opinion formation, which are often confused in the literature as the expected individual impacts of deliberation. Opinion change means holding a certain position in a moment A, and being convinced by another's arguments in a moment B, thus endorsing a different position. In contrast, opinion formation means that individuals who had weak preferences or no preference at all, formed their opinion in the course of the discussion, enlightened by the new arguments they heard.

The self-change process

Participatory budgets are ruled by implicit social norms, derived from the local enactment of the participatory grammar. Grammars are a set of rules individuals have to respect in order to act (and especially speak) meaningfully in a certain setting or community (see chapter one). These grammatical rules are conventions, derived from the implicit or explicit consensus between actors on the right and wrong moves in certain situations. Consensus on grammatical rules can emerge at different levels; it can be universal, but most of the time it is culturally specific, i.e., only shared by certain groups at national or local levels. From this perspective, it seems that there is a certain consensus around the world – mostly in Europe, Latin and North America – on the value of detachment and practicality (consensus coming from similar historical and structural evolutions) in the public realm (see chapter two). The participatory grammar, therefore, emerged as a new norm of contemporary public governance (see chapter three). Despite this first level of consensus on the value of participation – the ambiguity of the concept being probably at the roots of its rapid spread – different interpretations of the participatory grammar have been offered, given the specific historical trajectory, political tradition and civic habits of groups and communities. The different interpretations of a grammar are called 'styles' (Eliasoph and Lichterman 2003), which are derived from the consensus within a group on the specific meaning of the grammatical rules. Participatory institutions have therefore a certain style, not completely idiosyncratic, as it is shared with several other cases and recognisable as such (chapter three).

Different PB styles have therefore been distinguished, coming from the national enactment of the participatory grammar and its local filtering by the promoters of participatory institutions. The French case is embedded in 'proximity democracy', framed in a specific manner by the Communist municipality and is given their own ideological orientations and civic traditions. The Spanish and Italian cases emerged, on the contrary, in a less participatory environment, and were the offspring of radical political initiatives of Communist elected representatives. Morsang-sur-Orge has therefore been qualified as the 'bonded communist bastion', Rome Municipio XI the 'No-global in power', while the Seville PB process has been labelled 'social justice in practice'. The styles of these institutions attract different types of participants – more or less politicised and previously engaged – acting as specific PB characters, mobilising different types of skills and competences, mostly local knowledge, professional expertise and political competence (chapter four). The interactions between these different actors sometimes allowed for the emergence of deliberative sequences in public assemblies. Most of the time however, these collective discussions were monological (chapter five). The crucial moment in these public interactions was, therefore, the emergence of disagreement among the participants, allowing for the development of deliberation. Disagreement and dissent have also important consequences in terms of self-change.

The aim of this book is indeed not only to assess how participatory institutions can include new type of actors and competences in public decision-making processes, but also to evaluate whether citizens are affected by participation in such settings. Not only would they mobilise previously learned skills and knowledge, they could also acquire new democratic habits. Understanding the process of acquisition or transformation of civic competence through political participation leads to distinguishing the recurrent patterns of individual evolution, describing how citizens, given their previous political dispositions and socialisation, changed while participating in these institutions. The repeated observation of interactions allows distinguishing regularities as well as discontinuities, leading to a process model of self-change. This pattern, even if relatively similar from one case to the other on a formal level, is different in terms of substance. Having different styles, the cases offer different definitions of the good citizen, different speech norms and group bonds, which explain why actors are affected differently. The question of the effects of participation has therefore to be replaced in the broader (political, but also personal and professional) trajectory of actors by opting for a process analysis of civic engagement. This approach has already received a large echo in social movement scholarship through the study of activist careers; the concept of 'career' allowing the development of a dynamic understanding of identity construction processes (Becker 1963; Fillieule 2001). The mobilisation and acquisition of new competences can only be understood when replaced in the broader trajectory of actors, comparing their previous experiences to the new ones they lived in participatory institutions. Being certain characters at the beginning of the process (see chapter four) they might have become new ones once integrated in the PB institutions.

The recurrent pattern of self-change I observed is therefore the following. First, to exist and stabilise, participatory institutions need to create groups of regular participants, called 'groups of good citizens' (chapter three). Regular participants, as integrated in the process, are those who respect, recall and enforce the grammatical rules of the participatory bodies. The stabilisation of such groups is necessary for the institutionalisation of the PBs. These groups are therefore the primary agent of self-change. It is mostly through the scrutiny and analysis of the integration process of the group of good citizens that self-change can be explained. Once a newcomer starts participating, he/she has to respect the grammatical norms of the institution. The main stage to test one's ability to integrate into the group is the public assembly. If the newcomers immediately voice accurate arguments – given the discursive rules of the institution – they will not have problems integrating the group of good citizens. If, on the contrary, they make grammatical mistakes, as they do not know the rules of the game yet, they will be sanctioned. They can then either learn from their mistakes – and therefore change their arguments, adopting a language of the common good – and they will progressively integrate the group of good citizens, or remain at the margins of the institution, being granted a bad reputation.

The question of integration into the group of good citizens echoes classical sociological interrogations: why do people follow the rules? Why do they conform to the pressures of the group? What does following a group's (grammatical) rules mean and what impact has it on individuals? In some regards, these questions were already raised by Durkheim; when studying the move from organic to mechanical solidarity, he showed that social influence was experienced by individuals as exterior (encapsulated in the 'collective consciousness') and constraining. However, he offered a macro-sociological explanation, so that social conformity and integration remained a black box. Almost all of his arguments in *The Division of Labour in Society* concern the two types of solidarity, rather than the nature of solidarity as such (Durkheim 1893). Durkheim assumed social connectedness without examining this assumption empirically. Rule learning, conformity and integration have to be analysed as social processes, taking into account the length of such subtle interactions. Since Durkheim, different interpretations have been offered of this crucial sociological issue. Two of the main ones are evoked and evaluated in the description of the process of self-change. Conformity can first derive from influence – and even power – of the leaders of the group. Embodying a form of charisma and authority, leaders have the capacity to influence and persuade others – through arguments – that the rules of the game are right, and that they should therefore be respected. The sociology of influence as well as the deliberative democracy literature are therefore evaluated in light of the case-studies.

Then, conformity and integration can derive more directly from normative pressures. Elias showed convincingly how civilisation processes worked in modern institutions, through micro-sanctions and rewards having a direct impact on individual subjectivity, actors progressively integrating the social constrains of the pacification of mores (Elias 1939b). This approach can be translated to everyday life situations using Goffman's sociology (1969), who stressed the importance of the anticipation of embarrassment and shame in the regulation and normalisation of individual behaviour. Publicity, or interactions in front of an audience, can have a strong emotional impact on actors. Through symbolic sanction/reward mechanisms, groups foster or impede integration, and in so doing produce subjectivities (Foucault 1975).

In some regards, this second interpretation seems to fit better the processes I observed, where group pressure to conform – based on the grammars of public life and the norms of good citizenship derived from it – was immense and directly influenced people's self-change. Different consequences can derive from the sanctions. Shocked, ashamed or even humiliated by the sanction, incompetent newcomers might simply never come back, and exit the institution from the start. This is one of the main characters produced by PB institutions, the cynic: disappointed by his/her participatory experience he/she gets increasingly sceptical about politics. Apart from exit and cynicism, another option is to come back despite the public stigma (remain to be seen who, why and how), to reframe one's arguments, thus operating a discursive shift to respect the rules of the game and appear competent. This is the compelling power of the emotions: the pleasure of pride and fellow feeling on the one hand, and the punishment of embarrassment, shame or humiliation on the other, push people to change (Scheff 1989). Voicing grammatically correct arguments, these individuals can now be seen as good citizens, and get increasingly integrated in the institution, becoming members of the group of good citizens.

Being integrated in the group, good citizens participate regularly, and might get further affected by their participation. Regular public interactions with others might affect their civic behaviour in the long run. They might learn to organise a petition or a demonstration, to negotiate with local administrators or to launch a public campaign. They might as well learn more practical skills linked to the technical issues they had to deal with along with their PB participation. Fitting the PB style, and being only partially politicised, some good citizens might become the pillars of the PB institution. I call these characters the expert citizen. Others might reinvest the newly learnt skills and competences in other public arenas however. The actor's trajectory might therefore be further affected by adhesion to an association or a political party, or even by the election in municipal elections. I call these characters the civil society activist and the professional politician. I thus observed the emergence of four types of characters from the process of PB participation, usually present in the three case-studies: the cynic, the expert citizen, the civil society activist and the professional politician.

The process of self-change described here – and summed up in Figure 6.1 – raises important political and sociological questions that will be tackled at the end of the chapter. If the acquisition of civic competence, and more broadly the process of politicisation, requires following certain grammatical rules of good behaviour, enforced by powerful actors (the groups of good citizens), are the latter manipulating and dominating the lay citizens following these norms? The process of civic competence acquisition has been described as an educative one, but it could also be seen as manipulative, some actors playing a greater role than others in this process. As will be seen, education requires teachers, and often, they have influence, authority and even power on their pupils. Is this acceptable from a democratic point of view? Can this process still be qualified as deliberative or is this mere tutelage from politicised actors on naive lay citizens? Is the compelling force of the group – embodied in the rules of game – mere influence or does it represent a form of power and manipulation?

How people learn to speak the language of participation: a domestication process

A necessary condition to the integration in a PB institution is to learn public speaking. This requires two types of competence: mastering certain rhetorical skills, especially the art of argumentation, and mastering the implicit discursive norms (Eliasoph and Lichterman 2003) defining good and bad arguments in a specific context.

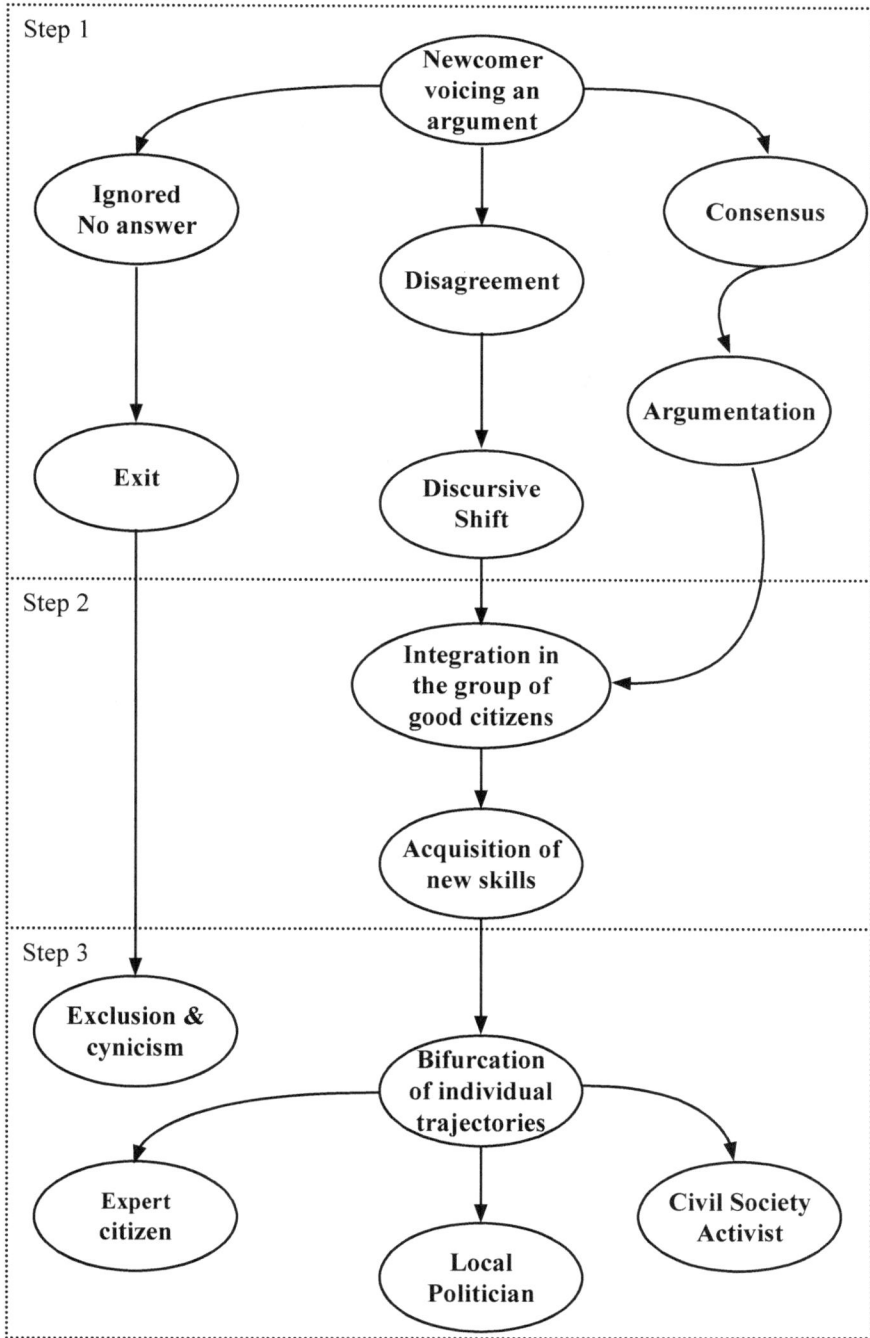

Figure 6.1: The process of self-change

The deliberative imperative: a strong cultural barrier to political inclusion

People have, first of all, to acquire the self-confidence to speak up and express themselves clearly in front of the assembly. This constitutes a first hurdle, as lower participation in the discussion meetings (working groups in Rome, delegate meetings in Seville) indicates. Thus, if 1498 persons participated in 2004 to the Roman PB, only about a hundred took part in the working group meetings.[1] While exit mechanisms cannot be explained only by the fear to speak in public – other factors such as the time required by participation, the limited interest granted to meetings only indirectly linked to decisions, and the implicit delegation towards 'PB delegates' plays also a role – it certainly constitutes a first filter to PB integration and therefore to self-change more broadly.

Then, even within the discussion meetings, everybody does not speak. Thus, 21 per cent of the Roman PB working groups' participants remained silent in the observed assemblies.[2] While this data does not reflect the inequalities between participants interventions – some actors speaking many time and for a few minutes, others only once and for a few seconds – it nevertheless stresses the importance of the procedural organisation of the meetings for access to public speech. In the two other cases, where meeting size is higher, the number of non-speakers is also higher (32 per cent in Morsang-sur-Orge, 60 per cent in Seville).

Those who remain silent are doomed to stay at the margins of the institution. Participating irregularly they might catch some information, but will not be significantly affected by such a superficial participatory experience. I never met a regular participant, truly integrated in the PB, who never spoke in a PB assembly.

Learning the grammatical rules of the institution: shame, exit or discursive shift

Not only should participants feel confident enough to speak up, but they have to do it by respecting the discursive norms of the group. They therefore have to learn the mastery of these imposed discursive standards. People cannot just say anything that passes through their mind in public; otherwise, they might be harshly sanctioned (Elster 1998a; Fearon 1998). Self-interested arguments were directly sanctioned in the PB assemblies, through the attribution of a negative reputation or direct public criticism and bashing. As seen in chapter three, PB discursive interactions are ruled by three main norms:

– Common-good orientation
– Non-political discourses
– Practicality

PB participants have therefore to express themselves in a general, but pragmatic manner, targeting public interest and linking it to concrete problems and possible solutions and projects. From this perspective, PB discursive rules might narrow down the political horizons of participants, by restraining political discussions.

Often, their personal request being rejected, or having even lost face publicly, newcomers do not come back. But some do. They can thereafter present their requests differently, in line with the ruling public grammar, which requires a discursive shift. As Goffman underlined, the will to avoid public embarrassment is indeed a strong driving force of human behaviour. Shame results from a wrong social performance, a violation of social and cultural conventions, that has been defined here as a grammatical mistake. Shame is merely the perception of a negative evaluation of the self by others (Scheff 1990; Harré and Parrott 1996) and, as Elster underlines (1999: 154), it is a strong drive for self-change:

> The anticipation of shame acts as a powerful regulator of behaviour. We avoid doing things that might otherwise benefit us because we fear that we might be discovered and put to shame. [...] Because avoidance of shame cannot take the easy option of self-deception, it has to use the hard option of behaviour modification.

The will to avoid shame, or more slightly, public embarrassment, appeared as a strong explanation of self-change in the studied cases. Christian, in Morsang-sur-Orge, participant who mobilised to obtain the rehabilitation of his street through the budget of his neighbourhood council offers a paradigmatic example. At the first meeting in which he participated, he did not express himself appropriately:

> The main issue on the agenda of the meeting was the evaluation of the new organisation of traffic near the school. Everyone was giving his/her opinion on the issue at stake, stressing the importance of kids' security. It was now Christian's turn to speak: 'Kids security is very important, we all agree on that, but you should know that this makes things complicated for residents on a daily basis. It's not Bayreuth, ok, it's not unliveable, but it's complicated on a daily basis [...] For instance, I cannot park my car in front of my house any more, as all the parking lots are taken by parents bringing their kids to school. And the pavements are really in a dire strait [...] maybe we could also invest in that.' Defending openly the interest of a group, the residents of his street affected by the reorganisation of traffic, he was sanctioned for not having respected the ruling public grammar, which makes 'kids' security' the highest value. Specific or group interests appear too particularistic and therefore antagonistic with the common good at the core of Morsang-sur-Orge public grammar. The remarks of Lucien, a regular participant of the neighbourhood council, were pretty clear from this perspective: 'the problem is that nowadays everybody has two or three cars, and we cannot ask the municipality to build a landing strip for everyone to park in front of his house [...] I don't target anybody, but [...]' These arguments were taken up by the elected official present that evening : 'At some point we need to decide what we want. Do we want comfort for the residents or security for the kids? I thought we agreed on the idea to give the priority to kids over cars.'

(Observation notes, Neighbourhood council Langevin,
Morsang-sur-Orge, 4th November 2005)

The personal request – even if supposed to embody the interests of the residents of a whole street – was rejected as inappropriate. Kids' security having been qualified for years as a priority, any argument trying to counter-balance such policies appeared suspect, biased and self-interested to the regular participants. As a newcomer, Christian was not aware of it, especially as his own request appeared 'absolutely legitimate' to him and his neighbours. This participant thus committed a pretty obvious grammatical mistake and was sanctioned for that, being ridiculed (the request was caricatured, qualifying the lack of parking spaces as requesting the creation of a 'landing strip') by a regular participant. At the following meeting however, a few weeks later, Christian presented his arguments in a different way, and obtained much better results:

'I speak in the name of the residents of Texel street, where the pavement is really in a bad shape. I have to tell you that people in the street don't understand, as it is really a strategic street [...] a lot of kids going to the school take it [...] so if we say that kids' security is the priority it would appear normal to rehabilitate it. And then you have a lot of public services around: the post office, the kindergarten, the House of Childhood, etc. These pavements are really used a lot. So we don't understand [...] pavements of deserted streets are rehabilitated, and this one that appears so evident is not!' The town councillor in charge of urbanism issues answered him immediately: 'Yes, it's true. We could put the pavement of this street on the list of priorities for 2006. We will have to discuss it collectively with the criteria and stuff, *but all this seems valid.*'

(Observation notes, Meeting of the workshop 'pedestrians, bikes, cars',
Morsang-sur-Orge, 12th December 2005)

This excerpt is paradigmatic of the importance of the form and modality of speech over its actual content, which appears rather trivial. Christian did not change his argument and proposition; he simply framed them differently. The claim – rejected at the first meeting – was reframed taking the ruling grammatical norms of the assembly into account. Christian – in this second excerpt – increased immediately the generality of his discourse, invoking a highly legitimising generalised other (Mead 1936) in Morsang-sur-Orge public meetings: 'kids'. He also invoked a valued public good for both the PCF municipality and the citizens: public services and their accessibility. Christian demodalised his speech, speaking more as a 'we' than as an 'I'. He invoked the risk created by the existent situation and the number of people using the pavement to justify his proposal. Expressing himself in a proper way, following the grammatical rules of the assembly, his argument was accepted ('all this seems valid') and the proposal integrated in the list of the potential investments of the 2006 budget, while it had been merely rejected at the first session. The main expression of symbolic rewards in a PB assembly is indeed the collective agreement on the importance of a proposal, and therefore its financing. Voicing the good argument is necessary for communication and persuasion, but it also allows social and emotional integration.

This example allows analysing further discursive shifts in PB assemblies. What happened between the two sessions? Did Christian change his mind? Did he realise, after the first discussion, that the arguments in favour of kids' security were better than his own resident's comfort? Hard to say. What can be assessed sociologically however is that he aligned his arguments on the public grammar of the institution. He evoked it in an interview conducted afterwards: 'But they don't give us the rules of the game at the beginning [...] I discovered the rules of game progressively, through two or three words slightly said at the end of a sentence'[3]. Christian's words echo almost perfectly the analysis of integration into new positions made by Goffman (1959: 72–3):

> When the individual does move into a new position in society and obtain a new part to perform, he is not likely to be told in full detail how to conduct himself. [...] Ordinarily he will be given only a few cues, hints and stage directions, and it will be assumed that he already has, in his repertoire, a large number of bits and pieces of performances that will be required in the new setting.

If they have not already mastered these 'pieces of performances', actors have to learn them through trial and error, sanctions and rewards. The sanctions attributed at the first meeting allowed Christian to discover the boundaries of the public grammar and thus to appear more competent at the following session. Christian took the role of the good citizen, caring about the common good – here framed as kids' security and the defence of public services.

A question needs nevertheless to be raised: should argumentative shifts – as in Christian's case – be qualified as strategic or rhetorical uses of argumentation? Did Christian increase the generality of his argumentation to appear more convincing or was he himself convinced of his own arguments? Do people take the role of good citizens for self-interested motivations? It seems to me that approaches in terms of 'interest for the universal' (Bourdieu 1998) or of the 'civilising force of hypocrisy' (Elster 1998a) are partly inappropriate in the study of the effects of deliberation. Beyond the fact that the 'true' motivations for action are inaccessible to the other interactants, such an approach above all misses the social efficiency of the justifications offered in a given public context. What matters in public arenas is not what people 'really think' but what they say.[4] This is all the more the case here, that in deliberative institutions it is indeed what is said, the actually voiced arguments and proposals, that influence collective decisions. The final decision has to be justified by arguments acceptable to all. If some arguments appear to the audience as too interested or too modalised, they will simply be rejected. Discursive shifts or 'versatility' presents indeed a risk for actors to 'raise suspicions about the engagement in each of the arguments' (Moody and Thévenot 2001: 278).

This does not mean that the issue of sincerity is irrelevant when it comes to public discussions, but that what matters is that the audience, the other interactants, feel the speaker is sincere. Contrary to Austin-Smith's thesis (1990), I argue that talk is rarely cheap in non-experimental and real life public discussions, simply because the speaker's reputation is at stake. People cannot say anything at will or switch from one argument to the other freely, as others will remember their formerly held position, and a reputation of 'weather vane' does not help convincing others. From this perspective, a parallel can be drawn with a crucial mechanism of representative government highlighted by Manin (1997: Ch.5). In representative government, the iteration of elections pushes representatives to keep their promises if they want to remain credible and get re-elected. Similarly, the iteration of participation and public discussions pushes actors to appear sincere, and to switch their arguments in a sensible way, only when they consider it worth it. As Habermas convincingly argued (1984: 303), sincerity can only be grounded on actors' deeds and consistency over time: 'That a speaker means what he says can be made credible only in the consistency of what he does and not through providing grounds.' Only consistency over time, granting a reputation of sincerity or truthfulness, makes a person sincere. The audience, without direct access to intentions, must rely on the speaker's reputation to infer his/her sincerity. Reputation, from this perspective, works as a proxy for sincerity, and the reiteration of participation and public interaction are the only grounds on which such a reputation can be built.

Having learnt the language of the institution, actors are increasingly integrated and can thereafter become regular PB participants. It has to be stressed, however, that many participants never pass this first step. Being discursively incompetent, they are doomed to remain at the margins of the institution.

When public participation excludes and fosters cynicism

Once the grammar of public life of the assembly has been defined and enforced by the group of good citizens, participants have only two options: adapting themselves through discursive shifts or leaving the institution. Many PB participants have indeed left the boat on the way, as the high turnover rates show. The only data available are for the Roman case, where turnover rates are extremely high. In 2004, 68.5 per cent of the participants declared they had not participated in the PB the year before. About half of 2003 participants stopped after one year. Turnover is also important within a PB cycle, as in 2004, 68.9 per cent of the participants in the final assembly declared they had not taken part in delegate elections at the beginning of the year (d'Albergo 2005).

Disappointed by an experience that did not match their expectations, many became cynical about participatory democracy in particular, and politics in general. Two types of criticisms are generally addressed to the PB: it only grants a limited (or illusionary) power to citizens as the slow pace of project realisation indicates, and it would be a way for elected representatives to manipulate citizens and calm down protest. As this Roman participant says: 'I feel like a fool. The PB is like a sweet in the mouth of citizens put by the Municipio to keep them quiet.'[5] For the cynic, the PB is just the reproduction of power politics under a new mask.

By definition, it is difficult to get in touch with those disappointed by the PB process. Criticisms and disappointments were hardly ever expressed publicly in the assembly. When criticisms were openly voiced however – this was generally the last step before exit – people were attributed a negative reputation as 'trouble makers'. The best way to scrutinise the growing cynicism towards the participatory process was therefore through interviews, with people who had previously expressed their discontent in the assemblies. The case of Christian, in Morsang-sur-Orge is extremely interesting from this perspective. He became indeed rapidly disappointed by the participatory process:

> The town councillors are participative as long as citizens make proposals that go in the direction of the municipality, then they say 'the citizens have decided, blah, blah, blah'. But when you propose something they don't agree with, hum [...] The dice are a bit loaded. I really think that the elected officials are not truly sincere, they don't tell us everything. [...] Because, who decides in the end? Elected representatives, because they have the budget. [...] It's clear, it's a way to get votes! [...] And in the end, the decisions taken in the assemblies, had to be taken anyway [...] They [the town councillors] take back their true role when you are taking a contentious posture. A guy told me at the beginning: 'as long as you'll go in their direction there won't be any problem, you'll decide. But when you won't go in the right direction, they'll take back the control.' They can't allow themselves [...]

> (Interview with Christian, Morsang-sur-Orge,
> 17th November 2005)

Christian takes therefore the classical posture of the cynic: irony and disillusion. Behind the nice participatory discourse lies the true face of power politics and special interests. The cynic typically makes an opposition between discourse and reality, public lies and private truth. The cynic, by his/her distance, shows he/she understands the game and is not a fool.

Two types of cynics can be distinguished however. On the one hand, the politicised cynic, often on the far-left of the political spectrum, who criticises the reformist taste of the PB, far from the direct democractic ambitions it had in the first place. I had the chance to follow the exit process of a once highly engaged participant, Fausto. Elected zone delegate in Seville, he got progressively disappointed by the PB and opted for exit:

> Interestingly, while I knew him well, Fausto refused to be interviewed, claiming, 'To remain uncertain about what to think about PB.' Despite his refusal, we talked a lot together. No doubt that his leftist trajectory and growing moderation – he was member of a Maoist party in the early 1970s, then of the PC, the PSOE at the beginning of the 1980s and is nowadays an 'independent leftist' as he defines himself – led him to participate in the PB process. The idea seemed neat to him. The first day, at the voting assembly, he presented proposals with his community association, and especially one about the rehabilitation of his street. He also ran for elections as district delegate, 'and was elected in front of all the PSOE and IU members', whereas as an independent he had no automatic support. Personally rewarded, he was pretty enthusiastic about the process.

He became, however, rapidly disappointed about it. He told me: 'I was thinking to do the revolution, and instead I take care of street cleaning.' In the end, he decided to stop participating.

Fausto's cynicism, resulting in his drop out, stems from his disappointment about the limited power of the PB. He first saw PB participation as a way to get back to political commitment after a twenty years parenthesis. As politically plural, the PB firstly satisfied him as it allowed going over the traditional sectarianism of political parties. This is precisely the roots of his disillusion: in the end, the PB would be just like traditional politics – about power – and worst, it is marked by IU 'Stalinist practices'. Fausto embodies the leftist cynicism type: having high expectations about the PB, he was soon disappointed. This form of cynicism was probably the most common in Seville, as most of the active participants were politicised actors. It was also present in Rome, many militants stopped participation in the first year of the PB process.

On the other hand, we find the apolitical cynic, for whom PB is just the reproduction of power politics. In this case, a negative participatory experience can lead from apoliticism to an anti-politics position, as is indicated in this pretty tensed sequence in a Roman assembly:

> The participants had been talking for some time about the difficulty for the municipal council not to respect the decisions of the zone assemblies, when Giovanna raised the tone and got literally outraged about the PB process, crying out for five minutes against the insufficiencies of the concrete achievements: 'The PB has not done anything yet since its creation! It's a shame! I feel I am a fool. Every time you [the facilitator] tell me not to say this or that, that it is not possible, that it's not in the competence of the Municipio, that it has already been accepted, etc. What is this all for, then? I really feel I am a fool! I made proposals ten times and they haven't changed anything!' People tried to calm her down, which worked after a few minutes. Most of them, explained to her that some projects had been achieved, even if they mostly told her to be patient. Their arguments did not seem to convince her however. Giovanna never came back.
>
> (Observation notes, Roma 70 Zone Assembly,
> Rome, 12th April 2005)

Many were indeed disappointed by the length and invisibility of the PB achievements. It is often considered that the 'demonstration effect' is crucial to spur mobilisation. In Porto Alegre, participation rates started to rise when the first PB achievements became visible (Baiocchi 2005).

While many citizens were disappointed by their participatory experience, others, motivated by a sense of civic duty or the will to benefit from PB decisions, kept on participating despite these initial difficulties. Mastering the discursive rules of the institution, they integrated the group of citizens and therefore learnt new skills and habits.

Learning new skills and competences from repeated participation

For those who acquired discursive competence, and who got increasingly integrated in the PB institution, the iteration of interaction with others, especially with already politicised and skilled actors, affected them significantly. In this regard, the learning of four types of skills and competences has been observed in PB institutions: practical know-how, technical skills, political competence, and local knowledge.

Practical know-how: PB engagement as a socialisation to collective action

PB participation implies the repetition of a certain set of actions, all requiring a specific know-how. The central stage of a PB is the public assembly. Participation therefore allows individuals learning to speak in public (see above), to facilitate a discussion, to help and give self-confidence to the less experienced speakers, to set up an agenda, to mitigate between different interests and sensibilities, and even sometimes to organise a negotiation between seemingly irreducible positions.

Repeated PB participation can also allow the learning of deliberation, as in this Roman neighbourhood assembly where a collective learning process took place through trial, error and imitation (see chapter five). After two messy meetings, Montagnola participants decided to split in small working groups, speakers lists were organised and discussion moderated by the participants themselves. It resulted in efficient deliberative interactions. Participants therefore learnt, in less than three meetings, how to organise themselves and discuss collectively. For many people, PB participation was their first experience of civic engagement (see chapter four). This new experience therefore led some of them – given the intensity of their participation – to learn certain skills and competences linked to collective action. Participants discovered how to write leaflets, to organise meetings, to launch petitions, to mobilise a community or to organise demonstrations. A striking example from this perspective comes from Wallon neighbourhood council in Morsang-sur-Orge, in the poorest zone of the city:

> For years, the neighbourhood council had known a small attendance, a lack of dynamism and enthusiasm from the population, few subaltern people participating at all. Considering this local apathy, the elected official in charge of the organisation of the neighbourhood council was extremely directive. She was the one who spoke the most over the meetings, who defined the agenda, and framed the discussions. In a word, Wallon neighbourhood council had little autonomy from the municipality.

> Things started to change in the fall of 2005, when the 'citizenry administration', and especially its boss, Marie, decided – in agreement with the Mayor – to give more autonomy to the city's neighbourhood councils, and especially to institutionalise the existence of organising committees, essentially composed of citizens. The aim was to lower the influence of elected officials – considered overwhelming – to empower participatory institutions and citizens in the meantime. Results were considered disappointing by the actors, apart from

a few cases, like in Wallon neighbourhood. Encouraged by the citizenship administration boss, a few participants started getting more involved in the organisation of the meetings. Preparation meetings were thus planned before each neighbourhood council, and at least five regular participants – the group of good citizens – attended, while the elected representative did not. These citizens were therefore able to define the agenda of the neighbourhood council meetings, to prepare small introductions on the issues to be discussed collectively, and in the end to moderate the meetings directly.

The change in the power-relationship of the neighbourhood council was exemplified by the very scenography of the meeting. While the elected official and the public functionary used to be at the centre, it was now this group of four or five good citizens at the centre, towards whom all the other participants were staring. The meetings were no longer introduced by the elected representatives, but by one of the members of the organising committee.

The evolution of the organisation of Wallon neighbourhood council is pretty telling on the type of collective learning and empowerment processes that can take place with reiterated participation. With time, encouraged by the administration, some citizens got enough self-confidence to play a bigger role in the neighbour-hood council. When one looks at the background of these good citizens however, the empowerment thesis has to be nuanced, as most of them were already mem-bers of either a PTA (FCPE), a trade union (CGT), or a resident association. Only Nicole – evoked below – had no previous civic experience. It can nevertheless be stressed that this dispositional thesis is also unsatisfying, as these actors, despite their previous political socialisation, were relatively passive in the neighbourhood council for years. Their political background cannot explain alone why at some point they started organising themselves in such a way as gaining autonomy from the municipality. The support from the citizenry municipal administration (close to the Communist Party) – against a town councillor member of the Socialist Party – created a situation that these actors, given their previous competences, could exploit. They thus collectively gained new competences in the organisation of meetings and public expression.

Interestingly, some citizens thus became able to endorse a role traditionally as-sumed by elected officials in Morsang-sur-Orge. These ordinary citizens, by gain-ing new competences, thus reached a form of professionalism. The acquisition of new competences by citizens can therefore be understood as a democratisation of the public sphere, but also as the emergence of new elites, embodying a new type of delegation (not legitimised by the electoral rule). Citizens themselves are aware of the risk, as Jean-Pierre, one of the members of Wallon neighbourhood council organising committee, acknowledged once in a preparation meeting: 'OK, we're voluntary citizens, but in people's minds it's always the same thing, it's power delegation. We're seen like a caste.'[6]

This is one of the central dilemmas for participatory democracy. While in-volved in participatory institutions citizens gain new skills and competences, but in so doing they specialise, professionalise, and in some regards become new experts of civic engagement. The circle of public decision-making is enlarged, but still remains in the hands of a minority. The acquisition of new competences seems therefore to contradict the inclusive thesis at the heart of participatory democracy initiatives. It can nevertheless be stressed that a collective learning and empowerment process took place – the group of good citizens gaining an increasing autonomy.

Citizens, by participating in PBs can also gain more radical political skills. Some previously disengaged individuals thus learned to mobilise their community and to organise a petition. Morsang's 'gang of mums' can be evoked again.[7] At first anonymous and atomised 'mothers', their support to a common cause – the rehabilitation of a public park in the neighbourhood – led them to organise a collective action. In Dewey's words, a public emerged from a common problem. By defining an 'us' – mums, good citizens, caring about kids' safety – and a 'them' – the wrong users of the park, smoking teenagers, dangerous dogs' owners, drug addicts, etc. – a public emerged, who lived a rich collective experience able to nurture new competences. Their participation in the PB process led these mums to canvass door-to-door the neighbourhood to get support for their rehabilitation project and also to create new links of sociability ('It allowed me meeting my neighbours, while I never had the occasion in years before'[8]). Their engagement also conducted them to write a petition in favour of the project – not defined as such by the actors however, who refused the term 'petition', considered overly political[9] – to aggregate support for the cause. This express formation to collective action was largely encouraged by the municipality, and especially the 'citizenry administration'. Reassuring the mums on the effects of such a mobilisation (elected officials supported the project from the beginning, while giving a certain autonomy to the 'gang of mums') the municipality made engagement interesting for actors. The crucial role of the participatory process from this perspective is to make mobilisation interesting, as it can translate into municipal investments and public policies.

It is through trial and error, due to problems faced in situation (shared analysis of the inefficiencies of discursive messiness, inequalities in a power relationship with elected officials, etc.), thanks to the positive influence of enlightened facilitators (stressing the importance of simple organisation procedures, encouraging autonomy, giving the material basis for organisation) that a collective learning mechanism can take place. Far from being a purely cognitive, discursive or rational process, the learning of democracy first requires mastering certain ways of participating, which can only happen in interaction. Even if extremely practical, these skills are decisive for PB participants, and can be reinvested in other public arenas.

Technical skills: reducing the technical gap between experts and citizens

Even if PBs are not highly technical institutions – to avoid excluding the individuals with less educational resources – participation can facilitate the learning of technical skills, that were up to that point the monopoly of experts. A crucial skill participants gained, was an increased understanding of the organisation of a public budget (composed of different taxes and sources, requiring an equilibrium, etc.). Furthermore, as PBs often deal with urban planning issues, participants increased their knowledge on the construction of roads and pavements, the judicial constraints surrounding the renovation of public parks or schools, etc.

Interested by an issue, a problem that emerged in their daily life, citizens might gather information or meet specialised associations. Internet plays a central role in this process of information seeking by democratising access to knowledge, even the most technical ones (Levrel 2008). Similar to the families of patients who became experts on some scientific questions thus creating a 'popular epidemiology' (Callon, Lascoumes and Barthe 2009), citizens engaged in PBs can become technicians able to bring an expertise in a public discussion. Facing a problem, they start an enquiry (Dewey 1927), leading an investigation to reconstitute causal chains. Thus, Alex, regular participant of Morsang-sur-Orge PB, confronted by the multiplication of digital antennas in his neighbourhood, started investigating their potential harm. He gathered information by surfing on the internet, 'swotted a whole weekend', got into contact with a regional association dealing with issues of new technologies and public health and, once equipped with this new knowledge, presented the issue in a public meeting of his neighbourhood council.

It was always the public justification constraint, the need and will to convince the audience of the seriousness of a problem that pushed actors to gain new knowledge and competences, to gather information to appear more convincing. In this case, participation can result in an increased individual and collective cognitive competence that might then be reflected in the quality of public policies.

The technical turn taken by the discussions, implied by the mobilisation of a newly acquired knowledge, can, however, create problems and tensions in PB assemblies. As PB participants, citizens have to take up the role of good citizen, without specific qualities or competences, ready to discuss and solve local political issues. The good citizen in PB institutions is expected to have a sense of the common good, not to become an expert. Once the good citizen role is adopted it might therefore, be difficult for actors to get away from it, to use a more technical language. Reactions to the problem raised by Alex – evoked above – were therefore contrasted:

> Michel thus claimed: 'for this kind of issue we have to rely on the municipal technical services. We can't know everything, we can't do everything as amateurs'. The town councillor in charge of the NC organisation, Francis, insisted however on the role of residents' local knowledge, at the roots of the city participatory initiative: 'We recognise an expertise right to the residents; because they live in the neighbourhood and see the problems on a daily basis. But it's true: we have also to rely on the technical services on that kind of issue.'

The question of citizen competence (practical and technical) was therefore at the centre of the debate. Participants did not appear as amateur however. Alex had obviously worked on the issue:

But you know, they are very powerful lobbies behind all that. I remember when I was 14, we already knew that asbestos was dangerous [...] Concerning the antennas, I think there is a legal weakness somewhere, because antennas used to transmit images (for TV or cell phones) depend on a specific legislation, they need a permit to install them. And I don't think the municipality has granted such a permit?

The member of the municipal technical office present that evening acknowledged Alex knew more than himself on the issue: 'You're more competent than me on this.' However, another participant, Roger, obviously upset, expressed his disagreement with the technical turn taken by the discussion: 'But all this is a technical issue, not a problem of the neighbourhood. We don't have to decide on this kind of questions!' Alex added a final argument against the antennas, relative to their impact on the value of private properties:

I met an association working on this issue and they told me that, in average, houses situated at less than hundred metres from this type of antennas lose 30 per cent of their value.

Roger appearing more and more upset, shouted:

But does this concerns the neighbourhood? What the neighbourhood council should talk about is whether or not we want these antennas. [...] We can talk about the aesthetic aspect, about health, etc. But we're not competent technically to decide what to do about these antennas.

(Observation notes, Cachin Neighbourhood council, Morsang-sur-Orge, 6th December 2005)

The expertise acquired by certain participants can therefore create conflicts as it redistributes the traditionally attributed roles. While, in general, citizens evoke personal troubles and propose solutions inspired by their local knowledge, municipal experts evaluate the technical and financial validity of the proposals, the acquisition of new competences changes the attribution of places and the distribution of power. Are ordinary citizens still profanes when they become more expert on an issue than the official experts themselves, who even acknowledge this fact? Is the expert still one, once he/she publicly recognises his/her incompetence? Is it the ordinary citizen's role to settle a dispute or to enrich the discussion cognitively? To some extent, the acquisition of new technical competences by some citizens might increase inequalities, some participants reaching the level of experts, while others, the majority, remain ordinary citizens basing their judgements on mere local knowledge. Once a role – that of good citizen mobilising his/her local knowledge for the common good – has been attributed, it is difficult and contentious to move to another one. Citizens' competence therefore risks being restricted and confined to an apolitical and non-technical posture.

Local knowledge: activists and lay citizens discovering the territory

PB engagement allows citizens to discover the territory of the city and gain local knowledge. Through the organisation of bus tours, 'pavements meetings', 'urban walks', or just by talking to other participants, actors increase their knowledge of the territory. Seville's bus tours appear especially efficient from this perspective. They are organised for PB delegates to evaluate the proposals made at the first general assembly, in order to apply the social justice criteria afterwards. The tours are therefore seen as a way to enrich the delegate's judgements. The experience of a group of participants in one of the poorest neighbourhoods of the city, is pretty telling of the discoveries made by participants.

After more than two hours going around *Torre del Agua* neighbourhood, and evaluating zebras, pavements, benches, speed bumps proposals in pretty well-off zones, the group moved to *El Esqueleto*, which appeared in a dire strait. Going around the zone we finally reached the famous '*3000 viviendas*', known as one of the poorest and more dangerous neighbourhoods of the city (drug dealing, traffic, violence, etc.) and with a high proportion of gypsy residents. The reactions of some of the participants were interesting. One of the delegates was from the neighbourhood and had to encourage the others to get off the bus to see the proposals, as some delegates appeared clearly reluctant to go there: 'Come on, let's go! They won't eat you!' The visual impression of the neighbourhood was crude: old and dirty buildings, young kids running and playing alone in the street, kids driving motorbikes, broken beer bottles on the floor, many empty lots all around the neighbourhood, etc. They nevertheless finally went off the bus, and at some point, they stopped and just looked at the neighbourhood with the kids, a group of men in the back (some delegates asserted it was a sect meeting ...), and a clear atmosphere of desolation and poverty.

> One of the delegates, Maria-Carmen said pretty frankly: 'It's the first time I come here! I had never seen such a thing, I didn't know it existed!'
>
> Elisabeth, her friend, added: 'A normal parent wouldn't leave her kids alone in the street like that.'
>
> Christina, the youngest of the group, who lived nearby: 'Here kids don't go to school you know. There is no authority.'
>
> Maria-Carmen: 'This really hurts me! What a pity! But [talking to me] I don't know, what can we do about it? We give apartments to these people, and they don't take care of them, they make fires inside, never clean.'
>
> Elisabeth: 'We have to start with the kids.'
>
> Maria-Carmen, obviously surprised and shocked: 'It's really hard, really difficult. I am aware of it now, I never came here before. I mean, seeing a two-year-old kid on a motorbike [...].'
>
> (Observation notes, Tour of the South District, Seville, 20th September 2006)

The discovery of the territory permitted by PB tours allows some group members to acquire knowledge on the social reality of the city. This knowledge is linked to a sensitive (especially sight in this case), and emotional (fear, surprise, disgust, etc.) experience. While in this case, the bus tour allowed white middle-class participants to discover the social situation of one of the most deprived neighbourhoods of the city, activists and politicised actors also acquired local knowledge thanks to their PB experience.

PB participation changed the 'vision' of many activists. The PB was, to a large extent, a new experience for the social movements' activists I met. PB assemblies, therefore, allowed them to encounter a form of otherness, embodied in ordinary citizens little concerned with politics. As highly politicised actors, activists were often committed to 'great causes' like global justice, environmental sustainability or international solidarity. When they had more practical commitments, these often concerned precarious groups like migrants, poor people or sexual minorities. They were far from the very practical and local concerns of the white working class participants of PB assemblies.

One of the main impacts of PB participation for activists was thus often framed as 'the rediscovery of the territory'. Participatory budgeting seems to give activists a new vision, a new glance at local problems and realities. The words of Alessandra in Rome, 33-year-old activist, member of the *International Civil Service* and PB participant in San Paolo neighbourhood, are telling from this perspective:

> The nicest thing is to rediscover the territory itself. [...] When I am in my car driving around the neighbourhood, now I look at the trees there, the building over there, etc. It's beautiful! You don't feel alone any more. And that's really an incredible added value. [...] All that there is behind the famous Urban Planning Project [that was discussed in PB assemblies], the parking over there, this thing here, [...] this gives you [...] It opens your mind with all the sensations [...] According to me, beyond money, beyond everything, this is it [the added value of the PB] [...] Rediscovering that you are part of something that belongs to you, that you're part of [...] that you could also be part of it in a different way. When we speak about active citizenship [...] it [PB] makes you feel alive, it gives you a will to speak with people in the street, with your neighbours [...] We speak of 'contacts' as if they were something cold and dead [...] But no, I'm not alone any more, I know with whom I can communicate, with whom I can share this thing in this territory.

(Alessandra, Rome, 29th March 2006)

PB allows activists going around the neighbourhood to check all the potential problems it faces, to look at maps and pictures, and above all to talk with people. Activists discovered the basic and almost daily needs of some part of the local population: the need to get better schools, better access to public transportation, better housing conditions, better recreational activities for the young, a more sustainable traffic management.

From this perspective, the learning processes observed in participatory budgeting institutions are not unidirectional, from activists to lay citizens only, as the former also learn, thanks to their local engagement.

Political competence

Political competence is traditionally defined as the capacity to understand the political system and to locate politicians and ideas on a left/right spectrum (Bourdieu 1984; Luskin 1990). Participatory arenas are not detached from the local political system, and participation is a way to increase one's knowledge on politics. Being in regular interactions with elected officials, participants can more easily identify their political orientation (which was far from being the case for most of them at the beginning), and put words and deeds on partisan decisions. They also learn to negotiate with elected officials and to play off the rivalries between parties to get things done. Participants also discover the way the administrative machine works, the distribution of competences among public bodies, as well as the conflicts between different institutions. The speeches made by certain activists can sometimes appear as lectures on the local power relationships or on the way the municipal institution works, thus embodying a great deal of knowledge for uninformed citizens. Apart from gaining knowledge about the political system, PB participation also allows individuals to increase their level of information on certain political issues. Party members evoke the latest municipal decisions, housing rights advocates tackle the homeless situation in the city, and environmentalists share their knowledge on global warming or urban planning. At a Roman working group meeting, Maurizio, an activist from *Legambiente*, the main Italian environmental organisation, made a very didactic intervention on the implications of the Kyoto protocol for the public transportation policies of Italian municipalities:

> You know that anyway, the Kyoto protocol has come into force in Italy since yesterday [15.02.2005] and Italy has to decrease its CO_2 emissions drastically in the following years [...] 30 per cent of the use of cars in this city regard trips of less than 3 km i.e., distances easily reachable by bike. It means we could decrease CO_2 emissions by 30 per cent just thanks to bikes! Anyway, [...] soon all the metro stations will be equipped with bike parking [...] it's a global trend.

> (Observation notes, Garbatella, mobility working group, Rome, 16th February 2005)

Through their engagement in PBs, participants are constantly acquiring new knowledge on the political system and on a variety of salient public issues. Given the exclusion of political discussions from public meetings, politicisation happens more often backstage than frontstage however. The group of good citizens appears indeed as a place of sociability, which plays a decisive role in this process. It is in the interpersonal discussions taking place after the assemblies, at the bar or in the street, that a relationship to politics and an interpretation of the collectively lived experience are built. The position of this or that participant is explained by his/her political affiliation, the latest municipal decisions are commented on, the evolution of issues is tackled, and sometimes formal party politics is evoked. PBs can therefore become arenas of individual politicisation and can generate stronger feelings of political efficacy, as this participant reports:

> I discovered a passion for politics. […] I enjoyed this experience in the PB so much that I wanted to keep on at a higher level. […] This is new for me, I always voted but I have never been really active in anything. But when the mayor offered for me to be on the list for the local elections, I was really honoured, and I said yes, of course.

> (Floriana, Rome, 28th March 2006)

The long-term consequences of participation: trajectory bifurcations

Certainly, many participants, as long as they were sufficiently engaged in PB processes, became more informed and competent after their participatory experience. They have learned technical, political and practical skills and knowledge. To what extent do these newly acquired competences translate into new civic practices, and in the bifurcation of individual trajectories? The findings from this study reveal significant modifications of individual trajectories. Three types of actors seem to be nurtured by PB institutions: (1) the expert citizen; (2) the civil society activist; (3) the professional politician.

The expert citizen

The newly acquired skills and habits of some participants can favour the institutionalisation of PBs, citizens carrying on participating at the local level for years. In some regards, PB engagement can be seen as a new form of civic commitment, different from political parties, unions and association membership. The expert citizen has been especially nurtured in Morsang-sur-Orge PB. The case of Nicole, woman in her 50s and regular PB participant, shows how a trajectory can be significantly affected by local engagement:

> Nicole evoked her own trajectory at the end of a NC meeting, reacting to the scepticism expressed by some newcomers: 'You know, I advise you to come at every neighbourhood council meeting […] it is in this way you get things done. You have to fight. […] Myself, at first, a long time ago already, I had come here to solve a problem we had in our street. I fought for four years, I mobilised my community, I came regularly at public meetings with town councillors, etc. and eventually we won!'[10]

This mobilisation starting with a personal trouble finally led her to integrate the group of good citizens of her neighbourhood council. She appears, since then, as the common good gatekeeper of her neighbourhood council:

> Starting from something rather narrow, at the neighbourhood level, we are then

able to discover [...] and to go further in terms of commitment [...] to improve one's city.[11]

Her good citizen status led her to be among the organisers of a 'Citizen Summit' launched by the municipality 'to boost the participatory process'. Such an official recognition of her competence was one of the final steps in her trajectory bifurcation, as she was then able to voice general and political arguments in her neighbourhood council assembly:

If we want our city to change we cannot stay on the side. We have to participate, because you never get anything just by yourself! We have to fight all together. We have the chance to express ourselves in Morsang so we have to take it.[12]

She was even clapped by the other participants at the end of her speech. What a change in comparison to her first steps in the neighbourhood council: 'Yes, I feel that this experience touched me [...] I feel more committed for my city now.'[13] It would nevertheless be misguided to interpret this bifurcation as the result of participation alone. Other factors, linked to her personal and professional trajectory played also a great role. Financial analyst for a bank in Paris for 15 years, she decided to put her professional career into brackets when her husband and herself adopted a son at the beginning of the 1990s. She has since then been in charge of the administrative management of the small firm created by her husband, but acknowledges the void created by this change: 'I have a less intense professional life today, and I miss it. That's why I find an interest in going there [to the PB], towards the other; It's like a need.'

In some regards, her commitment in Morsang-sur-Orge participatory institutions appeared as a compensation to the 'void' created by her professional bifurcation. She stresses in particular the cognitive ('I met many people full of ideas, rich in know-how, who know how to express themselves') and relational ('In these meetings you meet any social type [...] I really like being in contact and discovering new people'[14]) benefits she drew from participation. Interestingly, the language she used during the interview was relatively emotional: 'this experience touches me'; 'I feel more committed'; 'I have an attachment'. This highlights the emotional aspect of the symbolic integration into the group of good citizens. Participation obviously pleases her: 'I feel good in that kind of meetings'; 'I am happy to help people'; 'I am glad when these people participate'. Participation and integration gave her a form of public recognition that mattered a lot to her (Honneth 1995). This symbolic integration allowed by public rewards was made possible thanks to the biographical availability of this participant. Nicole was thus able to mobilise part of her previous professional skills in the realm of the public assemblies (ability to speak in public, to organise meetings, to set up projects with others, etc.). The participatory commitment of this woman, as relying on previous professional skills and satisfying a need of intellectual and relational investment, was intensive enough to lead her from the expression of a personal trouble to a minimal form of politicisation. This process took a few years however, and did not lead her to political activism as others: 'personally I wouldn't like to do politics'.[15]

It seems therefore that PB participation can produce new types of civic characters, namely expert citizens. Highly integrated in the process, member of the group of good citizens, these participants do not want to reinvest their newly acquired competences in other areas, as the PB goals and methods fit them perfectly. Being both open ideologically and plural in its social and cultural composition, the PB can constitute a relaxed mode of engagement for citizens with no previous experience of civic engagement. Self-change seems therefore possible when both biographical availability and normative pressure work in the same direction.

The local civil society activist

At odds with the previous character, PB participation also allows actors to reinvest their newly acquired competences in other political arenas: local civil society and the local political scene. One of the options for previously uncommitted citizens is therefore the adhesion to associations or the creation of new civic organisations. As they learn to speak in public, to mobilise the population, to organise demonstrations, to negotiate with local politicians, etc., highly committed PB members can then reinvest these competences in other associations. The most common bodies of recruitment for these actors were local community organisations, which in some regards have the same goals as the PB: promoting the interests of the local community (Della Porta 2004). Other organisations were specialised associations dealing with environmental issues or housing rights. This was especially the case in Rome and Seville, while in Morsang-sur-Orge boosting civil society did not seem to be on the political agenda of the promoters of the PB process. On the contrary, the nurturing of an 'active citizenship' was part of the goals of the inceptors of the Roman PB process. They saw the PB as a tool to boost local civil society by inspiring new forms of engagement.

One of the paradigmatic examples of Municipio XI PB's impact on local civil society is the creation of Roma 70 (one of the neighbourhoods of the district) youth social centre. In the first year of the PB experience, young people – teenagers between 16 and 22 – started participating in the PB and rapidly cooperated to push forward a proposal to create a youth social centre in the neighbourhood, as they were lacking a place to gather for social, political, cultural and leisure activities. The proposal was largely voted in at the end of the process, and, more interestingly, it translated rapidly into public policy and public works. A year and a half later, the youth social centre opened its doors, this rapid realisation being linked to the direct support of the administration and especially the PB councillor. The latter appeared indeed extremely satisfied with the project, directly fomenting active citizenship according to him:

> There is also the case of the young people of Roma 70. They were initiated to public life through their participation to the participatory budget in Roma 70, formulating ideas and proposals that became more and more interesting with time. These teenagers of the neighbourhood constituted themselves, autonomously, in a cultural association [that manages the centre]. Now,

they are organising projects on the territory and give autonomous vocational training classes. I think this is a typical example of how other processes of self-organisation, self-training and self-management, which are really important for me, can be created from the participatory budget. They build a competent citizenship.[16]

I had the chance to visit the centre, and saw how active it was locally, organising political debates (rather oriented on the left, most of its members being young leftist activists), local actions, concerts, private lessons, etc. The managing team – composed of the young students who had presented the project in the PB assembly – lived, therefore, its first associative experience. These teenagers were able to re-invest the competences they had learn while participating in the PB, in the framework of this newly created association. The realisation of a PB proposal therefore resulted in the creation of an association, and in the acquisition of new skills and competences for actors. On the other hand, it also translated in the exit from the PB process of these newly engaged association members. Roman PB therefore directly encourages (even financially) the bifurcation of individual trajectories in the sense of revitalisation of local civil society.

PB can also foster the professionalisation of an activist career. The trajectory of Joaquin in Seville (already evoked in chapter four) offers a good illustration. His mobilisation in the PB process appeared as a 'recycling' of his activism, a bifurcation in his militant career, due to his expulsion from the IU local directing board. Joaquin therefore invested himself fully in the PB process, so that he appeared transformed when I met him one year later after our first encounter. In the meantime, he had launched an association to defend the PB process – in case of electoral change at the coming elections – of which he rapidly became president. When I met him again, he appeared even physically changed, wearing a suit, with a new cell phone, and having a rather haughty attitude, in contrast with the more modest look he used to have. It was also difficult for me to meet him, as he now had a rather booked schedule. Joaquin had become a local notable.

The bifurcation of Joaquin's political career cannot be attributed to his PB experience alone. Experienced activist – long time union, political party and neighbourhood association militant – he had a stock of previous political skills and competences, he was able to mobilise in the PB framework as well as in the creation of his association. In this regard, he did not get many new competences by participating in the PB. His participatory experience allowed him, however, to meet other local leaders and therefore to build a wider political network, indispensable for his new political career. One of the effects of PB participation is, therefore, to both create social capital that actors can mobilise in other political arenas and to open new political opportunities for actors who do not fit with traditional party recruitment schemes.

The creation of a PB can therefore appear as a means to boost local civil society by fostering the creation of new civic organisation or reactivating weaker ones.[17] Local organisations – especially neighbourhood associations, such as the Italian *comitati di quartiere* – look in PBs for new potential members, individuals ready to commit their time and energy for the local common good. Modes of engagement and expression are indeed highly comparable between PBs and some local civic organisations. I therefore saw, a few times, leaders of local associations inviting – more or less publicly – active PB members they knew were free of all engagement. It has to be stressed however that this type of bifurcation is less common in Morsang-sur-Orge than in the two other cases, given the weakness of local civil society and thus the weakness of associative supply.

It should be noted however that without a clear (top-down) will of the administration to boost civil society it is not sure that such revitalisation would have occurred. In Seville and Rome, the promoters of the process decided to work hand in hand with associations and social movements, while they did not in Morsang-sur-Orge and civil society remained dull. PBs can also boost civil society by fomenting mobilisation against the participatory process. Threatened by the creation of a new body of participation, associations might mobilise (as they did in Cordoba, but also in Seville and Rome) and get stronger in reactions to the PB.

The professional politician: participatory budgeting as a political stepping-stone

In the three cases, I observed a growing professionalisation of the more committed PB actors. These new local elites were often contacted by elected representatives and political parties to be on the lists for the municipal elections. The civic skills they acquired – learning to speak in public, to organise a meeting, to mobilise the population, etc. – and the network they created, embody political resources parties try to catch, in search of political legitimacy and local embeddedness. Often, those who not only adhere to a political party, but get involved in local elections, were previously politicised. In this regard, the PB offered a stepping-stone towards a more institutional engagement, complementing a previous associational or political experience. This was especially the case in Rome and Seville. In Morsang-sur-Orge on the contrary, the PB participants who ended up on the electoral lists were mostly good neighbours, concerned parents and community leaders. They were especially contacted by the PCF, following a strategy of 'opening' to civil society and non-politicised citizens. It has indeed been a constant mode of recruitment for local governments to co-opt civil society leaders (Le Bart 2003).

In the three cases, some PB activists have been involved in the municipal administration. For instance, Françoise Lefebvre was recruited to be on the list of Morsang-sur-Orge Communist Party for the 2001 municipal elections. Member of a Third-World solidarity NGO, and working for social services, she had both previous political and professional skills she was able to reinvest in the local political scene.[18] As she argues: 'The mayor works to allow a growing number of people to participate in decisions. It appears to me fundamental for the life of our city. It was a decisive factor in my own involvement.' Being both a civil society activist and a regular participant to PB meetings, she constituted the typical character to be recruited by the administration. Once elected, she became one of the active organisers of the Langevin neighbourhood council. This trajectory cannot be entirely considered as the beginning of a political career however, the PB serving as a stepping-stone for broader political ambitions. Françoise Lefebvre sees her involvement in the municipal administration as something temporary (in fact just one term – she resigned in 2008) and surely not as a way to become a professional politician, as she kept on working as a social service manager all the way long.

For others, the PB can appear as a stepping-stone for a coming political career. The PB can indeed work as a space for notability for political activists willing to deepen their political commitment and reach some elective functions. The case of Floriana, active member of the Municipio XI PB from the beginning, and candidate on the electoral list of *Rifondazione Comunista* (RC) for the 2006 municipal elections, is rather telling from this perspective. Having always voted, without ever getting involved in a political party or an association, she acknowledges that she 'enjoyed her PB experience so much' that she 'discovered a passion for politics'.[19] At the beginning of her participation, she felt a sort of 'moral shock' (Jasper 1997) when discovering the problems the neighbourhood was facing:

> The first impact of my participation to this assembly was that it made me think [...] I remember, at the first meeting, we were talking about public parks, lightings, etc. and at some point a man I didn't know, who spoke Italian with a clear foreign accent, said, with a low voice: 'I understand that you speak about your gardens and all, but you know, in winter, people die of cold in the Rom camp nearby.' He was a representative of the gypsies, and it really got me to the guts [...] There were clearly two realities put next to the other. It really made me think, that PB really confronts you to reality. It is the representation of a true society, not a virtual one, who lives on the territory. It's really a super interesting laboratory. [...] And, I really had the impression to rebirth.

> (Interview with Floriana, Rome, 28th March 2006)

In this case, the direct presence and expression of a different and distant social reality in the PB assembly allowed Floriana to become aware of some crucial social problems the neighbourhood was facing and that were often overlooked in the public assemblies. Often, emotional shocks are at the roots of a more direct commitment, first step in a process of politicisation (Goodwin *et. al.* 2001). Even if in the case of Floriana her participatory experience did not politicise her – in the ideological sense of the term – it allowed her to acquire practical skills (speaking in public, setting up projects together with associations, bargaining with the administration and the municipal experts, playing on the rivalry between politicians, etc.) and a network of relationships with local notables, she was then able to reinvest on the local political scene. Such a bifurcation would have been impossible without the stock of previous experiences related to her professional career – she has been an accounting manager for 30 years at the Italian ministry of finance – and to her biographical availability. Like students engaged in social movements of the American New Left in the 1960s, who had enough free time for activism (McAdam 1988), Floriana used the time liberated by her retirement, and the feeling of 'idleness' that followed, to start participating in the PB.

All PB participants do not accept, however, the starting of a political career. Valentina – evoked in chapter four – was approached by *Rifondazione* and the Greens to be on their electoral lists, but refused for ideological and strategic reasons. In Morsang-sur-Orge, Alex, evoked earlier, one of the pillars of his neighbourhood council, and relatively independent politically, (while on the left) was contacted by the Communist Party; but he refused.

The observed bifurcations in trajectories linked to the acquisition of new competences, raise nevertheless questions on the effects of participation. While it offers a socialisation to civic engagement, participation then translates into the professionalisation of the most committed actors, and thus to a form of re-specialisation. Participatory institutions would therefore face a dilemma (Carrel 2006). The fragile politicisation acquired by certain actors would either get institutionalised in a political or associative milieu, or merely fade away when the initial cause of the mobilisation disappears. Supposed to open up the circle of representation by including non-professional actors in the production of public policies, participatory institutions would end up reproducing the traditional division of political labour at the heart of representative government. Ruse of reason, the participatory critique would end up reinforcing representative democracy by reducing its lack of legitimacy through the democratisation of the means of access to political positions. This is even clearer as the gap between participatory processes' insiders – who acquire new competences and thus professionalise – and outsiders – who participate less intensively – widens.

The process of elite production through PB participation seems to parallel the famous iron law of oligarchy, firstly analysed for political parties by Michels (1914). As in the case of the German Socio-Democratic Party (SPD) he observed, the very internal logic of participation creates insiders and outsiders, the former getting increasingly specialised and professionalised, and the latter ever more dispossessed. This process, mostly due to the internal logic of participation, the acquisition of a new language and diversified skills, cumulates with the over-representation in PBs of individuals with higher political and cultural capital. Cultural and political elites have, therefore, higher chances to become PB insiders, and thus members of the group of good citizens. The logic of social differentiation appears however less marked in PB institutions than in other representative arenas, as individuals with little political skills, or with little cultural capital, have nevertheless the opportunity of becoming local political elites too.

These conclusions are not entirely surprising, however, even if they contradict the initial participatory spirit of the studied cases. In the US, the aim of participatory democracy and community organising experiences is above all to form local leaders, able to mobilise their community, and to foster consciousness-raising activities (Alinsky 1946; Polletta 2002). Only the nurturing of community leaders can avoid the co-optation of urban social movements by external political organisations. The concept of *empowerment* has no other ambition than building local elites capable of raising up their community (Bachrach and Baratz 1970; Smock 2004; Bacqué 2005). This gives rise to a 'personalist' conception of social change: it is through individual biographical change and the production of community activists that deep social and political changes are possible. Renewing political elites – be they local or not – participatory democracy could not transform the way representative government works, but the content of public policies would be enriched by alternative perspectives from new actors.

By opening the local political scene to new actors and nurturing new political elites, participatory democracy could embody a way – not the only one to be sure – to renew representative government (Rosanvallon 2006; Sintomer 2007). Far from its radical political ambition to deepen democracy by offering a more direct voice to citizens in the production of public policies, it would institutionalise new intermediary bodies – complementing political parties in a role they nowadays fail to endorse perfectly – nurturing new local notables between professional politicians and the population. Increased – territorial, social and maybe cultural – proximity would thus be achieved, but the traditional alternative offered by representation to citizens, 'remaining silent or being spoken' (Bourdieu 1991), would remain at the core of the political system. A less cynical interpretation could nevertheless stress that the deliberative aspect of participation at the grassroots allows lay citizens to speak and collectively construct their claims, the new political elites being the mere voice of the assemblies.

How people learn democracy

Even if many PB participants stopped participating, it is worth assessing the sources of self-change observed for the remainders. What was the specific role of PB participation in the learning process? More precisely, what happened in this process that allowed participants to learn new skills and competences? Did people learn from deliberation? What was the role of their dispositions and previous experiences in this socialisation process?

Self-change as acculturation: sociability vs. deliberation, or the power of informal processes of politicisation

It can first be stressed that the role of deliberation has been relatively marginal in the actor's learning process. Contrary to our hypotheses and to the dominant trend in the literature, PB participants were not decisively affected by deliberation, understood as a reasoned exchange of arguments aimed at taking a collective decision. Mutual persuasion leading to preference change hardly ever happened in the public assemblies (see chapter five). Most of the time, people remained either silent or committed to their initial opinions. In a nutshell, the findings from this study suggest that self-change cannot only be attributed to a process of collective deliberation. Public discussion had an impact, in the sense that it allowed the transmission of new information and knowledge to individuals, and sometimes to opinion formation. The learning process usually took the form of oral transmission from more experienced activists to political amateurs.

It should nevertheless be stressed that the learning and self-change observed in the three PB processes was not merely cognitive. Participants learned new skills and competences from the interactions in which they were engaged with others in PB institutions. It was mostly the repeated engagement in an interactional setting, ruled by certain norms (e.g., commitment to the common good, promotion of concrete projects, exclusion of party politics and ideology) that had an impact on individuals, leading to trajectory bifurcations.

This self-change process could be compared to the 'politicisation by impregnation' evoked by Maurice Agulhon (1982). Similarly to the small Provence notable who played a role of cultural intermediary between national politics and French peasants in the nineteenth century – especially among '*chambrées*', i.e. local clubs and associations that made possible repeated interactions, interclass contacts and in so doing a mutual impregnation that politicised the social structure of small towns, affecting progressively all social classes (Agulhon 1982; Pécout 1994) – politicised actors in PBs, and especially militants, have played a decisive role in the politicisation of initially apolitical citizens. The knowledge they transmitted, the skills and habits learnt through imitation, sanctions and rewards, and more broadly, the space of sociability created around PBs, created interactions between politicised and non-politicised actors that affected the latter decisively, as long as they were sufficiently engaged.

This perspective of a unilateral and 'top-down' self-change process, from militants to amateurs, should be nuanced however, in so far as the influence was reciprocated, learning processes taking place in both directions. Militants acknowledge indeed that PB participation allowed 'rediscovering the territory' and acquiring a local knowledge they lacked at first, given their commitment for global causes. Similarly, initially non-politicised actors are not passive receptacles of politics, in the sense that they interpret as well the messages addressed to them, hybridising them, make them their own or rejecting them. In this regard, the self-change process observed seems closer to what Déloye (2007: 795) calls a politicisation by 'acculturation':

> Without denying the unequal nature of this relationship that can turn to conflict, the suggested notion of 'political acculturation' insists on the complexity, and above all on the non-unilateral and on the contrary diversified aspect (in its forms and places of actualisation) of this contact between two cultures (at least) that act and react one to and upon the other. Nothing would be more misguided than considering that one culture erases the other, shapes it at its image, as a soft wax.

By emphasising the heterogeneity of culture and the processes of mutual impregnation, of hybridising and resistance, the concept of 'political acculturation' adds complexity to the Agulhonian approach, and seems to fit better with what has been observed in PBs. Even if, given the heterogeneity of actors within PBs and of the more fragile and elusive nature of the politicisation observed, the concept of style – in the sense of Eliasoph and Lichterman (2003) – rather than that of culture seems to fit better participatory budgeting institutions. The group style permeates actors willing to integrate, and in so doing is also partly modified, negotiated by the inclusion of new members. In this regard, the process of integration to the group of good citizens, requiring the impregnation in interaction of its style, can be qualified as a process of acculturation.

Biographical availability and the role of socio-political dispositions

It has to be stressed however that not all participants were affected by their PB experience, and not everyone was affected in the same way. Individual dispositions also had an impact on the potential learning process actors could experience. From this perspective, a crucial factor to consider is biographical availability (McAdam 1986). One of the conditions for successful learning is repeated, and intense, participation. The intensity of commitment itself depends on the biographical availability of actors. For example, students and retired people – who have more time – are over-represented in PB institutions. However, biographical availability does not only mean free time. Participation also depends on the emotional and political availability of individuals. Some participants mentioned that the void created by children leaving home, a change in a professional career, or an unsatisfied need for commitment, had a direct impact on their engagement in PB.

The repetition of participation does not only depend on biographical availability, but also of the social and political dispositions of actors. Politicised actors, over-represented in PB assemblies (see chapter four), had higher chances to go through a learning process than non-politicised actors did, while the latter were primarily those in need of political socialisation.

Despite the role of biographical availability, and of initial political and social dispositions, it seems that PB institutions can have a decisive learning impact on individuals. In these case-studies, most of the affected participants were not from the more marginalised fringes of the population, but members of the middle-class. Through PB, they were able to acquire new cognitive, social and political resources which sometimes were reinvested in other public arenas. Such transformations could have an impact on the way representative government works.

Four scenarios for the future of participatory democracy and representative government

This research allowed observing the emergence of four types of civic characters in PB institutions: the cynic, the expert citizen, the local civil society activist and the professional politician. From these four characters, four scenarios for the future of participatory democracy, and democracy *tout court*, can be drawn, the success of one over the other depending on the type of subjectivity it will mostly produce.[20]

If the majority of PB participants exit these institutions rapidly – as the high turnover rates indicate – and become cynical, it will mean the failure of participatory democracy to re-enchant politics. Participatory democracy, failing to do politics differently, falls back in citizens' view into the traditional traps of representative government. Far from reducing the distance between citizens and politics, participatory democracy will have burnt one of the last chances against the growing specialisation of politics and the eclipse of the public.

If, on the contrary, participatory democracy manages to produce a majority of expert citizens and PB activists (but the same can be true for other institutions), it will become increasingly autonomous, a specific realm between civil society and the state emerging. This, however, requires firstly, a greater institutionalisation of these participatory bodies. If they manage to do so, participatory democracy might be able to embody new intermediation bodies between society and the political sphere, between citizens and the *res publica*. One of the drawbacks of such a scenario is that participatory democracy might embody depoliticised intermediation arenas, offering a consensual definition of the common good. This largely depends on the relationship of these new institutions to social movements.

A third scenario makes of participatory democracy a producer of local civil society activists. Participatory institutions could work as arenas of politicisation and acquisition of critical political skills that could be reinvested in other fields. Given its inclusiveness, participatory institutions could embody arenas of empowerment and consciousness-raising for ordinary citizens. By nurturing new activists for local associations and social movements, participatory democracy could boost the critical potential of local civil society (Fung 2005). The risk, however, is the fading of participatory democracy, if all the activists it produces exit the institution to participate in other civic arenas. If participatory institutions constantly lose their leaders, they will need to be in a constant renewal, capable of attracting new recruits, which is difficult, as the concern about the low levels of participation in these institutions attest. Hence the interest of mixing two of these paths together, the production of expert citizens and local civil society activists, the two enriching themselves mutually.

Finally, in the last scenario, participatory institutions can mostly produce local professional politicians. The political field manages to co-opt the most skilful citizens, thus integrating the municipal lists for the elections. It would allow diversifying the recruitment of local political elites and increasing their (social, territorial and political) proximity with citizens. In this regard, participatory democracy could foster the regeneration of representative government. Participatory institutions cannot be a substitute to political parties in their function of production and selection of political elites, but can nevertheless complement them given the crisis they undergo. In this case, far from the radical alternative to representative government some make of participatory democracy, the critique it embodies would merely be internalised, making representation stronger and more legitimate.

The point of drawing these different scenarios was to stress the unfailing relationship between the quality of the citizenry and the nature of the political regime. As Tocqueville rightly emphasised (1835 [2000]: 321, vol. 2.):

> It is difficult to conceive how men who have entirely given up the habit of self-government should succeed in making a proper choice of those by whom they are to be governed; and no one will ever believe that a liberal, wise and energetic government can spring from the suffrages of a subservient people.

NOTES

1   More precisely, 278 persons participated to the working groups in 2004. However, this data takes into account participants each time they assisted a working group meeting, so well that it can be estimated that about a hundred participated regularly to these discussion meetings.

2   Only working groups' speakers are taken into account here, as the other meetings are not aimed at organising a collective discussion. Thus, 340 of the 430 participants to the observed working groups spoke at one moment or the other (see chapter four).

3   Interview with Christian, Morsang-sur-Orge, 17th January 2005.

4   For a similar argument, rejecting the importance of sincerity and hypocrisy for the analysis of deliberation, see Thompson 2008: 504.

5   Observation notes, Montagnola Zone Assembly, Rome, 29th March 2006.

6   Wallon NC organising committee, Morsang-sur-Orge, 22nd February 2006.

7   See chapter four for a presentation of this group, and especially their self-definition as 'mothers'.

8   Interview with Tatiana, Morsang-sur-Orge, 8th December 2005.

9   Thus Tatiana, while presenting the project in the NC, said clearly: 'But I insist, this is not a petition.' Robespierre NC, Morsang-sur-Orge, 26th November 2005. This meant it was not a political act to her, and that it was not to be understood as a mobilisation against the municipality, which was seen as highly supportive of the project from the beginning to the end, but as a constructive project. When asked why she did not want to use the word petition she answered: 'I don't know, it sounds too political.' Interview with Tatiana, Morsang-sur-Orge, 8th December 2005.

10 Observation notes, Wallon neighbourhood council, Morsang-sur-Orge, 10th January 2006.

11 Interview with Nicole, Morsang-sur-Orge, 24th February 2006.

12 Intervention in Wallon neighbourhood council, Morsang-sur-Orge, 23rd February 2006.

13 Interview with Nicole, Morsang-sur-Orge, 24th February 2006.

14 Nicole, Morsang-sur-Orge.

15 Nicole, Morsang-sur-Orge.

16 Interview with Luciano Ummarino, 9th January 2005.

17 This effect is even stronger in Porto Alegre, Brazil. See Baiocchi 2005.

18 Interview with Françoise Lefebvre, Morsang-sur-Orge, 5th December 2005. See as well the article, 'Morsang-sur-Orge: un féminisme au source de la citoyenneté', *L'humanité*, 1st March 2001, dedicated to women in Morsang-sur-Orge municipal council.

19 Interview with Floriana, Rome, 28th March 2006.

20 These scenarios are partly inspired from Bacqué, Rey and Sintomer 2005: conclusion.

| conclusion

Are participatory institutions schools of democracy? Do they teach people to act as good citizens, nurture democratic skills and habits, transforming them into public-spirited actors? I would have liked to answer these questions in a straightforward manner, to give a final solution to this crucial political dilemma. The answer this research brought is: it depends. One of the central conclusions of this book is indeed that when people are given the adequate social, cultural and institutional means, they can act competently in the public sphere and take enlightened public decisions. Civic competence is not primarily a resource, but a product of interactions; if it adequately arose, it therefore becomes accessible to the less armed citizens. I therefore tried to concentrate on some specific explanatory factors, to see how and when people trajectories were affected by their participatory experiences. I especially tried to go beyond the slogan 'institutions matter', to enter the black box of participatory procedures and see the interactions and social processes that emerged. It allowed reaching some important conclusions that point towards four decisive factors in the explanation of self-change.

First of all, the bifurcation of individual trajectories – or on the contrary their stability – depends on the previous political and personal experiences of the participants. The degrees of politicisation or depoliticisation as well as their biographical availability play crucial roles in self-change processes. Second, public discussion is decisive in the learning processes taking place in participatory institutions. More precisely, the emergence of disagreement and dissent in discussion appear as a necessary step in the process of politicisation and change. Third, as self-change is largely a matter of the type of interactions developing in participatory institutions, the role of the dominant grammatical norms ruling participatory institutions appear decisive in re-orienting individual behaviours. More precisely, a particular emotion, shame felt under the eyes of a public, appears as a powerful social mechanism in influencing actors performances. This nevertheless raises some normative questions in terms of the legitimacy of such processes that can be seen as manipulative or even as crude forms of symbolic domination. This is even more the case, as the role of leaders – this is the fourth point – appears critical in defining and enforcing the groups' norms, exerting the power of shame, and disciplining others' conduct.

Empowerment and the production of new civic characters

One of the critical conclusions of this book is in some regards a disillusion. Participatory institutions are not magic; they cannot transform any individual into a skilful democratic citizen. Past experiences matter too much, and PB institutions do not offer interactions intensive enough to allow such a radical process of change. The research allowed distinguishing different types of trajectories given the previous experiences of actors however. One of the crucial factors from this perspective is unsurprisingly previous political participation. Politicised actors were not radically affected in terms of politicisation. Two main consequences of participation have nevertheless been noticed. Either PB participation led to an extension of activists' understanding of politics (like the 'rediscovery of the territory' of Roman activists, who included local concerns and embeddedness in the territory in their understanding of politics) or it conducted on the contrary to an increased political professionalisation, PB participation being thus seen as a necessary step towards a local political career (this happened in the three case-studies). The difference between these trajectories depends on the type of politicisation (more or less institutionalised or radical) and on the biographical availability of actors. Politicisation happened through socialisation to collective action (in Morsang-sur-Orge, but also in Rome). More often, it took the form of a discursive change, actors taking the role of the good citizen in the assembly, and becoming like expert citizens, the PB being their main arena of participation. The skills and competences learned in the process of participation were sometimes reinvested in other public institutions, mostly associations and political parties. Most of the time, participants for whom such reinvestment occurred had a certain biographical availability which allowed them to invest themselves sufficiently to be affected by the experiences they lived. In other words, empowerment requires time and emotional commitment.

These conclusions are not sufficient however. They just point out that some participants have higher opportunities for self-change – the most available – and that their previous experiences might explain the process of change they underwent. This does not tell how the process actually works in participatory governance institutions. The role of public discussion and especially disagreement appear from this perspective crucial.

The democratic role of dissent

One of the central activities of participatory institutions is public discussion. People talk to find agreements on what to do about public funding. These discussions might be a succession of proposals, monologically stated, written down, and not collectively debated. This type of discussions had little impact on individuals. Participants might feel at best that they 'are heard' or that they 'can make a difference', but will remain immune from such conversations. Only when discussions become collective, when people listen to other's arguments and answer each other, can people be affected. This kind of discussion – defined as deliberation – can only emerge when disagreement is voiced. But disagreement is scarce, because it is risky. It might however be expressed, as seen in chapter 5, when a public decision is at stake, the discussion is well organised, and when some leaders – often activists – consider worth voicing dissent. Disagreement pushes actors to justify their claims, to make explicit their assumptions and aims, and it therefore creates cleavages. Such contentious situations do not let people unaffected. Some speakers, stigmatised or ashamed, might exit the institution and never come back. Others will come back and either accept the others' counter-arguments or convince them of the soundness of their own. Some actors will in any case modify their public standings. They will then integrate the group of good citizens of the institution, which might have a further impact on their personal and political trajectory.

Despite its importance, dissent is rare in modern societies. It was rare as well in PB public meetings. Most of the time people kept their grievances and disagreements private. However, once the stakes of the discussion increased, people voiced their arguments more easily. Fostering the logic of voice over exit or silence requires encouraging dissent at all the stages of the process with, for instance, micro-decisions being taken regularly rather that at the end of the cycle. The Roman case, where micro-decisions were constantly taken – probably overly implicitly, the power to decide whether a proposal was kept or not resulting from subtle influence game between the actors – is a good example of how deliberative sequences can emerge when procedurally encouraged. The type of dissent that is created is however crucial as well. The dynamic or Morsang-sur-Orge and Roman disagreements were different. In the French city, citizens mostly criticised town councillors' actions and engaged in conflictive talk about past bad practices. On the contrary, in Rome, people disagreed on what should be done, on future potential projects and public investments.

Finally, the stress put on the value of disagreement for deliberation – that may clash with some more consensus-oriented conceptions of deliberation – should incite researchers to offer contextualised or situated analysis of communicative practices in contemporary societies. As most democratic innovations – apart from one-shot ones, based on random sampling – take place at the local level and are territorially-based, we also know from urban sociology that there is a growing tendency towards territorial homogeneity (Bacqué *et al.* 2010). In a word, the structural and social conditions for the expression of disagreement in public arenas are vanishing. From this perspective, reflections on democratic innovations cannot focus on procedural designs and institutions only, but should also be combined with investigations on new ways of fostering (social, cultural, ethnic) heterogeneity or 'social mix' in the urban space, which appear as a prerequisite for the deliberative success of democratic innovations.

Emotions, publicity and social norms

Arguing that disagreement is crucial in the process of self-change is not sufficient however. I tried to go further in the analysis by investigating the role of a powerful social emotion like shame felt under the scrutiny of others. Disagreement is important in the process of self-change because it might be a shock, a trauma, for people. Change hardly occurs from routine. Something has to happen – a crisis, an '*épreuve*' – for people to reconsider their routinised behaviour. I scrutinised the different types of shocks experienced by PB participants over this research. The 'moral shocks' felt by Sevillan participants discovering the living conditions of some of the poorest residents of the city did not left them immune. While Seville PB did not leave much room for public discussion, disagreement and shame occurred as well as participants were provided direct sensitive experiences that affected their judgements and eventually their trajectories. In Rome and Morsang-sur-Orge, where public discussion was central, disagreement marked people. Confronted to the social norm of an existing group embodied by powerful and charismatic leaders, people felt ashamed to have made grammatical mistakes. They felt ridiculed to have been regarded as egoistic and self-interested. They could not stand being seen as racists or conservatives. For some, this experience was too hard, and they simply left. For others, motivated by the chance to make a difference, to impact local public policies, or simply 'to do good', they stayed, changed their arguments, and got integrated into the group.

Shame felt in public had therefore a deep civilising function, as Norbert Elias had already underlined. The process of civilisation has mainly occurred through the progressive internalisation by actors of social norms through self-control mechanisms to avoid experiencing shame in public (Elias, 1939b). The desire to get others' approval and the fear of conflict push people towards conformity. It seems however that the hypothesis of the internalisation of such norms – that is merely unverifiable – is unnecessary in the case of PBs. It is sufficient to see they are respected in situation.

Once the power of shame identified, the issue of its legitimacy arises immediately. It implies at least two important problems. First, rules respected due to the power of shame are not good per se. As we saw (chapter three), they stem from the complex interplay between national political culture, customary civic practices and actors' peculiar styles. The grammatical rules therefore varied a great deal from one case to another. While they all praised the value of citizen participation, and made of the promotion of the common good the highest political value, different meanings were given to concepts such as common good or citizenship. Legitimating a social process like the anticipation of shame by actors in the regulation of their behaviour in public cannot come from the intrinsic value of some norms over others. The legitimacy of such social processes depends on the origin of the grammatical rules and especially on the way they became dominant in the institution. Only a collective deliberation on the norms regulating the interactions in these institutions can grant them legitimacy. It partly happened in Seville – with the collective definition of the *Autoreglamento* – but the implicit norms regulating public behaviour were not discussed as such. In all the cases, shame was experienced because a dominant group was able to make the rules accepted, and make outsiders feel bad about not respecting them. In a word, shame implied authority. The group of good citizens had the authority to impose certain norms on others, to attribute rewards and sanctions, to integrate or exclude. Leaders appeared central in all the cases in the enforcement of the rules, and therefore in the process of self-change itself; this raises the question of influence, authority and domination over others however.

The role of leaders: influence, authority and instrumentalisation

The boundary is thin between learning and instrumentalisation, both appearing as two ways of interpreting influence of some over others. The distinction between instrumentalisation and learning could mostly come from the intentions of actors while exerting their authority. Having opted for a non-mentalist perspective, it appears unsuitable to sever out between interested influence – instrumentalisation being defined as influence exerted in the aim of secretly promoting one's self-interest – and disinterested influence, i.e. aimed at the others' welfare, that is learning. It is however possible to observe the consequences of influence processes. The cases of Rome Municipio XI and Morsang-sur-Orge appear from this perspective different. In Rome, leaders were mostly activists and politicised actors, belonging to local or national associations, political parties, unions and social movements. They nevertheless participated as individual actors and not as representatives of their organisations. It was therefore difficult to induce what kind of personal or interested gains these actors could obtain from their influence over the discussion, the group norms and others in general. At best, they managed to have an ideological influence on others, to expand their political views. The PB assemblies offered activists a scene to express their political positions.

On the contrary, in Morsang-sur-Orge, leaders were most of the time elected officials. Even if this changed over time in some neighbourhoods (like in this neighbourhood council where a group of citizens managed to get progressively empowered and to put the elected official on the side), town councillors had a decisive influence on the grammatical rules prevailing in Morsang-sur-Orge participatory institutions. In this case, observable gains could more easily be noticed: legitimating one's policy by including citizens in the policy process, gaining support and even votes from citizens. Once, over my participant observation experience in Morsang-sur-Orge 'House of the citizenry' I was surprised to hear some members of the administration say, while discussing among themselves: 'In the end, we're here to make them win the elections.' Even though these observations can be biased by the fact participant observation was conducted in only one of the cases, the strategic motivations, backed up by ideological ones as well, appear nevertheless clearly. Broadly speaking, it is hard to distinguish between strategic oriented actions and disinterested ones in the case of political parties, which have an interest (winning the elections, getting administrative positions, etc.) in having their disinterested ideological orientations promoted. This is probably why the participation of elected officials in participatory institutions is mostly detrimental, as their influence might always remain overwhelming and easily turn into instrumentalisation.

The democratisation of the public sphere

Paradoxically, along with the recent emergence of the participatory imperative a true 'hatred of democracy' (Rancière 2007) has arisen, confining the masses to an ontological incompetence. Controversies around citizen juries in France (Sintomer 2007), or referendum and direct democracy in Switzerland are always rooted in the belief that citizens are too ignorant to decide for themselves, or worst, that participatory democracy would foster irrational or dangerous decisions. The aim of this book was to show that ordinary citizens can become politically competent – they are not so naturally or automatically – once provided the adequate institutional, procedural and political conditions. If actors can become sufficiently competent, a more participatory system of government is no longer a chimera and can become a political ambition. In a word, the justification of delegation of power towards the elites does not hold anymore, once proven the masses are not naturally born uninterested with politics and unable to articulate their views and interests. On the contrary, a more participatory system of government could both foster the construction of civic competence and, in the meantime, the promotion of social justice through a wider opening to the claims coming from the subaltern classes. While participatory democracy has remained, so far, aloof from such ambitions, even risking deligitimising them, it seems that the focus put on institutional and procedural devices as they frame interactions and foster learning, allows raising the essential political question: who can speak, and therefore, govern.

appendix | towards a comparative ethnographic method

Evaluating the impact of participation on individuals could have been achieved through survey research, assessing before and after the participatory experiences whether participants had changed their minds. This is the dominant approach for measuring the effects of deliberation, which focuses mostly, however, on preference change rather than on practice transformation. Why opt for an ethnographic approach then? Three main reasons justify this choice. First, ethnographic research appears complementary to the more positivist approaches adopted so far in the literature, allowing the offering of a praxeologic insight on a phenomenon generally regarded from a purely cognitive perspective. Then, it also allows the evaluation of the impact of participation in the long-run; even if this would also be possible with surveys and questionnaires, but has hardly been conducted so far. Last but not least, the ethnographic method can show not only that people were affected by their participatory experiences, but also leads to an understanding of why and how they were. In a nutshell, it gives an entry to the black box of the construction of the civic competence mechanisms. I could, therefore, construct what I called a process model of self-change; offering explanatory factors for the bifurcation of individual trajectories. This has led to the argument that actors and their environment were mutually shaped in interaction. Actors produce an environment, which in return affects them. It appeared therefore indispensable to scrutinise the norms regulating interaction in the institutions studied. This was achieved by comparing discursive interactions in time and between sites. Each assembly being composed of dozens of discursive sequences, this research is thus based on the comparison of hundreds of discursive sequences among ordinary citizens in PB institutions. The comparison between them allows the severing out of rules – that people respect systematically – and deviations. Regularity appears indeed as a strong marker of normativity. This methodological approach is inspired by analytical induction (Strauss and Corbin 1997), building working hypotheses and potentially theories from the comparison of different interactional sequences. Each new observation should either confirm, or inflect, the conclusions drawn from the previous observations, in a movement towards generality and typification (Schutz 1970).

I therefore spent twenty-two months on the field, between December 2004 and September 2006. This ethnographic approach included different methodological tools: direct observation of public meetings, life history interviews with participants, participant observation in the PB administration for one of the cases.

The central tool I used all along my fieldwork was direct observation of public meetings in PB assemblies. As collective discussions play an important role in the decision-making process of these public bodies, and that the neighbourhood assembly is the central institution of participation, most of my empirical work was just to take notes about the discursive interactions taking place in these assemblies. This allows 'hearing' citizens voices directly, while they generally remain strangely mute in the research interested in communicative phenomena in the public sphere. Overall, I assisted in fifty-four public meetings in Rome Municipio XI, forty-nine in Morsang-sur-Orge and twenty-nine in Seville. In the observation of the meetings, I was attentive to many different features. The scenography, i.e., how is the room organised, where does the meeting take place, is there a spatial separation between the speakers and the audience, etc. I also focused on the participants, evaluating the number of participants attending, the number of males and females, the number of speakers over the meetings, etc. But the vast majority of my observations were simply notes on the actual conversations between the participants. I focused on both what was said and how it was said. Then, reporting these notes, I followed a detailed observation guide, which helped to make sense of this blurred reality. It allowed systematising the observations and to start analysing them, focusing on the motives used by the participants along the discussions. This constituted the core empirical material of the research, as I was above all interested in public interaction and discussion among lay citizens.

I then conducted many interviews, of different types. I first conducted interviews with the administration, to get basic information about the cases, their history, organisation and political context. In general, I interviewed the local councillor in charge of the participatory budget – for Rome and Morsang-sur-Orge, while in Seville I interviewed members of the organising administration. Then, in the French case, I also conducted many interviews with the administration during the internship I had at the House of Citizenry (see below). I thus conducted eleven interviews with the heads of these municipal departments (the cultural service, the administration in charge of youth policies, the urban management service, the sport administration, the environment service, etc.), which permitted getting a richer grasp of the diversity of the participatory practices of the city and of the relationships between the administration, the politicians and the citizens. I was however unable to reach such an in depth knowledge of the administrations for the two other cases.

Most of the interviews were nevertheless conducted with PB participants. I thus interviewed about ten citizens for each case. I managed to interview some of them more than once, to scrutinise the evolution of their relationships to politics. These interviews were relatively loosely structured in practice, as the aim was to let citizens reconstruct their personal and political trajectory, which led them to get involved in a PB institution. I therefore opted for life-history interviews, focusing on their previous experiences of participation – if any – their political socialisation, to reach progressively their experience in the PB, their motives for participating, their impressions, deceptions and hopes about it. The main questions I asked were therefore:

- Why did you start participating in a participatory budget? And have you ever had such an experience before?
- Was it easy to participate and speak up during the meetings?

- Do you have the feeling that you have learned anything from it?
- Are you participating since then, in other civic groups?

Finally, I decided to take an internship in one of the three cities I studied; understood as an experience of participant observation, which allowed me to see the process backstage and eventually to observe better power relationships in these institutions. I thus spent four months in the 'House of Citizenry' of Morsang-sur-Orge during the fall of 2005, living participatory democracy on a daily basis, writing letters or notes, calling citizens, preparing meetings. As I researched participatory democracy institutions, it appeared to me that being on the side of the organisers would provide a lot of interesting insights on how it actually worked in practice. Participant observation thus allowed getting both 'intimacy' with the participants and to grasp better the power relationships shaping the participatory process. Interacting backstage with the inceptors of the participatory institutions did not allow a better evaluation of how citizens were affected by their experiences of participation, but it gave me day-to-day contact with the participatory process and its participants that was incredibly rich. I therefore saw people not only for participatory meetings, but also for informal gatherings, private discussions or small convivial moments, thus grasping better who they were and understanding better how they performed on the participatory scene. I got informal information, thanks to my colleagues who were always ready to gossip about people. I was thus able to know what were people's jobs, political orientations, reputations, etc.

This experience convinced me that participant observation is especially useful for studying power relationships in institutional settings. Even if it was not directly at the core of this research at first, I got enough interesting material to use it fruitfully. As a matter of fact, I got along very well with my colleagues, and especially my boss, who was the director of the House of Citizenry, and her partner, the director of Cabinet of the Mayor. I therefore got a lot of political conversations with them, which helped me understand better how things really worked, and especially the actual decision-making process of the institution. This appears all the more interesting while dealing with a participatory institution, i.e., a public body claiming 'to give power back to citizens', 'to empower people', or 'to share power'. Being backstage allowed the understanding that this was much more complex in practice indeed. The point is not to argue about the biased nature of participatory democracy – once again ruled by realpolitik and power behind good intentions – but as several actors are involved in the process, with different motives and dispositions, a complex decision-making process is created, where power is shared by different groups fighting insidiously for it, while pretending to be all allied for the common good.

These types of analyses could not have been reached without participant observation, and without paying attention to what is said, both frontstage and backstage. In this case, interviews would have been useless (even if I conducted some on other issues) as actors would have presented a much brighter picture. Only being considered part of the group, and not as 'the researcher' to whom only nice things have to be shown or said, allowed me to go further in my analysis of the actual power relationships in these institutions.

Table: Observations and interviews for each case-study

	Rome	Morsang	Seville
Direct observation of public meetings	54	49	21
Interviews with participants	10	8	8
Interviews with the administration	2	13	2

| bibliography

Agulhon, M. (1982) *The Republic in the Village: The People of the Var from the French Revolution to the Second Republic*, Cambridge: Cambridge University Press.

Alexander, J. C. and Smith, P. (1993) 'The discourse of American civil society: a new proposal for cultural studies', *Theory and Society*, 22 (2): 151–207.

Alexander, J. C. Mast, J. L. (2006) 'Introduction: Symbolic Action in Theory and Practice: the Cultural Pragmatics of Symbolic Action', in J. C. Alexander, B. Giesen and J. L Mast (eds) *Social Performance: Symbolic Action, Cultural Pragmatics, and Ritual*, Cambridge: Cambridge University Press.

Allegretti, G. and Herzberg, C. (2005) 'Participatory Budgets in Europe: Between Efficiency and Growing Local Democracy', Transnational Institute and the Centre for Democratic Policy-Making, TNI Briefing Series, 2004/5.

Alinsky, S. (1971) *Rules for Radical: A Pragmatic Primer for Realistic Radicals*, London: Random House.

Arendt, H. (1965) *On Revolution*, London: Pelican Books.

⸻   (1995) *Qu'est-ce que la politique?* Paris: Seuil.

Aristotle (1993*) Rhetoric*, Princeton: Princeton University Press.

Aristotle (1995) *Politics*, Oxford: Clarendon.

Arnstein, S. (1969) 'A ladder of citizen participation', *JAIP*, 35/4: 216–224.

Associazione Progetto Laboratorio Onlus (APLO) (2005) 'Il progetto Sensiblizzando', in M. Smeriglio, G. Peciola and L. Ummarino (eds) *Pillola rossa o pillola blu? Pratiche di Democrazia Partecipativa nel Municipio Roma XI*, Rome: Intra Moenia Edition: 148–167.

Austin, J. (1975) *How to Do Things With Words*, Cambridge: Harvard University Press.

Austin-Smith, D. (1990) 'Strategic models of talk in political decision-making', *International Political Science Review*, 13: 124–152.

Bachrach, P. and Baratz, M. (1970) *Power and Poverty: Theory and Practice*, New York: Oxford University Press.

Becker, H. (1963) *Outsiders: Studies in the Sociology of Deviance*, New York: Free Press.

Bacqué, M.-H. (2005) 'Dispositifs participatifs dans les quartiers populaires, héritage des mouvements sociaux ou néo-libéralisme? Empowerment zones aux Etats-Unis et politique de la ville en France', in M-H. Bacqué, H. Rey, and Y. Sintomer, (eds) *Gestion de Proximité et Démocratie Participative: une Perspective Comparative*, Paris: La Découverte.

Bacqué, M.-H. and Sintomer, Y. (1999) 'L'espace public dans les quartiers populaires d'habitat social', in C. Neveu (ed.) *Espace public et engagement politique, Enjeux et logiques de la citoyenneté locale*, Paris: L'Harmattan.

—   (2001) 'Affiliations et désaffiliations en banlieue. Réflexions à partir des exemples de Saint-Denis et d'Aubervilliers', *Revue Française de sociologie*, 217–249.

—   (eds) (2011) *La démocratie participative: Histoire et généalogie*, Paris: La Découverte.

Bacqué, M-H., Rey, H. and Sintomer, Y. (eds) (2005) *Gestion de Proximité et Démocratie Participative: Une Perspective Comparative*, Paris: La Découverte.

Bacqué, M.-H., Fijalkow, Y., Flamand, A. and Vermeersch, S. (2010) 'Comment nous sommes devenus HLM. Les opérations de mixité sociale à Paris dans les années 2000', *Espaces et sociétés*, 140–141.

Baiocchi, G. (2001) 'Participation, activism, and politics: the Porto Alegre experiment and deliberative democratic theory', *Politics & Society,* (29)1: 42–73.

—   (2005) *Militants and Citizens: The Politics of Participatory Democracy in Porto Alegre*, Princeton: Princeton University Press.

Barber, B. (1984) *Strong Democracy, Participatory Politics for a New Age,* Berkeley: University of California Press.

Beck, U. (1992) *Risk Society: Towards A New Modernity* [1986] London: Sage.

Bellah, R. *et al.* (1985) *Habits of the Heart: Individualism and Commitment in American Life,* New York: Harper and Row.

Benedicto, J. (2003) 'Démocratie, citoyenneté et culture politique: la transition démocratique en Espagne', in D. Céfaï (ed.) *Cultures Politiques*, Paris: PUF: 485–501.

Benhabib, S. (1996) 'Toward a Deliberative Model of Democratic Legitimacy' in S. Benhabib (ed.) *Democracy and Difference: Contesting the Boundaries of the Political,* Princeton: Princeton University Press.

—   (ed.) (1996) *Democracy and Difference: Contesting the Boundaries of the Political,* Princeton: Princeton University Press.

Berry, J. M., Portney, K. E. and Thomson, K. (1993) *The Rebirth of Urban Democracy,* Washington: The Brookings Institution.

Bettin Bates, G. and Magnier, A. (1995) 'I nuovi sindaci: come cambia une carriera politica, *Rivista Italiana di Scienza Politica*, XXV: 1: 91–118.

Bickford, S. (1996) 'Beyond friendship: Aristotle on conflict, deliberation, and attention', *The Journal of Politics,* 58 (2): 398–421.

Blanc, M. (1999) 'Participation des habitants et politique de la ville', in L. Blondiaux, G. Marcou and F. Rangeon (eds) *La démocratie locale. Représentation, participation et espace public,* Paris: PUF.

Blanco, I. (2001) 'Les jurys citoyens en Espagne: vers un nouveau modèle de démocratie locale?', *Mouvements,* 18.

Blatrix, C. (1999) 'Le maire, le commissaire enquêteur et leur 'public'. La pratique politique de l'enquête publique', in CURAPP/CRAPS (eds), *La Démocratie locale,* Paris: PUF: 188–202.

Blatrix, C. (2000) *La 'démocratie participative', de mai 1968 aux mobilisations anti-TGV. Processus de consolidation d'institutions sociales émergentes,*

Ph. D thesis, Paris: Université Paris 1- Panthéon Sorbonne.

— (2003) 'The Changing French Democracy: Patchwork Participatory Democracy and Its Impact on Political Participation', paper presented at the ECPR Joint Sessions of Workshops, Edinburgh, March 28 – April 2, 2003.

Blondiaux, L. (1996) 'Mort et résurrection de l'électeur rationnel: Les métamorphoses d'une problématique incertaine', *Revue Française de Science Politique*, 46 (5).

— (2000) 'La démocratie par le bas: Prise de parole et délibération dans les conseils de quartier du vingtième arrondissement de Paris', *Hermes*, 26–27.

— (2005) in 'L'idée de démocratie participative: Enjeux, impensés et questions récurrentes', in M-H. Bacqué, H. Rey, and Y. Sintomer (eds) (2005) *Gestion de Proximité et Démocratie Participative: une Perspective Comparative*, Paris: La Découverte.

— (2008) *Le nouvel esprit de la démocratie: Actualité de la démocratie participative*, Paris: PUF.

Blondiaux, L., Marcou, G. and Rangeon F. (eds) (1999) *La démocratie locale. Représentation, participation et espace public,* Paris: PUF.

Blondiaux, L. and Lévêque, S. (1999) 'La politique locale à l'épreuve de la démocratie. Les formes paradoxales de la démocratie participative dans le XXème arrondissement de Paris' in C. Neveu (ed.) *Espace public et engagement politique: Enjeux et logiques de la citoyenneté locale,* Paris: L'Harmattan

Blondiaux, L. and Michel L. (2007) 'L'expertise en débat : jeux d'acteurs et conflits de savoirs autour d'un débat public local dans le Lot', in F. Cantelli, S. Jacob, G. Genard and V. de Visscher (eds), *Les constructions de l'action publique,* Paris: L'Harmattan: 181–201.

Blondiaux, L. and Sintomer, Y. (2002) 'L'impératif délibératif', *Politix*, 15 (57).

Bloor, D. (1997) *Wittgenstein: Rules and Institutions*, London: Routledge.

Bohman, J. (1996) *Public Deliberation: Pluralism, Complexity and Democracy,* Cambridge: The MIT Press.

Boltanski, L. (1993) *La souffrance à distance. Morale humanitaire, médias et politique,* Paris: Editions Métailié.

Boltanski, L. and Thévenot, L. (1991) *De la justification. Les économies de la grandeur,* Paris: Gallimard.

Boltanski, L. and Chiapello, E. (1999) *Le nouvel esprit du capitalisme,* Paris: Gallimard.

Bourdieu, P. (1984) 'L'opinion publique n'existe pas', in Bourdieu, P. *Questions de sociologie,* Paris: Minuit.

Bourdieu, P. (1991) *Language and Symbolic Power*, Harvard: Harvard University Press.

— (1998) *Practical Reason: On the Theory of Action*, Stanford: Stanford University Press.

— (2002) 'Le mystère du ministère. Des volontés particulières à la volonté générale', *Actes de la recherche en Sciences Sociales,* 140 (5): 7–11.

Boy, D., Donnet Kamel, D. and Roqueplo, P. (2000) 'Un exemple de démocratie participative. La "conférence de citoyens" sur les organismes génétiquement modifies', *Revue Française de Science Politique,* 50 (4–5): 779–810.

Braconnier, C. and Dormagen, J.-Y. (2007) *La démocratie d'abstention: Aux origines de la démobilisation électorale en milieu populaire,* Paris: Gallimard.

Briquet, J-L. (2003) 'Les territoires imaginaires de l'Europe du Sud: Constructions savantes et productions politiques', in D. Céfaï (ed.) *Cultures Politiques,* Paris: PUF: 397–398.

Button, M. and Mattson, K. (1999) 'Deliberative democracy in practice: challenges and prospects for civic deliberation', *Polity,* vol. XXXI (4).

Caciagli, M. (1988) 'Quante Italia? Persistenza e trasformazione delle culture politiche subnazionali', *Polis* (3): 429–457.

Caddy, J. and Peixoto, T. (2006) *Beyond Public Scrutiny: Stocktaking of Social Accountability in OECD Countries,* Paris: OECD.

Callon, M., Lascoumes, P. and Barthe, Y. (2009) *Acting in an Uncertain World: An Essay on Technical Democracy,* Cambridge: The MIT Press.

Cantelli, F., Jacob, S., Genard, J.-L. and Visscher, C. (eds) (2006) *Les constructions de l'action publique,* Paris: L'Harmattan.

Cardon, D., Heurtin, J.-P. and Lemieux, C. (1995) 'Parler en public', *Politix,* 31: 5–19.

Carrel, M. (2006) 'Politisation et publicisation: les effets fragiles de la délibération en milieu populaire', *Politix,* 75: 33–51.

Castel, R. (1995) *Les métamorphoses de la question sociale: Une chronique du salariat,* Paris: Fayard.

Castells, M. (1983) *The City and the Grassroots: A Cross-Cultural Theory of Urban Social Movements,* Berkeley: University of California Press.

Castoriadis, C. (1998) [1975] *The Imaginary Institution of Society,* Cambridge: The MIT Press.

Céfaï, D. (2001) 'Les cadres de l'action collection: Définitions et problèmes', in D. Céfaï and D. Trom (eds) (2001) *Les formes de l'action collective: Mobilisations dans des arènes publiques,* Paris: Editions de l'EHESS.

——— (2002) 'Qu'est-ce qu'une arène publique? Quelques pistes pour une approche pragmatiste', in D. Céfaï and I. Joseph (eds) (2002) *L'héritage du pragmatisme: Conflits d'urbanité et épreuves de civisme,* Paris: Editions de L'aube.

——— (ed.) (2003) *Cultures Politiques,* Paris: PUF.

Céfaï, D. and Joseph, I. (eds) (2002) *L'héritage du pragmatisme. Conflits d'urbanité et épreuves de civisme,* Paris: Editions de l'Aube.

Chambers, S. (2005) 'Measuring publicity's effect: reconciling empirical research and normative theory', *Acta Politica,* 40 (2): 255–266.

Checkoway, B. (1986) 'The politics of public hearings', *Journal of Applied Behavioral Science,* 17 (4): 566–582.

Chomsky, N. (1977) *Dialogues avec Mitsout Ronat*, Paris: Flammarion.

Cohen, Je. (1999) 'Trust, Voluntary Association, and Workable Democracy: The Contemporary Discourse of Civil Society', in M. Warren (ed.) *Democracy and Trust,* Cambridge: Cambridge University Press.

Cohen, Jo. (1989) 'Deliberation and Democratic Legitimacy' in A. Hamlin and P. Pettit, (eds) *The Good Polity,* Oxford: Basil Blackwell.

—   (1997) 'Deliberation and Democratic Legitimacy' in J. Bohman and W. Rehg (eds) *Deliberative Democracy: Essays on Reason and Politics,* Cambridge: MIT Press.

Cole, R. L. and Caputo, D. A. (1984) 'The public hearing as an effective citizen participation mechanism: a case study of the general revenue sharing program', *American Political Science Review,* 78: 404–416.

Conover, P. J., Searing, D. and Crewe, I. M. (2002) 'The deliberative potential of political discussion', *British Journal of Political Science,* 32.

Converse, P. (1964) 'The Nature of Belief Systems in Mass Publics' in D. E. Apter (ed.) *Ideology and Discontent,* New York: Free Press.

Coote, A. and Lenaghan, J. (1997) *Citizens' Juries: Theory into Practice,* London: Institute for Public Policy Research.

Crosby, N. (1995) 'Citizen Juries: One Solution for Difficult Environmental Questions', in O. Renn, T. Webler, and P. Wiedemann (eds) *Fairness and Competence in Citizen Participation: Evaluating Models for Environmental Discourse,* London: Kluwer Academic Publisher.

Crozier, M. (1995) *La Crise de l'intelligence*, Paris: Interéditions.

Crozier, M., Huntington, S. and Watanuki, J. (1975) *The Crisis of Democracy: Report on the Governability of Democracies to the Trilateral Commission,* New York: New York University Press.

d'Albergo, E. (ed.) (2005) *Pratiche partecipative a Roma. Le osservazioni al piano regolatore e il bilancio partecipativo*, Rome: Sapienza University.

Dalton, R. (2007) *The Good Citizen: How a Younger Generation is Reshaping American Politics*, Washington: CQ Press Americans.

Dante, B. (1997) 'Sub-national governments in the long Italian tradition', *West European Politics*, 20.

Delap, C. (2001) 'Citizens' juries: reflections on the UK experience', *PLA Notes,* 40.

Della Porta, D. (ed.) (2004) *Comitati di cittadini e democrazia urbana*, Soveria Mannelli: Rubbettino editore.

Della Porta, D. *et al.* (2006) *Globalization from Below: Transnational Activists and Protest Networks*, Minneapolis: University of Minnesota Press.

Delli Carpini, M. X., Lomax Cook, F. and Jacobs, L. R. (2004) 'Public deliberation, discursive participation, and citizen engagement: a review of the empirical literature', *Annual Review of Political Science,* 7.

Déloye, Y. (2007) 'Pour une sociologie historique de la compétence à opiner "politiquement". Quelques hypothèses de travail à partir de l'histoire électorale française', *Revue française de science politique,* 57 (6): 775–798.

Déloye, Y. and Ihl, O. (2008) *L'acte de vote*, Paris: Presses de Sciences Po.

Derrida, J. (1990) *Limited Inc.*, Paris: Galilée.

Dewey, J. (1997) [1927] *The Public and Its Problems,* Athens: Ohio University Press.

— (1938) *Experience and Education,* in *The Later Works*, 1925–1953, Carbondale: Southern Illinois University Press.

Dewitt, P., Pilet, J.-B., Reynaert H. and Steyvers K. (2007) (eds) *Towards DIY-Politics: Participatory and Direct Democracy at the Local Level in Europe,* Bruges: Vanden Broele.

Downs, A. (1957) *An Economic Theory of Democracy,* New York: Harper Collins.

Druckman, J. N. and Lupia, A. (2000) 'Preference formation', *Annual Review of Political Science, 3.*

Dryzek, J. (2000) *Deliberative Democracy and Beyond,* Oxford: Oxford University Press.

Dryzek, J. and List, C. (2003) 'Social choice theory and deliberative democracy: a reconciliation', *British Journal of Political Science,* 33: 1–28.

Dryzek, J. and Goodin R. (2006) 'Deliberative impacts: the macro-political uptake of *mini-publics'*, *Politics and Society,* 34 (2): 219–224.

Duchesne, S. and Haegel, F. (2006) 'Avoiding or accepting conflict in public talk', *British Journal of Political Science,* 37 (1): 1–22.

Durkheim, E. (1893) *The Division of Labour in Society,* New York: Free Press [1997].

Edles, L. (1995) 'Rethinking the democratic transition: A culturalist critique and the Spanish case', *Theory and Society,* 24 (3): 355–384.

Elias, N. (1939a) [1991] *The Society of Individuals*, Oxford: Basil Blackwell.

— (1939b) [1994] *The Civilizing Process*, Oxford: Blackwell.

Eliasoph, N. (1998) *Avoiding Politics: How Americans produce apathy in everyday life,* Cambridge: Cambridge University Press.

— (2002) 'Raising Good Citizens in a Bad Society: Moral Education and Political Avoidance in Civic America', in R. Madsen, W. Sullivan, A. Swidler and S. Tipton (eds) *Meaning and Modernity: Religion, Polity, and the Self,* Berkeley: University of California Press.

Eliasoph, N. and Lichterman, P. (2003) 'Culture in interaction', *American Journal of Sociology,* 108 (4).

Elkin, S. and Soltan, K. (eds) (1999) *Citizen Competence and Democratic Institutions*, Philadelphia: The Pennsylvania University Press.

Elster, J. (1994) 'Argumenter et négocier dans deux assemblées constituantes', *Revue Française de Science Politique,* 44 (2).

— (1995) 'Strategic Uses of Argument', in K. Arrow, *et al.* (eds) *Barriers to Conflict Resolution,* New York: Norton.

— (1997) [1986] 'The Market and the Forum' in J. Bohman and W. Rehg (eds) *Deliberative Democracy: Essays on Reason and Politics,* Cambridge: MIT Press.

— (ed.) (1998a) *Deliberative Democracy*, Cambridge: Cambridge University Press.

— (1998b) 'Deliberation and Constitution Making', in Elster, J. (ed.)

Deliberative Democracy, Cambridge: Cambridge University Press.

— (1999) *Alchemies of the Mind: Rationality and the Emotions*, Cambridge: Cambridge University Press.

Escalera, J. (ed.) (2002) *Contrapuntos sobre politica y democracia: cultura, sociedad y regimen democratico,* Granada: Junta de Andalucia.

Evans, S. and Boyte, H. C. (1986) *Free Spaces,* New York: Harper & Row.

Fagotto, E. and Fung, A. (2006) 'Empowered participation in urban governance: the minneapolis neighbourhood revitalization program', *International Journal of Urban and Regional Research*, 30: 638–655.

Fearon, J. (1998) 'Deliberation as Discussion', in Elster, J. (ed.) (1998) *Deliberative Democracy*, Cambridge: Cambridge University Press.

Ferejohn, J. and Kuklinski, J. (eds) (1990) *Information and Democratic Processes*, Urbana: University of Illinois Press.

Fernandez-Llebrez Gonzàlez, F. (1999) *La indiferencia democratica. Democracia y abstencion en Andalucia. 1982–1996,* Granada.

Ferrara, A. (2001) 'Alcuni fattori di debolezza della cultura politica democratica in Italia', in F. Crespi and A. Santambrogio (eds) *La cultura politica nell'Italia che cambia,* Rome: Carocci.

Fillieule, O. (2001) 'Pour une analyse processuelle de l'engagement individuel', *Revue française de science politique*, 51 (1–2): 199–217.

Fine, G. A. (1979) 'Small groups and culture creation: The idioculture of little league baseball teams', *American Sociological Review*, 44 (5): 733–745.

Fine, G. A. and Kleinman, S. (1979) 'Rethinking subculture: an interactionist analysis', *The American Journal of Sociology*, 85 (1): 1–20.

Finley, M. (1973) *Democracy: Ancient and Modern,* New Brunswick: Rutgers University Press.

Fiorino, D. (1990) 'Citizen participation and environmental risk: a survey of institutional mechanisms', *Science, Technology and Human Values,* 15 (2).

Fischer, F. (2000) *Citizens, Experts, and the Environment: The Politics of Local Knowledge*, Durham: Duke University Press.

Fishkin, J. S. (1997) *The Voice of the People: Public Opinion and Democracy,* New Haven: Yale University Press.

Fishkin, J. S., Luskin, R. C. and Jowell, R. (2002) 'Considered opinions: deliberative polling in Britain', *British Journal of Political Science,* 32 (3): 455–487.

Foley, M. W., Edwards, B. and Diani, M. (eds) (2001) *Beyond Tocqueville: Civil Society and the Social Capital Debate in Comparative Perspective,* London: University Press of New England.

Font, J. (de) (2001) *Ciudadanos y decisionas publicas*, Barcelona: Editorial Ariel.

Font, J. and Blanco, I. (2007) 'Procedural legitimacy and political trust: the case of citizen juries in Spain', *European Journal of Political Research*, 46 (4): 557–589.

Forman-Barzilai, F. (2005) 'Sympathy in space(s): Adam Smith on proximity', *Political Theory,* 33 (2):189–217.

Forster, M. (2004) *Wittgenstein on the Arbitrariness of Grammar,* Princeton: Princeton University Press.

Foucault, M. (1975) *Discipline and Punish: The Birth of the Prison*, New York: Random House.

French Political Culture and Society (2006) 'Lost the Banlieues of the Republic?'.

Fung, A. (2004) *Empowered Participation: Reinventing Urban Democracy*, Princeton: Princeton University Press.

—— (2005) 'Deliberation before the revolution: towards an ethics of deliberative democracy in an unjust world', *Political Theory*, 33 (2): 397–419.

—— (2006) 'Varieties of participation in complex governance', *Public Administration Review*, 66: 66–75.

Fung, A. and Wright, E. O. (eds) (2003) *Deepening Democracy: Institutional Innovations in Empowered Participatory Governance*, London: Verso.

Gambetta, D. (1998) 'Claro! An Essay on Discursive Machismo' in J. Elster (ed.) *Deliberative Democracy*, Cambridge: Cambridge University Press.

Gamson, W. A. (1992) *Talking Politics*, Cambridge: Cambridge University Press.

Gannette, R. (2003) 'Bowling ninepins in Tocqueville's township', *American Political Science Review*, 97 (1): 1–16.

Garsten, B. (2006) *Saving Persuasion: A Defence of Rhetoric and Judgement*, Cambridge: Harvard University Press.

Gastil, J. and Levine, P. (eds) (2005) *The Deliberative Democracy Handbook: Strategies for Effective Civic Engagement in the Twenty-First Century*, San Francisco: Jossey-Bass.

Gaxie, D. (1977) 'Economie des parties et rétributions du militantisme', *Revue Française de Science Politique*, 27 (1).

—— (1978) *Le cens caché : inégalités culturelles et ségrégation politique*, Paris: Seuil.

—— (2002) 'Appréhensions du politique et mobilisations des expériences sociales', *Revue française de science politique*, 52 (2–3): 145–178.

Gelli, F. and Pinson, G. (2001) 'Federalization process, participation and democracy in Italy. The examples of the Veneto region Constitutional Chart and of the City of Turin new urban policies', paper presented at the ECPR Joint Session of Workshops, Grenoble, April 2001.

Gigone, D. and Hastie, R. (1993) 'The common knowledge effect: information sharing and group judgement', *Journal of Personality and Social Psychology*, 65: 956–974.

Goffman, E. (1959) *The Presentation of the Self in Everyday Life*, New York: Doubleday Anchor books.

—— (1961) 'Role-Distance' in E. Goffman, *Encounters: Two Studies in the Sociology of Interaction*, Indianapolis: Bobbs-Merrill: 85–152.

—— (1971) *Relation in Public: Microstudies of the Public Order*, London: Penguin Books.

—— (1981) *Forms of Talk*, Philadelphia: University of Pennsylvania Press.

Goodin, R. E. (2003) *Reflective Democracy*, Oxford: Oxford University Press.

—— (2004) 'Representing diversity', *British Journal of Political Science*, 34: 453–468.

Goodin, R. E. and Niemeyer, S. J. (2003) 'When does deliberation begin? Internal reflection versus public discussion in deliberative democracy', *Political Studies*, 51: 627–649.

Goodwin, J., Jasper, J. and Polletta, F. (2001) *Passionate Politics: Emotions and Social Movements*, Chicago: The University of Chicago Press.

Gordon, C. and Jasper, J. (1996) 'Overcoming the "NIMBY" label: rhetorical and organizational links for local protestors', *Research in Social Movements, Conflicts and Change*, 19.

Gunther, R., Montero, J. R. and Botella, J. (ed.) (2004) *Democracy in Modern Spain*, Yale: Yale University Press.

Gurr, T. (1970) *Why Men Rebel?* Princeton: Princeton University Press.

Gutmann, A. and Thompson, D. (1996) *Democracy and Disagreement*, Cambridge: Harvard University Press.

Habermas, J. (1962 trans 1989) *The Structural Transformation of the Public Sphere: An Inquiry into a Category of Bourgeois Society*, Cambridge: Polity.

—   (1971) 'Technology and science as ideology', in J. Habermas, *Toward a Rational Society: Student Protest, Science, and Politics*, Boston: Beacon Press.

—   (1984) *The Theory of Communicative Action*, vol. 1, Boston: Beacon Press.

—   (1992) 'Further Reflections on the Public Sphere', in C. Calhoun (ed.) *Habermas and the Public Sphere*, Cambridge: the MIT Press.

—   (1996a) 'Three Normative Models of Democracy' in S. Benhabib (ed.) *Democracy and Difference*, Princeton: Princeton University Press.

—   (1996b) *Between Facts and Norms: Contributions to a Discourse Theory of Law and Democracy*, Cambridge: The MIT Press.

Hamidi, C. (2010) *La société civile dans les cités. Engagement associatif et politisation dans les associations de quartier*, Paris: Economica.

Hamilton, A., Madison, J. and Jay, J. (1937) *The Federalist Papers* [1787], New York: The Modern Library.

Hansen, K. H. (2002) 'Real Attitude Change Through Deliberation', Paper presented at the 30th Joint Session of Workshop, ECPR, Turin, March 22–27, 2002.

Hansen, K. H. and Andersen, N. (2007) 'How deliberation makes better citizens: The Danish deliberative poll on Euro', *European Journal of Political Research*, 46.

Harré, R. and Parott, G. W. (1996) *The Emotions: Social, Cultural and Biological Dimensions*, London: Sage.

Hastings, M. (2003) 'Les filigranes du communisme français' in D. Céfaï (ed.) *Cultures Politiques*, Paris: PUF.

Hatzfeld, H. (2006) *Faire de la politique autrement. Les expériences inachevées des années 1970*, Rennes: Adels/Presses Universitaires de Rennes.

Hedbige, D. (1979) *Subculture: The Meaning of Style*, London: Routledge.

Hibbing, J. R., and Theiss-Morse, E. (2002) *Stealth Democracy: Americans'*

Beliefs About How Government Should Work, Cambridge: Cambridge University Press.

Hirschman A. (1983) *Shifting Involvement, Private Interest and Public Action*, Princeton: Princeton University Press.

Honneth, A. (1995) *The Struggle for Recognition: the Grammar of Moral Conflicts*, Cambridge: Polity Press.

Hooghe, M. (2003) 'Voluntary Associations and Democratic Attitudes: Value Congruence as a Causal Mechanism', in M. Hooghe and D. Stolle (eds) *Generating Social Capital: Civil Society and Institutions in Comparative Perspective*, New York: Palgrave McMillan.

Huckfeld, R. and Sprague, J. (1995) *Citizens, Politics and Social Communication: Information and Influence in an Election Campaign*, New York: Cambridge University Press.

Huckfeld, R., *et al.* (2004) *Political Disagreement: The Survival of Diverse Opinions within Communication Networks*, Cambridge: Cambridge University Press.

Jacobs, L., Lomax Cook, F. and Delli Carpini, M. (2009) *Talking Together: Public Deliberation and Political Participation in America*, Chicago: The University of Chicago Press.

Jasper, J. (1997) *The Art of Moral Protest: Culture, Biography, and Creativity on Social Movements,* Chicago: Chicago University Press.

Joas, H. (1987) 'Symbolic Interactionism', in A. Giddens and J. Turner (eds) *Social Theory Today*, Stanford: Stanford University Press, 82–115.

— (1993) *Pragmatism and Social Theory*, Chicago: The University of Chicago Press, 55–77.

Joss, S. and Durant, J. (eds) (1995) *Public Participation in Science: The Role of Consensus Conferences in Europe*, London: Science Museum Editions.

Kertzer, D. (1980) *Comrades and Christians: Religion and Political Struggle in Communist Italy*, Cambridge: Cambridge University Press.

Kinder, D. and Sears, D. (1985) 'Public Opinion and Political Action', in Lindzey, G. and Aronson, E. (eds) *Handbook of Social Psychology*, New York: Random House.

Knight, J. and Johnson, J. (1994) 'Aggregation and deliberation: on the possibility of democratic legitimacy', *Political Theory*, 22 (2).

Koehl, E. and Sintomer, Y. (2002) *Les jurys de citoyens berlinois*, Rapport final pour la Direction Interministérielle de la Ville.

Koff, S. and Koff, S. (2000) *Italy: From the First to the Second Republic*, London: Routledge.

Kuklinski, J. (ed.) (2001) *Citizens and Politics: Perspectives from Political Psychology*, Cambridge: Cambridge University Press.

Kuklinski, J. H., Riggle, E., Ottati, V., Scharz, R. and Wyer, R. S. (1991) 'The cognitive and affective bases of political tolerance judgements', *American Journal of Political Science*, 35 (1).

Lafaye, C. and Thévenot, L. (1993) 'Une justification écologique? Conflits dans l'aménagement de la nature', *Revue Française de Sociologie*, 34 (4).

Lamont, M. and Fournier, M. (eds) (1992) *Cultivating Differences: Symbolic Boundaries and The Making of Inequality*, Chicago: The University of Chicago Press.

Lamont, M. and Thévenot, L. (eds) (2001) *Rethinking Comparative Cultural Sociology: Repertoires of Evaluation in France and the United States*, Cambridge: Cambridge University Press.

Lang, A. (2007) 'But is it for real? The British Columbia Citizens' Assembly as a model of state-sponsored citizen empowerment', *Politics & Society*, 35 (1): 35–69.

Latour, B. (1993) *We Have Never Been Modern*, Cambridge: Harvard University Press.

Le Bart, C. (2003) *Les Maires. Sociologie d'un rôle*, Villeneuve d'Ascq: Presses Universitaires du Septentrion.

Le Bart, C. and Lefebvre, R. (eds) (2005) *La proximité en politique. Usages, rhétoriques, pratiques,* Rennes: Presses Universitaires de Rennes.

Lefebvre, R. (2005) 'La proximité à distance', in C. Le Bart and R. Lefebvre (eds) (2005) *La proximité en politique. Usages, rhétoriques, pratiques,* Rennes: Presses Universitaires de Rennes: 103–127.

—— (2011) 'Retour sur les années 1970. Le parti socialiste, l'autogestion et la démocratie locale', in M.-H. Bacqué, Y. Sintomer (eds) *La démocratie participative. Histoire et généalogie*, Paris: La Découverte.

Lefebvre, R. and Roger, A. (eds) (2009) *Les partis politiques à l'épreuve des procédures délibératives*, Rennes: Presses Universitaires de Rennes.

Lemieux, C. (2009) *Le devoir et la grâce*, Paris: Economica.

Levi, M. (1996) 'Social and unsocial capital: a review essay of Robert Putman's *Making Democracy Work'*, *Politics and Society*, 24: 45–55.

Levrel, J. (2008) 'L'écriture encyclopédique ouverte à tous', in S. Topçu, C. Cuny and K. Serrano-Velarde (eds) *Savoirs en débat. Perspectives franco-allemandes*, Paris: L'Harmattan.

Lichterman, P. (1995) *The Search for Political Community: American Activists Reinventing Commitment*, Cambridge: Cambridge University Press.

—— (2005) *Elusive Togetherness: Church Groups Trying to Bridge America's Divisions*, Princeton: Princeton University Press.

Lindeman, M. (2002) 'Opinion Quality and Policy Preferences in Deliberative Research', in M. Delli Carpini *et al.* (eds) *Research on Micro-Politics: Political Decision Making, Deliberation and Participation,* vol. 6.

Linz, J. (1972) 'An Authoritarian Regime: The Case of Spain', in S. Eisenstadt (ed.) *Political Sociology: A Reader*, New York: Basic Books: 521–530.

Lippmann, W. (1925) *The Phantom Public*, New York: Transaction Publisher.

Lipset, S. M. (1960) *Political Man: The Social Bases of Politics,* New York: Doubleday.

Loughlin, J. (ed.) (2004) *Subnational Democracy in the European Union: Challenges and Opportunities*, Oxford: Oxford University Press.

Luskin, R. (1990) 'Explaining political sophistication', *Political Behavior*, 12(4): 331–361.

Lyotard, J.-F. (1979) *La Condition Postmoderne*, Paris: Minuit.

McAdam, D. (1986) 'Recruitment of high-risk activism: the case of Freedom Summer', *American Journal of Sociology*, vol. 92.

— (1988) *Freedom Summer*, Oxford: Oxford University Press.

— (1989) 'The biographical consequences of activism', *American Sociological Review*, 92: 64–90.

Macedo, S. *et al.* (2005) *Democracy at Risk: How Political Choices Undermine Citizen Participation, and What We Can Do About It*, Washington D.C.: Brookings Institution Press.

Madison, J. *et al.* (1790) *The Federalist no. 10*, Middletown, Conn.: Wesleyan University Press, 1961.

Magone, J. M. (2004) 'The Main Features of Contemporary Political Culture', in R. Gunther, R. J. Montero and J. Botella (eds) *Democracy in Modern Spain*, Yale: Yale University Press.

Manin, B. (1987) 'On legitimacy and political deliberation', *Political Theory*, 15: 338–368.

— (1997) *The Principles of Representative Government*, Cambridge: Cambridge University Press.

— (2005) 'Democratic Deliberation: Why We Should Promote Debate Rather than Discussion', Paper delivered at the Program in Ethics and Public Affairs Seminar, Princeton University, October 13th 2005.

Mansbridge, J. (1980) *Beyond Adversary Democracy*, New York: Basic Books.

— (1999a) 'On the Idea that Participation Makes Better Citizens', in S. Elkin and K. Soltan (eds) *Citizen Competence and Democratic Institutions*, Philadelphia: The Pennsylvania University Press.

— (1999b) 'Everyday Talk in the Deliberative System' in S. Macedo (ed.) *Deliberative Politics: Essays on Democracy and Disagreement*, Oxford: Oxford University Press.

Maravall, J. A. (1982) *The Transition to Democracy in Spain*, London: Croom Helm.

Marcou, G. (1999) 'La démocratie locale en France: Aspects juridiques', in L. Blondiaux, G. Marcou, and F. Rangeon (eds) *La démocratie locale. Représentation, participation et espace public*, Paris: PUF.

Marcus, G. E. and Hanson, R. L. (eds) (1993) *Reconsidering the Democratic Public*, Philadelphia: The Pennsylvania State University Press.

Mayer, I., de Vries, J. and Geurts, J. (1995) 'An Evaluation of the Effects of Participation in a Consensus Conference', in S. Joss and J. Durant (eds) *Public Participation in Science. The Role of Consensus Conferences in Europe*, London: Science Museum Editions.

Mead, G. H. (1934) *Self, Mind and Society*, Chicago: The University of Chicago Press.

Mendelberg, T. (2002) 'The Deliberative Citizen: Theory and Evidence' in M. Delli Carpini *et al.* (eds) *Research on Micro-Politics: Political Decision Making, Deliberation and Participation*, vol. 6, Elsevier Press.

Merkle, D. M. (1996) 'The polls – review: the national issues convention deliberative poll', *Public Opinion Quarterly,* 60: 588–619.

Michels, R. (1914) [1999] *Political Parties: A Sociological Study of the Oligarchic Tendencies of Modern Democracy*, New Brunswick: Transaction.

Mill, J. S. (1958) [1861] *Considerations on Representative Government* New York: Bobbs-Merrill.

Minaldi, G., Riolo, C. (2005) 'Electoral Systems, Forms of Government and the Local Political Class in Italy' in H. Reynaert *et al.* (eds) *Revolution or Renovation? Reforming Local Politics in Europe*, Brugge: Vanden Broele: 131–153.

Mitofski, W. (1996) 'It's not deliberative and it's not a poll', *Public Perspective*, 7 (1): 4–6.

Moody, M. and Thévenot, L. (2000) 'Comparing Models of Strategy, Interests, and the Common Good in French and American Environmental Disputes', in M. Lamont and L. Thévenot (eds), *Rethinking Comparative Cultural Sociology: Repertoires of Evaluation in France and the United States*, Cambridge: Cambridge University Press: 273–306.

Morales, L. (2003) 'Ever Less Engaged Citizens? Political Participation and Associational Membership in Spain', Barcelona, WP 220: Institute of Social and Political Sciences.

Moscovici, S. (1976) *La Psychanalyse, son image et son public*, Paris: PUF.

—   (1992) *Dissension et Consensus: Une Théorie Générale des Décisions Collectives*, Paris: PUF.

Mouffe, C. (2000) *Deliberative Democracy or Agonistic Pluralism*, Vienna: Institute for Advanced Studies.

Mutz, D. (2002) 'Cross-cutting social networks: Testing democratic theory in practice', *American Political Science Review*, 96: 11–126.

Mutz, D. and Martin, P. (2001) 'Facilitating communication across lines of political difference: the role of mass media', *American Political Science Review,* 95: 97–114.

Narayan, D. (1999) *Bonds and Bridges: Social Capital and Poverty*, Washington DC: World Bank, Poverty Reduction and Economic Management Network, Poverty Division.

Neveu, C. (2003) *Citoyenneté et espace public. Habitants, jeunes et citoyens dans une ville du Nord*, Lille: Editions du Septentrion.

Newton, K. (1999) 'Social Capital and Democracy in Modern Europe', in J. Van Deth *et al.* (eds), *Social Capital and European Democracy*, London: Routledge.

Nez, H. and Talpin, J. (2010) 'Généalogie de la démocratie participative en banlieue rouge. Un renouvellement du communisme municipal en trompe-l'oeil?', *Genèses,* 79: 97–115.

Noelle-Neumann, E. (1993) *The Spiral of Silence: Public Opinion – Our Social Skin* 2nd Ed, Chicago: University of Chicago Press.

Nonjon, M. (2005) 'Professionnels de la participation: savoir gérer son image militante', *Politix*, 18 (70): 89–112.

Norris, P. (ed.) (1999) *Critical Citizens: Global Support for Democratic Government*, Oxford: Oxford University Press.

—— (2002) *The Democratic Phoenix: Reinventing Political Activism*, Cambridge: Cambridge University Press.

Nylen, W. (2002) 'Testing the empowerment thesis: the participatory budget in Belo Horizonte and Betim, Brazil', *Comparative Politics* 34(2) : 127-145.

OECD (2001) *Citizens as Partners: Information, Consultation and Public Participation in Policy Making*, Paris: OECD.

Offe, C. (1997) 'Micro-aspects of Democratic Theory: What Makes for the Deliberative Competence of Citizens?' in A. Hadenius (ed.) *Democracy's Victory and Crisis,* Cambridge: Cambridge University Press.

—— (2006) 'Political Disaffection as an Outcome of Institutional Practices? Some Post-Tocquevillean Speculations', in M. Torcal, and J. R. Montero (eds) *Political Disaffection in Contemporary Democracies: Social Capital, Institutions, and Politics*, London: Routledge.

Page, E. and Goldsmith, M. (eds) (1987) *Central and Local Government Relations: a Comparative Analysis of West Europeans Unitary States*, London: Sage.

Paoletti, M. (2007) *Décentraliser, d'accord, démocratiser, d'abord*, Paris: La Découverte.

Pasquier, R. and Pinson, G. (2004) 'Politique européenne de la ville et gouvernement local en Espagne et en Italie', *Politique européenne,* 12: 42–65.

Passeron, J. C. (1989) 'Biographies, flux, itinéraires, trajectoires', *Revue française de sociologie*, XXXI: 3–22.

Pateman, C. (1970) *Participation and Democratic Theory*, Cambridge: Cambridge University Press.

Pécout, G. (1994) 'La politisation des paysans au 19e siècle. Réflexions sur l'histoire politique des campagnes françaises', *Histoire et sociétés rurales*, 2: 91–125.

Peirce, C. S. (1934) 'Some Consequences of Four Incapacities', in C. Hartshorne, and P. Weiss (eds) *Collected Papers, vol. 5,* Cambridge: Harvard University Press.

Pelletier, D., Kraak V., McCullum, C., Usitalo U., and Rich, R. (1999) 'The shaping of collective values through deliberative democracy: An empirical study from New York's North Country', *Policy Sciences,* 32.

Phillips, A. (1995) *The Politics of Presence,* Oxford: Clarendon Press.

Piechaczyk, X. (1997) 'Instruire ou construire l'intérêt général? Radiographie d'une population de commissaires enquêteurs', *Ecologie et Politique,* 21: 43–60.

Polletta, F. (1999) 'Free spaces in collective action', *Theory and Society,* 28: 1–38.

—— (2002) *Freedom is an Endless Meeting: Democracy in American Social Movements,* Chicago: The University Press of Chicago.

—— (2005) *It Was Like a Fever: Story Telling in Protest and Politics*, Chicago: The University Press of Chicago.

Porras, A. J. and Soria, E. (1993) 'Elections et vie politique dans l'actuelle Séville', in B. Vallé (ed.) *Séville: Vingt siècles d'histoire,* Collection de la Maison des Pays Ibériques, Institut d'études Ibériques et Ibéro-Américaines, 196–214.

Powell, W. and DiMaggio, P. (1991) *The New Institutionalism in Organizational Analysis,* Cambridge: Cambridge University Press.

Putnam, R. D. (1993) *Making Democracy Work: Civic Traditions in Modern Italy,* Princeton: Princeton University Press.

— (1995) 'Bowling alone: America's declining social capital', *Journal of Democracy,* 6: 65–87.

— (2000) *Bowling Alone: The Collapse and Revival of American Community,* New York: Simon and Schuster.

Quéré, L. (2002) 'La structure de l'expérience publique d'un point de vue pragmatiste', in D. Céfaï and I. Joseph (eds) *L'héritage du pragmatisme. Conflits d'urbanité et épreuves de civisme,* Paris: Editions de l'Aube.

Rancière, J. (1995) *La mésentente. Politique et philosophie,* Paris: Galilée.

— (2007) *Hatred of Democracy,* London: Verso.

Rawls, J. (1971) *A Theory of Justice,* Cambridge: Harvard University Press.

— (1997) 'The Idea of Public Reason' in J. Bohman and W. Rehg (eds) *Deliberative Democracy: Essays on Reason and Politics,* Cambridge: MIT Press, 131–144.

Remer, G. (2000) 'Two models of deliberation: oratory and conversation in ratifying the constitution', *The Journal of Political Philosophy,* 8 (1): 68–90.

Reynaert, H., Steyvers, K., Delwit, P. and Pilet, J.-B. (eds) (2005) *Revolution or Renovation? Reforming Local Politics in Europe,* Brugge: Vanden Broele.

Riker, W. H. (1982) *Liberalism against Populism,* San Francisco: Freeman.

Rodriguez Alvarez, J. M. (2005) 'Local Democracy Reforms in Spanish Cities', in H. Reynaert *et al.* (eds) *Revolution or Renovation? Reforming Local Politics in Europe.* Brugge: Vanden Broele, 155–184.

Rokkan, S. and. Eisenstadt, S. (eds) (1973) *Building States and Nations,* Beverly Hills: Sage.

Rosanvallon, P. (1976) *L'âge de l'autogestion,* Paris: Seuil.

— (2004) *Le modèle politique français: la société civile contre le jacobinisme de 1789 à nos jours,* Paris: Seuil.

— (2006) *La contre-démocratie: La politique à l'age de la défiance,* Paris: Seuil.

— (2008) *La légitimité démocratique. Impartialité, réflexivité, proximité,* Paris: Seuil.

Rosanvallon, P. and Viveret, P. (1977) *Pour une nouvelle culture politique,* Paris: Seuil.

Rosenberg, S. W. (ed.) (2008) *Deliberation, Participation and Democracy: Can the People Govern?* London: Palgrave Macmillan.

Rostboll, C. (2005) 'Preferences and paternalism: On freedom and deliberative Democracy', *Political Theory,* 33 (3): 370–396.

Rouban, L. (1991) 'Le client, l'usager et le fonctionnaire : quelle politique de modernisation pour l'administration française?', *Revue française d'administration publique*, 59: 435–444.

—— (ed.) (1999) *Citizens and the New Governance: Beyond New Public Management*, Amsterdam: IOS Press.

Rui S. (2004) *La Démocratie en débat. Les citoyens face à l'action publique*, Paris: Armand Colin.

Ryfe, D. (2005) 'Does deliberative democracy work?', *Annual Review of Political Science*, 8: 49–71.

Sabbioni, P. (1999) 'La démocratie locale en Italie', in L. Blondiaux, G. Marcou and F. Rangeon (eds) *La démocratie locale. Représentation, participation et espace public*, Paris: PUF.

Sanders, L. M. (1997) 'Against Deliberation', *Political Theory*, 25(3) : 347–376.

Sartori, G. (1962) *Democratic Theory*, Detroit: Wayne State University Press.

Scheff, T. (1989) *Microsociology: Discourse, Emotion and Social Structure*, Chicago: The University Press of Chicago.

Schmitt, C. (1939) *The Concept of the Political*, Chicago: Chicago University Press.

Schmitter, P. and Trechsel, A. (2004) *The Future of Democracy in Europe: Trends, Analyses and Reforms*, Strasbourg: Council of Europe.

Schulz-Hardt, S., Frey, D., Lüthgens, C. and Moscovici S. (2000) 'Biased information search in group decision making', *Journal of Personality and Social Psychology*, 78: 660–669.

Schumpeter, J. (1942) *Capitalism, Socialism and Democracy*, New York: Harper and Brothers.

Schutz, A. (1970) *On Phenomenology and Social Relations* (ed. Wagner, H.), Chicago: The University of Chicago Press.

Segatori, R. (2001) 'La cultura politica degli amministratori dei Communi italiani', in F. Crespi and A. Santambrogio (eds) *La cultura politica nell'Italia che cambia*, Roma: Carocci.

Segatti, P. (2006) 'Italy, Forty Years of Political Disaffection: A Longitudinal Exploration', in M. Torcal and J. R. Montero (eds) *Political Disaffection in Contemporary Democracies: Social Capital, Institutions, and Politics*, London: Routledge.

Selle, P. and Stromsnes, K. (1999) 'Membership and Democracy', in J. W. Van Deth *et al.* (eds) *Social Capital and European Democracy*, London: Routledge.

Sintomer, Y. (1996) 'Le corporatisme de l'universel et la cite', *Actuel Marx*, 20: 92–104.

—— (1998) 'Sociologie de l'espace public et corporatisme de l'universel', *L'homme et la société*, 7–19.

—— (2007) *Le pouvoir au peuple. Jury citoyens, tirage au sort et démocratie*, Paris: La Découverte.

—— (2008) 'Du savoir d'usage au métier de citoyen?', *Raisons politiques*, 31: 115–133.

Sintomer, Y. and Allegretti, G. (2009) *I bilanci partecipativi in Europa. Nuove esperienze democratiche nel vecchio continente*, Rome: Ediesse.

Sintomer, Y. and Gret, M. (2005) *The Porto Alegre Experiment: Learning Lessons for a Better Democracy,* New York: Zed Books.

Sintomer, Y. and de Maillard, J. (2007) 'The limits to local participation and deliberation to the French "politique de la ville"', *European Journal of Political Research*, 46 (4): 503–529.

Sintomer, Y., Herzberg, C. and Röcke, A. (2008a) 'From Porto Alegre to Europe: potential and limitations of participatory budgeting', *International Journal of Urban and Regional Research*, 32 (1): 164–178.

— (2008b) *Démocratie participative et modernisation des services publics: des affinités électives? Enquête sur les expériences de budget participatif en Europe*, Paris: La Découverte.

Sintomer, Y., Röcke, A. and Talpin, J. (2009) 'Démocratie participative ou démocratie de proximité? Le budget participatif des lycées du Poitou-Charentes' , *L'Homme et la société*, 172–173 : 303–319.

Sintomer, Y. and Talpin J. (eds) (2011) *La démocratie participative au-delà de la proximité. Potiou-Charentes et l'échelle régionale*, Rennes: Presses Universitaires de Rennes.

Sirianni, C. (1993) 'Learning Pluralism: Democracy and Diversity in Feminist Organizations', in J. Chapman, and I. Shapiro (eds) *Democratic Community, NOMOS XXXV,* New York: New York University Press.

Skinner, Q. (1981) *Machiavelli: A Short Introduction,* Oxford: Oxford University Press.

— (1998) *Liberty before Liberalism*, Cambridge: Cambridge University Press. Smeriglio, M., Peciola, G. and Ummarino, L. (eds) (2005) *Pillola rossa o pillola blu? Pratiche di Democrazia Partecipativa nel Municipio Roma XI,* Rome: Intra Moenia Edition.

Smith, A. (1759) [2002] *The Theory of Moral Sentiments*, K. Haakonsen (ed.) Cambridge: Cambridge University Press, .

Smith, G. (2005) *Beyond the Ballot: 57 Democratic Innovations from around the World*, London: The POWER Inquiry.

— (2009) *Democratic Innovations*, Cambridge: Cambridge University Press.

Smith, G. and Wales, C. (2002) 'Citizens' Juries and Deliberative Democracy', in M. Passerin d'Entrèves (ed.) *Democracy as Public Deliberation: New Perspectives,* Manchester: Manchester University Press.

Smock, K. (2004) *Democracy in Action: Community Organizing and Urban Change*, New York: Columbia University Press.

Sniderman, P., Brody, R. and Tetlock, P. (1991) *Reasoning and Choice: Exploration in Political Psychology*, Cambridge: Cambridge University Press.

Sommier, I. (2001) *Les nouveaux mouvements contestataires à l'heure de la mondialisation*, Paris: Flammarion.

Stasser, G. and Titus, W. (1985) 'Pooling of unshared information in group decision making: biased information sampling during discussion', *Journal of*

Personality and Social Psychology, 48: 1267–1278.

Steiner, J., Bachtiger, A., Spörnli, M. and Steenbergen, M.R. (2005) *Deliberative Politics in Action: Analysing Parliamentary Discourse*, Cambridge: Cambridge University Press.

Stoker, G. (2006) *Why Politics Matters: Making Democracy Work*, London: Palgrave Mcmillan.

Strassoldo, R. (1992) 'Globalism and Localism: Theoretical Reflections and Some Evidence', in Z. Mlinar (ed.) *Globalization and Territorial Identities*, Avebury: Aldershot and Brookfield.

Strauss, A. and Corbin, J. (eds) (1997) *Grounded Theory in Practice*, London: Sage.

Sunstein, C. (1991) 'Preferences and politics', *Philosophy and Public Affairs*, 20 (1):3–34.

— (2003a) *Why Societies Need Dissent*, Cambridge: Harvard University Press.

— (2003b) 'The Law of Group Polarization' in J. S. Fishkin and P. Laslett (eds) *Debating Deliberative Democracy*, Oxford: Blackwell.

Talpin, J. (2006) 'Jouer les bons citoyens. Les effets contrastés de la participation à des dispositifs participatifs', *Politix*, 75: 13–31. (2007) 'Who Governs in Participatory Governance Institutions? The Impact of Citizen Participation in Municipal Decision-Making Processes in a Comparative Perspective' in P. Dewitt *et al.* (eds).

— (2007) *Towards DIY-Politics: Participatory and Direct Democracy at the Local Level in Europe*, Bruges: Vanden Broele.

Talpin, J. and Wojcik, S. (2010) 'Deliberating environmental policy issues: comparing the learning potential of online and face-to-face discussions on climate change', *Policy & Internet*, 2(2) 4.

Thévenot, L. (2006) *L'action au pluriel. Sociologie des régimes d'engagement*, Paris: La découverte.

Thompson, D. (1970) *The Democratic Citizen*, Cambridge: Cambridge University Press.

— (1976) *John Stuart Mill and Representative Government*, Princeton: Princeton University Press.

— (2008) 'Deliberative democratic theory and empirical political science', *Annual Review of Political Science*, 11: 496–520.

Tocqueville, A. de (2000), *Democracy in America* [1835 and 1940], Chicago: The University of Chicago Press, t. 1 and 2.

Torcal M. and Montero J. R. (2006) (eds) *Political Disaffection in Contemporary Democracies: Social Capital, Institutions, and Politics*, London: Routledge.

Tossutti, L. (2002) 'Between globalism and localism, Italian style', *West European Politics*, 25 (3): 51–76.

Turner, V. (1982) *From Ritual to Theatre: The Human Seriousness at Play*, New York: PAJ Publications.

Urbinati, N. (2002) *Mill on Democracy: From the Athenian Polis to Representative*

Government, Chicago: The University of Chicago Press.

Van Deth, J. W., Maraffi M., Newton, K. and P. F. Whiteley (eds) (1999) *Social Capital and European Democracy,* London: Routledge.

Verba, S., Lehman Schlozman, K. and Brady, H.E. (1995) *Voice and Equality: Civic Voluntarism in American Politics,* Cambridge: Harvard University Press.

Viroli, M. (1990) 'Machiavelli and the Republican Idea of Politics', in G. Bock, Q. Skinner and M. Viroli (eds) *Machiavelli and Republicanism*, Cambridge: Cambridge University Press.

Warren, M. (2001) *Democracy and Association,* Cambridge: Cambridge University Press.

Warren, M. and Pearse, H. (eds) (2008) *Designing Deliberative Democracy: The British Columbia Citizen Assembly*, Cambridge: Cambridge University Press.

Weber, M. (1978) *Economy and Society: An Outline of Interpretive Sociology*, Berkeley: University of California Press.

Winquist, J. and Larson, J. (1998) 'Information pooling: when it impacts group decision making', *Journal of Personality and Social Psychology*, 74: 371–377.

Wittgenstein, L. (1978) *Philosophical Grammar*, Berkeley: University of California Press.

—   (2005) *The Big Typescript: TS 213*, Malden: Blackwell.

Wuthnow, R. (1992) *Vocabularies of Public Life*, London: Routledge.

—   (1998) *Loose Connections: Joining Together in America's Fragmented Communities*, Cambridge: Harvard University Press.

Young, I. M. (1990) *Justice and The Politics of Difference,* Princeton: Princeton University Press.

—   (1996) 'Communication and the Other: Beyond Deliberative Democracy', in S. Benhabib (ed.) *Democracy and Difference: Contesting the Boundaries of the Political,* Princeton: Princeton University Press.

—   (1997) 'Asymmetrical Reciprocity: On moral respect, wonder, and enlarged thought', *Constellations* 3(3): 340-363.

—   (2000) *Inclusion and Democracy,* Oxford: Oxford University Press.

—   (2001) 'Activist challenges to deliberative democracy', *Political Theory,* 29 (5: 670–688).

Zaller, J. (1992) *The Nature and Origins of Mass Opinion*, New York: Cambridge University Press.

Zask, J. (2002) 'Ethiques et politiques de l'interaction. Le self-government à la lumière du pragmatisme', in D. Céfaï and I. Joseph (eds) *L'héritage du pragmatisme. Conflits d'urbanité et épreuves de civisme*, Paris: Editions de l'Aube.

| index

Moscovici, S. 2, 108
Mouffe, C. xvi
Mutz, D. 144, 146

Napoleon I 40
Narayan, D. 33
neighbourhood councils 38, 42–3, 44
    under-representation in 42
    see also under Morsang-sur-Orge;
       Rome; Seville
neo-institutionalism 14, 17
neo-republicanism 1
Netherlands, The, participatory
    budgeting in 44
Neveu, C. 123
Newton, K. 13
Nez, H. 25
Niemeyer, S. J. 2, 5, 6, 41, 137
No Global movement 32
Noelle-Neumann, E. 7
Nonjohn, M. 71, 84
Norris, P. 34
Nylen, W. 44

OECD 33, 71
Offe, C. 16, 28 n.7, 155, 156
opinions 3, 4, 151, 152
    change of 6, 150–1, 152–4, 155,
       158 n.19
    study of 18
    see also preference change

Page, E. 44
Paoletti, M. 37
Parrott, W. G. 165
participation, political
    conformity and 161
    ethnographic research, use of 197
    grammars of *see* participatory
       grammar
    influence, sociology of 161
    integration and 161, 168
    internal logic of 185
    leaders, influence of 161, 191,
       194–5

recognition and 108
rule learning and 161, 162
self-change and 2–3, 14, 19, 160,
    191
    action, theories of 15
    cognitive hypothesis 6–8
    deliberative hypothesis 4–6
    disagreement, role of in 193
    emotional hypothesis 12–14
    interest hypothesis 8–10
    pragmatist perspective of 15, 20
    praxeologic perspective 20
    process model of 160, *163*, 197
    processes of 3–4
    publicity hypothesis 10–12, 14
    see also participatory budgeting,
       self-change and
shame and 165, 191, 193–4
sincerity and 167–8
see also citizen participation;
    participatory democracy
participatory budgeting (PB) xii, 32,
    43–4
as a 'school of democracy' 44, 54,
    191
case study selection/ presentation
    criteria 44–5, 67, 82, 197–200
    'House of Citizenry' internship
       199
    life-history interviews and 198–9
    participant observation, use of
       199
comparative ethnographic method,
    use of ix, xvi, xvii, 24, 27, 99,
    138, 139, 140, 144, 197–200
circles of participation in 107–9,
    131 n.15, 185
citizen competences and 124,
    127–8, 129, 162, 175, 178,
    186–7, 191
elite creation 185–6
legitimacy and 129–30
local knowledge and 124, 171,
    176–8, 187
new skills, types of 170, 171,

www.ingramcontent.com/pod-product-compliance
Lightning Source LLC
Chambersburg PA
CBHW072102020426
42334CB00017B/1598